# BANKING THEORY, LAW AND PRACTICE

*(Prepared Strictly in accordance with the Revised Syllabus of Banking Theory, Law and Practice, Semester III of the Madras University, B.Com. Degree Course)*

# BANKING THEORY, LAW AND PRACTICE


**Dr. K. Nirmala Prasad**

*Principal, M.O.P. Vaishnav College for Women, Chennai.*

**J. Chandradass**

*Former Professor of Commerce,*
*Madras Christian College, Chennai.*



Himalaya Publishing House

ISO 9001:2008 CERTIFIED

First Edition : 2005
Edition : 2012
Edition : 2013
Edition : 2014
Edition : 2016
Edition : 2017
Edition : 2025

**Published by** : Mrs. Meena Pandey for **Himalaya Publishing House Pvt. Ltd.**, "Ramdoot", Dr. Bhalerao Marg, Girgaon, Mumbai - 400 004.
**Phone:** 022-23860170, 23863863; **Fax:** 022-23877178
**E-mail:** himpub@vsnl.com; **Website:** www.himpub.com

**Branch Offices** :

**New Delhi** : "Pooja Apartments", 4-B, Murari Lal Street, Ansari Road, Darya Ganj, New Delhi - 110 002.
Phone: 011-23270392, 23278631; Fax: 011-23256286

**Nagpur** : Kundanlal Chandak Industrial Estate, Ghat Road, Nagpur - 440 018.
Phone: 0712-2738731, 3296733; Telefax: 0712-2721216

**Bengaluru** : Plot No. 91-33, 2nd Main Road Seshadripuram, Behind Nataraja Theatre, Bengaluru - 560 020.
Phone: 08041138821; Mobile: 09379847017, 09379847005

**Hyderabad** : No. 3-4-184, Lingampally, Besides Raghavendra Swamy Matham, Kachiguda, Hyderabad - 500 027.
Phone: 040-27560041, 27550139

**Chennai** : New No. 48/2, Old No. 28/2, Ground Floor, Sarangapani Street, T. Nagar, Chennai - 600 012. Mobile: 09380460419

**Pune** : First Floor, "Laksha" Apartment, No. 527, Mehunpura, Shaniwar Peth (Near Prabhat Theatre), Pune - 411 030.
Phone: 020-24496323, 24496333; Mobile: 09370579333

**Lucknow** : House No. 731, Shekhupura Colony, Near B.D. Convent School, Aliganj, Lucknow - 226 022.
Phone: 0522-4012353; Mobile: 09307501549

**Ahmedabad** : 114, "SHAIL", 1st Floor, Opp. Madhu Sudan House, C.G. Road, Navrang Pura, Ahmedabad - 380 009.
Phone: 079-26560126; Mobile: 09377088847

**Ernakulam** : 39/176 (New No. 60/251), 1st Floor, Karikkamuri Road, Ernakulam, Kochi - 682011.
Phone: 0484-2378012, 2378016; Mobile: 09387122121

**Bhubaneswar** : 5 Station Square, Bhubaneswar - 751 001 (Odisha).
Phone: 0674-2532129; Mobile: 09338746007

**Kolkata** : 108/4, Beliaghata Main Road, Near ID Hospital, Opp. SBI Bank, Kolkata - 700 010. Phone: 033-32449649; Mobile:07439040301

Printed at : M/s Sri Sai Art Printer, Hyderabad. On behalf of HPH.

# PREFACE

Indian Financial system has undergone a tremendous change in recent years. The entry of large number of private sector banks (both Indian and foreign) with advanced technology have created great element of competition which has paved the way for innovations in the banking sector. The new market oriented trend in the Indian Banking system has a multiplier effect on the economy.

We have discussed the latest techniques in banking services like e - banking and also the banker and customer relationship in detail. The topics have been arranged as per the latest syllabus of the University of Madras to facilitate easy reference. Every effort has been made to bring out this book in a simple language to cater to the needs of students belonging to urban and rural areas.

We take the opportunity to express our thanks and gratitude to Ms. N. Meenakshi, S.Geetanjali Jindger, Ms.K.Malarvizhi and Mr.P. Gopalakrishnan who have helped us in revising this book.

We are thankful to Messers Himalaya Publishers for publishing this book.

**Dr.K.Nirmala Prasad**
**Prof. J. Chandradass**

# SYLLABUS OF MADRAS UNIVERSITY BANKING THEORY, LAW AND PRACTICE

**UNIT I**

Origin of banks—Banking Regulation Act, 1949 (Definition of Banking, Licensing, Opening of branches Functions of Banks Inspection)—Role of Banks and Economic development—Central Banking and Role of RBI and their functions.

**UNIT II**

Commercial Banks—Functions—Accepting Deposits—Lending of funds, E-Banking—ATM Cards, Debit cards, Personal Identification Number—Online enquiry and update facility—Electronic Fund Transfer—Electronic Clearing System.

**UNIT III**

Opening of an Account—Types of Deposit Account—Types of customers (Individuals, firms, Trusts, and Companies)—Importance of customer relations—Customer grievances and redressal—Ombudsman

**UNIT IV**

Principles of lending—Types of Borrowings—Precautions to be taken by a banker.

**UNIT V**

Negotiable Instruments—Promissory Note—Bills of Exchange -, cheque, Draft—Definitions, Features—Crossing—Endorsement—Material Alteration—Paying Banker- Rights and Duties—Statutory protection—Dishonour of cheques—Role of collecting Banker.

# CONTENTS

# 1

# ORIGIN AND KINDS OF BANK

The word "Bank" is derived from the word "Bancus or Banque", that is bench. Jews, who were considered to be the early bankers, transacted their business on benches in the market. Some people trace the origin of the word "Bank" from the German word "back" meaning a joint Stock Fund. This seems to be a better derivation.

## Early History of Banking

According to history, Babylonians had developed a Banking system. The great temples were powerful of the Greek Banking Institutions. In ancient Greece and Rome, the practice of granting credit was widely prevalent. People used cheques and drafts to settle their accounts.

During the early periods, although banking business was mostly done by private individuals, many countries established private banks. A public bank was established in Barcelona in 1941. During 1407, the Bank of Genoa was established. The Bank of Amsterdam was established in 1609 to meet the needs of the merchants of the city. It accepted deposit which could be drawn on demand.

English Banking may correctly be attributed to the London gold smiths. They received their customer's valuables and funds for safe custody and issued receipts. These notes, in course of time, became payable to bearer on demand and hence enjoyed considerable circulation. However, in the course of time, gold smiths were ruined. This led to the growth of private banking and establishment of "Bank of England" in 1694.

In India, banking existed even during Vedic period. Manu, the ancient Hindu law giver, has written exhaustive regulations governing credit. He talks about credit installments, interest on loans and commercial papers. The books of Manu contain references regarding deposits, pledges, and policy of loans and rate of interest.

Although, the business of banking is old, Banking Institutions have since changed in character and content.

Banks play an important role in the economic development of the country. The entire commercial and industrial activities are well knit with the banks. One cannot imagine the cessation of the banking activities even for a day. There will be an economic crisis in the country if the banks stop functioning for some days.

In the early days, the banking business was confined to receiving of deposits and lending of money. But the modern bankers undertake wide variety of functions to assist their customers. In countries like United Kingdom, Banking development preceded industrial development and in United States of America, the Banking development followed the industrial development. But in many other countries including India, the development has almost been simultaneous. The peculiarity of Indian Banking is that the banks were started, funded and managed by industrialists to enable them get adequate finance for their businesses or industries. We can see a direct relationship between banks and the business houses. The Tata group was associated with Central Bank of India, House of Birla with United Commercial Bank and similarly Rajahs of Chettinad with Indian Bank etc.

Most of the traditional bankers were interested in developing their industries and business units. So there has been an organised development in such banking activities. Such banks were concentrating in the urban areas. The vast majority of the rural population was governed only by unorganised group of bankers like indigenous banks and moneylenders. It would be easier to classify the banks on the basis of their functions:

(1) Central Bank.
(2) Commercial Banks.
(3) Co-operative Banks.
(4) Industrial Banks.
(5) Development Banks.
(6) Exchange Banks.
(7) Agricultural Banks.
(8) Indigenous Banks.
(9) Regional Rural Banks.

## CENTRAL BANK

The Central Bank of a country is that institution which is vested with certain prerogative powers by an Act of Parliament to regulate the monetary system in the country. It occupies a central position in the monetary and banking structure of the country. It acts as the leader of the money market in supervising, controlling and regulating the activities of all commercial banks and other financial institutions. Central Banking has become an entirely separate branch of banking as it is distinct from the functions of other banks. It is very difficult to give an accurate definition of Central Bank, as the functions performed by the Central Bank are multifarious. Many authors have tried to define a Central Bank briefly; but these definitions are not widely accepted as every author has emphasised one function or the other. The main functions of a Central Bank are broadly the same all over the world. M.H. Dekock's definition of Central Bank, although it is too long, is widely accepted as he brings in all the important functions of the Central Bank. According to him, a central bank is a bank which constitute the apex of the monetary and banking structure of its country and performs as best as it can in the national economic interest.

The following are the functions of the Central Bank :

(1) The regulation of currency in accordance with the requirements of business and the general public, for which purpose it is granted either the sole right of note issue or at least a partial monopoly thereof;

(2) The performance of general banking and agency services for the State;

(3) The custody of the cash reserves of the commercial banks;

(4) The custody and management of the nation's reserves of the international currency;

(5) The granting of accommodation in the form of rediscounts or collatera. advances to commercial banks, bill brokers and dealers, or other financial institutions, and the general acceptance of the responsibility of lender of the last resort;

(6) The settlement of clearance balances between the banks; and

(7) The control of credit in accordance with the needs of business and with a view to carry the broad monetary policy adopted by the State.

Historically, all the central banks were originally started as privately owned and privately managed joint-stock banks. But gradually they have become the Government organisations and their main objective is to support the economic policy of the Government.

### Objectives and Functions

*(a)* The objectives of the Central Bank are to control the banking system without making profit and to support the economic policy of the Government. The scope and content of policy may vary from country to country and from period to period depending on the stage of development, the structure of the economy and the goals to which the Government is committed. *(b)* The central bank is vested with certain prerogative powers to control and regulate the working of commercial banking system. It acts as government machinery and co-ordinates with other government departments, particularly with the Department of Finance and Treasury. The central bank is managed by the Government officials or those closely connected with the Government. *(c)* The central bank has the sole right of issuing currency notes. *(d)* It also acts as a banker to the commercial banks and to some financial institutions including state co-operative banks. *(e)* The central bank is the custodian of cash reserves. *(f)* The bank is empowered with the power of controlling the credit, using measures like bank rate, open market operations and extensive and selective credit methods. *(g)* One of the important functions of the central bank is to conduct the banking and financial operations of the Government. *(h)* In addition to this, the banks should maintain the exchange value of a rupee. *(i)* It acts as an agent of the Government in respect of India's membership of the International Monetary Fund.

The functions of the Central Bank are slowly widening. The Bank is performing a variety of developmental and promotional functions, which were unheard in the past.

## COMMERCIAL BANKS

As the name indicates, the primary objective of the commercial banks is to earn profit. A commercial bank receives money from the depositors and lends it to trade, industry and commerce. When the bank borrows money from the depositors through various deposit schemes, it allows interest on such deposits. Similarly, when the banker lends money to the industry or business by way of overdraft, cash credit, loans and advances or by any other means, he charges interest on such borrowings. The difference between the lending rate and the borrowing rate is his profit. The interest rates are governed by the Reserve Bank of India.

The commercial banker allows the customer to draw cheques against their credit balances and honours such cheques as and when they are presented in the bank. In addition to the primary function of receiving deposits and lending to others, he undertakes a wide variety of functions to assist their customers by performing agency services and general utility services. *Some of the important agency services performed by the commercial banks are the collection of cheques, bills etc., on behalf of the customer, payments of insurance premium, subscription, rent, etc., on behalf of the customer, purchase and sale of securities, transfer of funds, etc.* The agency functions are carried out by the banker, as they are incidental to his banking transaction with the customer, although they are not statutory functions. The banker charges the customer for the services rendered to him.

Apart from this, the banker provides certain general utility services like safe custody deposit and safe deposit locker facilities; issuing of traveller's cheques, circular notes, gift cheques and credit cards. He acts as a referee by giving information about his customers to third parties. He also gives professional advice to his customers on financial matters.

Now a modern commercial bank is expected to go beyond the conventional banking functions and to take up challenging tasks of achieving economic growth, combined with stability and social justice.

## CO-OPERATIVE BANKS

India is an agricultural country. About 70% of our country's population depends upon agriculture for their livelihood. The Indian farmer is poor, illiterate and heavily indebted. Non-availability of adequate and timely agricultural credit results in low productivity and makes agriculture more capital intensive. As there is no agency to supply credit, farmers are the ready victims of the moneylenders and indigenous bankers who charge exorbitant rates of interest. In order to protect them from the economic evils and moral degeneration, the co-operative movement in India was encouraged.

The co-operative movement in India began with the passing of the Cooperative Credit Societies Act of 1904. The Act provided for the formation of credit societies, emphasising on rural credit. Unlimited liability was the rule in rural societies. These credit societies slowly paved the way in the formation of co-operative banks.

The Co-operative banks are institutions established with principle of co-operation. The objective of such organisations is to facilitate rural credit and to promote thrift and self-help among the economically weaker sections of the society. Like commercial banks the co-operative banks also receive deposits and lend money. But they lend money to their members and make incidental profits, although their sole objective, is not profit earning.

The co-operative banking in India has grown in size and volume. A special feature of co-operative banks in India is its federal structure, the units ranging from primary level to national level. Co-operative Banking in India can be divided into two important areas, namely, agriculture and non-agriculture. The agricultural co-operative banks are primary co-operative banks at the village level, Central co-operative banks at the district level and the State co-operative bank at the state level. The non-agricultural cooperative banks include urban co-operative banks, employee credit cooperative banks and housing co-operative banks.

## INDUSTRIAL BANKS

The economic development of a country depends on the development of its industries. The advanced countries like United Kingdom, United States of America, Japan and Germany are the pioneers in the field of industrial development. Some countries like Japan and Germany started banks exclusively to meet the needs of industries.

The industrial banks provide long-term loans and supply fixed capital to industrial concerns by subscribing to the shares and debentures floated by the companies. As they have financed the share capital, the industrial banks play an important role in the management and administration of the companies. The industrial banks have acted as underwriters in the floatation of new industrial concerns. In addition to this, they also arrange for medium term loans. But in India, we have a number of financial corporations, development corporations and investment corporations acting as industrial development banks.

## DEVELOPMENT BANKS

Development Banking is a new concept to cater to the needs of industrial and agricultural finance in the country. Most developing countries were faced with scarcity of capital. They needed such development banks urgently as the existing financial agencies could not co-ordinate and integrate with the financial requirements. Development banks were established in different underdeveloped countries to suit the social, political and economic environment of each country.

In India, Development Banks were set up to cater to the needs of agriculture and industries. They provide long-term and medium term loans. They also play an important role in promoting investment projects, undertaking project reports and providing technical advice and managerial services. In short, the Development banks play the role of "Finance Corporation" and "Development Corporation". A number of financial corporations and banks have been set up at the central and state level to promote agricultural and industrial development in our country.

## LAND DEVELOPMENT BANKS

India, being an agricultural country, need to develop the agricultural operations. The funds needed by Indian farmers are classified into short-term, medium-term and long-term loans. Short-term loans are needed by them to buy seeds, fodder and to pay wages for the agriculture labourers. Short-term loans are needed for a period of six months. Normally they repay the short-term loan immediately after the harvest. Medium-term loans are needed for buying cattle, agricultural implements and for the reclamation of land. Medium-term loans range from 2 to 5 years. Periodical repayment may be possible. Finally, they require long-term loans to make permanent improvements in the land or even to purchase additional land. These loans are for long periods ranging from 10 to 20 years.

Although the requirement of short and medium-term agricultural loan are met by various agencies including commercial banks, there seems to be no agency for financing long-term loans. Land Development Banks play an important role in financing long-term loans to agriculturists. Previously they were known as Land Mortgage Banks. Land Development Banks are organised primarily on co-operative basis. The banks in the taluk and district levels granting long-term loans for cultivation are known as primary land development banks. Their main objectives are:

*(i)* To grant long-term loans with land as a security.

*(ii)* To get finance from the State Land Development Banks and help the members.

*(iii)* To grant loans for buying tractors, digging wells, constructing fence, repayment of old debts.

*(iv)* To start farms, improving the land for cultivation, construction of fence, etc.

*(v)* To encourage saving habit among the public.

The Land Mortgage Banks raise finance through share capital, reserve fund, and issue of bonds or debentures. The Development Banks issue debentures, which are subscribed by the Co-operative Banks, Commercial Banks, State Bank of India, Reserve Bank of India and the public.

During the early years, when it was known as "Land Mortgage Banks" loans were also granted for redemption of debts. It was stressed that the Land Development Banks should grant loans especially for productive purposes other than liquidating earlier loans. During the recent years, loans for land improvement and cultivation have been actually encouraged.

## EXCHANGE BANKS

Exchange Banks are also commercial banks engaged in the foreign exchange transactions. They also receive deposits and lend money. They build up balances abroad by purchasing claims to foreign currencies. They also sell these proceeds to the importers. They act as businessmen in buying and selling foreign currencies or claims to foreign exchange. In the case of international trade, the exporter draws a foreign bill of exchange which is accepted by the importer's bank. The exporter sells them to the exchange bank. The banker, on the due date, presents the bill at his bank or importer's bank situated in the exporter's country and gets the full value. He may also discount them in the London or New York money market. The Exchange Bank grants direct loans to the exporters or importers. Sometimes instead of discounting the bill, the exchange banks may grant loans to the exporter on the strength of the bill of exchange. The proceeds of the bill are used for settling the loan. The bank may also open a letter of credit in favour of the importer, which enables him to meet his financial needs in foreign currency. In India, some of the commercial banks are the authorised dealers in foreign exchange. State Bank of India and all the foreign banks functioning in India transact foreign exchange business.

## INDIGENOUS BANKS

The indigenous bankers are the earliest bankers in India and are still occupying an important place in the Indian financial system. It is strange to note that some communities have taken up the indigenous banking as a profession. For instance, the Chettiars of Tamil Nadu, Shaukars in Uttar Pradesh, Shroffs and Marwaris in Mumbai, and so on. The indigenous banking is not taken up by most of the South Indians because of the existence of certain traditional stigma attached to this profession. They carry on the banking business combined with trading activities. In fact, the indigenous bankers established perfect monopoly in the field of banking prior to the establishment of modern joint stock commercial banks.

The Indian Central Banking Enquiry Committee has defined an indigenous banker as "an individual or private firm receiving deposits and dealing in hundis or lending money." They distinguish the indigenous bankers from moneylenders. The Central Banking Enquiry Committee presumed that an indigenous banker would accept deposit in addition to his lending business. Nowadays, the indigenous banks do not accept money at all. They rely on their own capital. The indigenous bankers are more popular in urban and semi-urban areas.

The indigenous bankers have formed their associations such as the Shroff's Association in Mumbai, Ahmedabad and Calcutta, the Marwari chamber of commerce, etc. These associations are responsible in uniting most of the indigenous bankers who are working in different parts of the country. They meet periodically and discuss their common problems. However, they do not adopt uniform policy and accounting procedures. There is no co-ordination between the various groups of indigenous bankers. Although attempts were made to bring the indigenous bankers within the ambit of Reserve Bank of

India, still now it is a mirage. The indigenous bankers are not willing to accept the Banking Commission's recommendations such as not to engage themselves in trading activity; to maintain minimum capital; preparation and submission of annual accounts to Reserve Bank of India.

The indigenous bankers have their own code of conduct. They don't follow the Reserve Bank of India's directives and procedures. The indigenous bankers deal with agriculturists and small businessmen. There is no need for the submission of application form in many cases. The indigenous bankers, if satisfied with the borrower and the purpose of the loan, do not hesitate to lend them immediately. But the rate of interest is quite high compared with that of commercial banks. Although the indigenous bankers do not follow the double entry system of book-keeping, their accounts are simple and accurate. Like moneylenders, they are readily accessible. But they lend money on the basis of certain securities.

In spite of large-scale expansion of commercial banks in India, the indigenous banks are still playing a predominant role in the field of agriculture, industry and commerce. It would be good if their activities are regulated by the Reserve Bank of India so that they could develop on the right lines.

## REGIONAL RURAL BANKS

The Regional Rural Banks were set-up by the Government by promulgating an ordinance in September 1975. The Ordinance was replaced by the Regional Rural bank Act, 1976. The Regional Rural Banks were set-up on the recommendations of a working group headed by Mr. Narasimhan. To start with, there were only 5 Regional Rural Banks on October 2, 1975, with an authorised capital of Rs.1 crore each. Every rural bank is expected to cover a population of one crore through 100 branches.

The share capital of the Regional Rural Banks were subscribed by the Central Government, State Government and, the Sponsor bank in the ratio of 50:15:35 respectively. The sponsor bank is a commercial bank. The sponsoring commercial bank provides them with funds, guidance, direction and managerial skill. The Regional Rural Banks raise their resources through : *(a)* Owned capital; *(b)* Deposits from the public; *(c)* Borrowings from sponsor banks; and *(d)* Refinance from NABARD.

The objective of establishing the Regional Rural Banks was to develop the rural economy by developing agriculture, trade, commerce, industry and other productive activities in the rural areas. Apart from this, the Regional Rural Banks are expected to help the small and marginal farmers, agricultural labourers, artisans and small entrepreneurs. The RRB's are managed by the Board of Directors consisting of nominees of the Government of India, State Government and Sponsoring Banks.

In short, the Regional Rural Banks are to act as an alternative agency to provide institutional credit in the rural areas and to replace the moneylenders in course of time. At the same time, the RRBs should supplement the activities of co-operative banks.

## MODEL QUESTIONS

**Section - A**

1. What do you mean by the term 'Bank'?
2. Classify the banks on the basis of their functions.
3. What is the main objective of a central bank of a country?
4. Write about the principle and the objectives of Co-operative banks.
5. Write few lines on Industrial Banks.

**Section - B**

1. Write notes on Indigenous Banker.
2. Why are Development banks established?
3. What are the main objectives of Land Development Banks?
4. Write short notes on Exchange Banks.

**Section - C**

1. Explain the evolution of Banking in India.
2. Explain the classification of banks on the basis of their functions.
3. Define an Indigenous Banker. Point out the role of Indigenous Banks as special lending units in India.

# 2

# THE BANKING REGULATION ACT, 1949

Banks' play a vital role in the economic development of a country. They are distinct from other business units. It is said that a banker is a businessman who deals with other people's money. They collect large sums of working capital from the depositors. Even their paid-up capital is less than 1 % of their current and demand liabilities. Since they are dealing with other's money, they should be regulated without allowing them to abuse such funds. Moreover, the business of banking has been regarded as a public service.

## NEED FOR LEGISLATION

From time to time attempts were made to attract the attention of the Government to enact a comprehensive legislation for protecting the interest of the depositors. There had been instances of misadministration of banks-like: *(i)* combining trading with banking, *(ii)* bad and speculative investments *(iii)* unrestricted loans to the directors or to the industries/businesses in which the directors were interested, *(iv)* injudicious advances, *(v)* utilisation of short-term funds etc. These unfair banking practices combined with dishonest management and inefficiency of the directors paved the way for many bank failures which brought untold agony to the depositors, particularly to the retired personnel, middle-class wage earners, small businessmen etc. Such sporadic bank failures necessitated the enactment of a separate banking legislation. The Government appointed a Central Banking Enquiry Committee in 1929 to study the functions of the banks with a view to protect the interest of the depositors. The recommendations of the Central Banking Enquiry Committee was mainly concerned with the organisation, management, audit and liquidation of the banks.

### The Indian Companies (Amendment) Act, 1936

The Central Banking Enquiry Committee felt that the provisions of the Companies Act governing banking companies were inadequate and recommended for the enactment of a comprehensive legislation. However, the foreign experts who were also the members of the committee favoured an amendment of the Indian Companies Act for the incorporation of their recommendations. As such the law relating to banking companies was first enacted as Part X A of the Indian Companies Act with an amendment in 1936. Prior to this amendment, the banks were governed by the Indian Companies Act, 1913.

Some of the important provisions of the Indian Companies (Amendment) Act, 1936 (relating to banking) are:

(1) Definition of a banking company.

(2) Prohibition of banking companies from carrying on businesses other than specified in the definition.

(3) Provision for a minimum paid-up capital (Rs. 5 lakhs).

(4) Restriction on Managing Agency System.

(5) Provision for the maintenance of reserve fund and cash reserve by non-scheduled banks.

(6) Prohibition of charge on unpaid capital.

(7) Provision for the grant of moratorium by the court to a bank in temporary difficulties.

Although there were amendments in the Indian Companies Act, considerable difficulties were experienced by the administrators. Even the registrar of companies experienced difficulty in identifying a banking company as there was ample scope for ambiguity. A number of banking and finance companies claimed that they were banking companies within the scope of the definition given in the Companies (Amendment) Act, 1936.

Some of the bank failures, particularly the failure of the Travancore National and Quilon Bank Ltd. in 1938 created public awareness for enabling a comprehensive legislation. Finally in 1939, the Central Board of Directors of Reserve Bank of India submitted their draft proposal to the Government of India for separate bank legislation. In the mean time the Government agreed to take certain interim measures to reinforce the administration of the banking companies and amended the Act in 1942. According to this amendment, any company which used as part of its name the word 'bank', 'banker' or 'banking' would be deemed to be a banking company whether they accepted deposits or not. This became easier to identify/classify a banking company.

The Indian Companies Act was again amended in 1944, which contained the following important provisions:

(1) No banking company incorporated on or after 1st Jan. 1937 could carry on business unless its subscribed capital was not less than half of the authorised capital and the paid-up capital not less than half the subscribed capital.

(2) The voting rights of all shareholders shall be proportionate to the shares held by them depending upon the paid-up capital of the company.

### Post-war Period

During the post-war period there was an increase in the number of bank offices and bank deposits. It was felt that adequate care was to be taken to keep away undesirable forces from exploiting the situation. Therefore, the earlier bill submitted by the RBI was revised and resubmitted. The Government, however, scrutinised the bill and introduced it in the Legislative Assembly in 1944. However, the bill could not be passed due to the impending elections, and the consequent failure to extend the term of the Assembly beyond lst Oct. 1945.

However, after the formation of the new Assembly in 1945, the new Banking Companies Act, 1945 was introduced based on 1944 bill, with several modifications. However, the priority for the Government was to check the mushrooming expansion of branches in a few cities. For controlling this, the Government passed another Act known as the Banking Companies (Restriction of Branches) Act, 1956. As per this amendment, any bank which intends to open a new office/branch or change of location should get prior permission from the RBI.

### The Banking Companies Act, 1949

The long awaited comprehensive banking bill was introduced on March 1948. This historical bill was passed and came into effect from March 1949. Some of the important provisions of this Act are as follows:

## IMPORTANT PROVISIONS

### Definition of Banking

The term 'Banking' or 'Banker' was not defined by any statute until the passing of the Indian Companies Act, 1936. Even the definition given in the Negotiable Instruments Act, 1881 was not satisfactory. According to Section 3 of the Negotiable Instruments Act, 1881, the term 'Banker' includes a person acting as a banker. This definition is a mere tautology saying the same thing in different ways without making one's meaning clearer or more forceful.

According to Section 5(c) of the banking Regulation Act, 1979,'Banking Company' means "any company which transacts the business of banking in India." Section 5(b) defines the word 'banking' as "the accepting, for the purpose of lending or investment, of deposits of money from the public, repayable on demand or otherwise and withdrawable by cheque, draft, order or otherwise." The above definitions reveal certain special characteristics:

(1) A banker should accept deposits from the public with a view to lend them to others or to invest;

(2) He should return the money to the depositors on demand or after some time, as per the agreement;

(3) He should allow them to withdraw their money by cheque, draft or order. The banker, by himself, will not return the money to the depositors. This means that the depositor should demand payment as per the withdrawal procedure even, in the case of fixed deposits.

(4) The explanation of Section 5(c) of Banking Regulation Act states that any company which is engaged in the manufacture of goods or carries on any trade and which accepts deposits of money from the public merely for the purpose of financing in business as such manufacturer or trader shall not be deemed to transact the business of banking.

(5) In the same way, any one who carries on the business of lending alone cannot be termed as 'Banker.'

Mere power of granting loan does not make a company a 'banking company'. Power of receiving money or deposits from customers and honouring their cheques is an essential character of banking. *(Mahalaxmi Bank Ltd. Vs. Registrar of Companies, AIR 1961 Cal. 666).*

Another important character of the banking business is that no firm, individual or group of individuals can run a banking business. According to Section 7 (2).* No company other than a banking company shall use as part of its name, any of the words 'bank' 'banker' or 'banking' and no company shall carry on the business of banking in India unless it uses as part of its name atleast one of such words.

In case of change in the name of any banking company, the Central Government's approval is necessary. The Central Government shall not give the approval to the change in name of any banking company unless the Reserve Bank of India certifies in writing that it has no objection to such change.

* The business of banking can be undertaken by a company registered under the Indian Companies Act, 1956 or a co-operative bank or a foreign bank registered outside India or a Government sponsored bank.

## Forms of Business in which Banking Companies may engage

Section 6 gives an exhaustive list of businesses undertaken by a banking company. In addition to the banking business a banking company may undertake one or more of the following functions :

### Main Functions

1. The borrowing, raising or taking of money;
2. The lending or advancing of money either upon security or without security;
3. The drawing, making, accepting, discounting, buying, selling, collecting and dealing in bills of exchange, hundis, promissory notes, coupons, drafts, bill of lading, railway receipts, warrants, debentures, certificates, scrips and other instrument and securities whether transferable or not;
4. The granting and issuing of letters of credit, traveller's cheque and circular notes;
5. The buying, selling and dealing in bullion and specie (money in the form of coins);
6. The buying and selling of foreign exchange including foreign bank note
7. The acquiring, holding, issuing on commission, underwriting and dealing in stock, funds, shares, debentures, debenture stock, obligations, securities and investments of all kinds;
8. The purchasing and selling of bonds, scrips and other forms of securities on behalf of constituents or others;
9. The negotiating of loans and advances;
10. The receiving of all kinds of bonds, scrips or valuables on deposits or for safe custody or otherwise;
11. The providing of safe deposit vault;
12. The collecting and transmitting of money and securities.

### Miscellaneous Functions

1. Acting as agents for any Government or Local Authority or any other person or persons;
2. Carrying on of agency business of any description including the clearing and forwarding of goods, giving of receipts and discharges and otherwise acting as an attorney on behalf of customers but excluding the business of a managing agent or secretary and treasurer;

3. Contracting for public and private loans and negotiating and issuance of the same;
4. Effecting, insuring, guaranteeing, underwriting, participating in, managing and carrying out any issue of State, Municipal or other loans or shares, stocks, debentures of companies and may lend money for the purpose of any such issue;
5. Carrying on and transacting every kind of guarantee and indemnity business;
6. Managing, selling and realising any property, which may come into their possession in satisfaction of any of their claims;
7. Acquiring, holding and dealing with any property on any right, title or interest in any such property which may form the security for any loan or advance;
8. Undertaking the administration of estates as executor, trustee or otherwise;
9. Undertaking and executing trusts;
10. Establishing, supporting or aiding in the establishment and support of associations, institutions, funds, trusts calculated to benefit employees or ex-.employees of the company or the dependents or connections of such persons;
11. Granting pensions and allowances and making payment towards insurance;
12. Subscribing for guaranteeing money for charitable or benevolent objects or for any exhibition or for any public or general or useful object;
13. Acquiring, constructing and maintaining any building for its own purpose;
14. Selling, improving, managing, developing, exchanging, leasing, mortgaging, disposing of or turning into account or otherwise dealing with all or any part of the property and rights of the company.
15. Acquiring and undertaking the whole or any part of the business of any person or company when such business is of a nature described in Section 6.
16. Doing all such things which are incidental or conducive to the promotion or advancement of the business of the company or any other business specified by the Central Government as the lawful business of a banking company.

## Prohibition of Trading

Section 8 prohibits a banking company from trading activities like buying or selling or exchanging of goods except in connection with the realisation of security given to or held by it. In this context 'goods' means any kind of movable property, other than actionable claims, stocks, share, money, bullion and specie and all instruments referred to in clause *(a)* of subsection *(i)* of Section 6. However, a banking company may buy or sell or barter for others in connection with:

(1) Bill of exchange received for collection or negotiation; and

(2) Undertaking the administration of estates as executors, trustee etc.

Section 9 deals with disposal of non-banking asset. A banker is restricted from holding any immovable property except for his own use. He might also possess certain immovable property during the course of his business. If so, such assets should be disposed off within seven years. However, the RBI may extend the term for another five years if it is satisfied that such extension would be in the interest of the depositors.

## Minimum Capital

One should not be carried away by an impressive figure of authorised or issued capital. The paid-up capital and reserves are the real capital in any business. The minimum capital for any bank incorporated in India after the commencement of this Act is Rs. 5 lakhs. However, this provision does not apply to banks, which were incorporated prior to 1962. If no minimum capital is prescribed for a banking company, a large number of banking companies may spring up without adequate financial backing, leading to easy liquidation, which would ultimately affect the stability of the economy of the country.

There are two advantages of having larger amount of paid-up capital and reserves. First of all, directors should take adequate care in dealing with funds as their own funds are in stake. Secondly, the paid-up capital would act as additional security for the depositors in addition to the guarantee given by the Deposit Insurance Credit Guarantee Corporation (DICGC).

Section 11 states about the minimum paid-up capital and reserves of a banking company. The Act has clearly fixed the minimum capital on the basis of incorporation and territorial area of operation as indicated below:

| **Banks Incorporated in India** | *Rs.* |
|---|---|
| 1. If it has places of business in more than one state. | 5 lakhs |
| 2. If it has any such place or places of business situated in Mumbai, Calcutta or both. | 10 lakhs |

3. If it has all its places of business in one state none of which is situated in the city of Mumbai or Calcutta in respect of :

| | |
|---|---|
| *(a)* its principal place of business | 1 lakh Plus |
| *(b)* in respect of each of its other place of business situated in the district of its principal place of business | 10,000 Plus |
| *(c)* in respect of each place of business situated elsewhere in the state outside the same district | 25,000 |
| Subject to a total of | 5 Lakhs |
| *(d)* if it has only one place of business | 50,000 |
| *(e)* if it has all its places of business in one state or one or more of which is or are situated in the city of Bombay or Calcutta | 5 lakhs plus |
| *(f)* In addition to the above, in respect of each place of business situated outside the city of Mumbai or Calcutta as the case may be | 25,000 |
| Subject to a total of | 10 Lakhs |

The above provisions are applicable to those banks, which were established before 1962. The Banking Companies Amendment Act, 1962 raised the minimum amount of the paid-up capital to Rs. 5 lakhs for any Indian bank after the commencement of the Act. The "value" in this connection, means the real or exchangeable value or networth of the business (Assets outside Liabilities) and not the nominal value which may be shown in the books of the banking company (Section 11(5) (b)). In case of any dispute in computing the minimum capital and reserves, the RBI's assessment is final.

*Foreign Banks :* Banks incorporated outside India (Foreign Companies) have the following capital structure :

(1) MinimumCapitalRs.15 Lakhs.

(2) If it has a place of business in the city of Mumbai or Calcutta Rs. 20 Lakhs.

An amount equal to the minimum capital either in cash or in the form of unencumbered approved securities should be deposited with the Reserve Bank of India. A foreign bank should also deposit each year with RBI 20% of its profits in respect of all businesses transacted through its branches in India. The Central Government may, on the recommendation of the RBI and the adequacy of the amount already deposited with it in relation to its deposit liabilities, exempt any foreign company from the above provision of depositing profits. Recently the RBI has given new guidelines for starting new private banks.

## Regulation of Capital

Section 12 brings the relationship between the authorised, subscribed and paid-up capital of a banking company. Accordingly, the subscribed capital should not be less than one-half of the authorised capital and the paid-up capital should not be less than one-half of the subscribed capital.

The capital of the company consists of ordinary shares only or ordinary shares and preference shares issued at par prior to 15th January 1944. This means the preference share issued after 1944 cannot be taken into consideration for the purpose of computing minimum capital of a banking company.

## Licensing of Banking Companies

Every banking company should obtain a license issued on its behalf by the RBI before commencing its banking business.

The RBI will issue the license if it is satisfied with the following conditions:

*(a)* A company is or will be in a position to pay its present or future depositors in full as their claims accrue.

*(b)* The affairs of the company are not being, or are not likely to be, conducted in a manner detrimental to the interests of the present or future depositors.

*(c)* The general character of the proposed management of the company will not be prejudicial to the public interest or the interest of its depositors.

*(d)* The company has adequate capital structure and earning prospects.

*(e)* The public interest will be served by the grant of a license to the company to carry on banking business in India.

*(f)* Having regard to the banking facilities available in the proposed principal area of operations of the company, the potential scope for expansion of banks already in existence in the area and other relevant factors, the grant of the license would not be prejudicial to the operation and consolidation of the banking system consistent with monetary stability and economic growth.

*(g)* Any other condition, the fulfillment of which would, in the opinion of the Reserve Bank, be necessary to ensure that the carrying on the banking business in India by the company will not be prejudicial to the public interest or the interest of the depositors.

*(h)* The RBI should also be satisfied that - *(i)* The Company would carry on the banking business in the public interest. *(ii)* The Government or law of the country does not discriminate the banking company in any way; and *(iii)* The Company would comply with all the provisions of the law applicable to banking companies.

## Opening of Branches

Primarily any bank which intends to open a new branch or to transfer the existing place of business in India or outside India should obtain prior permission from RB I (Section 23). But no permission is required for:

(a) A change of location within the same city, town or village (in India or abroad), and

(b) Opening of temporary place of business within a city for a maximum period of one month for providing banking facilities on the occasion of an exhibition, a conference or a mela or any other like occasion.

Before granting any permission to open branches or transfer of a branch, the RBI should be satisfied with the financial condition and history of the company, the general character of its management, the adequacy of its capital structure, its earning prospects and public interest. The RBI may impose certain conditions to any particular bank.

If any banking company fails to comply with any of the conditions imposed on it, the RBI, by an order in writing and after affording reasonable opportunity to the banking company for showing cause against the action proposed to be taken against it, revoke any permission granted to it earlier.

## Statutory Liquidity Ratio and Cash Reserves

Deposits from public constitute a major demand liability for a banking company. In order to inspire public confidence and to meet their demands, it is absolutely necessary to maintain a reasonable liquid position. According to Section 24, every banking company shall maintain gold or unencumbered approved securities, valued at a price not exceeding the current market price, an amount which shall not, at the close of business on any day be less than 20% of the total of the demand and time liabilities.

In addition to the statutory liquidity ratio, (as per Section 42 of the RBI Act) every schedule bank should maintain cash reserve ratio with RBI at an average minimum daily balance of the total demand liabilities. The RBI, after notification in the official gazette, may increase up to a maximum of 15%.

## Submission of BSR and other Returns

1. The Basic Statistical Returns (BSR) showing particulars of a bank's assets maintained in accordance with the provisions and its demand and time liabilities should be submitted to RBI on each alternate Friday during the month. The return should be submitted within 20 days after the end of the month. Besides, the RBI may also require a banking company to submit a return showing these figures on each day of the month.

2. In addition to the above statistical returns, a bank should submit quarterly statement to the RBI regarding the assets and liabilities of the bank in the

prescribed form. It should be noted that the assets owned by a banking company in India should not be less than 75% of its time and demand liabilities in India. 'Liabilities' in this context does not include the paid-up capital and reserves or any credit balance in the profit and loss account of the banking company (Section 26).

3. The commercial banks should also submit a return in the prescribed form to the RBI at the end of the calendar year specifying all accounts in India which have not been operated for a period of 10 years. The banker should submit such returns within 30 days after the close of each calendar year.

4. According to Section 27 (i), every banking company should submit to the RBI a return in the prescribed form and manner showing its assets and liabilities in India at the close of business on the last Friday of every month.

5. The RBI at any time direct a banking company to furnish certain statements and information relating to the business affairs of the banking company as it may consider necessary. The RBI may also call for half-yearly statements regarding its investments, classification of advances in respect of agriculture, industry and commerce (Section 27 (2)).

6. The RBI has the power to publish information obtained by it under the Banking Regulation Act in such consolidated form as it may think fit (Section 28).

## Reserve Bank's Power of Inspection

In order to protect the interest of the depositors, the officers of RBI, at any time, may inspect on the direction of RBI, any banking company and its books and accounts. A copy of such inspection report will be supplied to the banking company. Every director or officer or employee of a banking company should furnish the necessary information or documents to any officer making such inspection. The officer of the RBI is also empowered to examine on oath any director or officer or employee of the banking company in relation to its business.

If the Central Government after scrutinizing the report, is of the opinion that the affairs of the banking company are being conducted to the detriment of the interests of the depositors, it may, after giving reasonable notice and opportunity to make representations, order in writing to:

*(a)* Prohibit the banking company from receiving fresh deposits.

*(b)* Direct the RBI to apply under Section 38 for winding up of the company.

The Central Government may defer, cancel or modify any such order upon such terms and conditions as it may think fit to impose.

## Power of the RBI to Give Directions

The RBI can give directions from time to time to the banking companies :

*(a)* In the public interest;

*(b)* In the interest of banking policy;

*(c)* To prevent the affairs of any banking company being conducted in the manner detrimental to the interest of the depositors or in a manner prejudicial to the interest of a banking company; or

*(d)* To secure the proper management of any banking company generally.

Any person making an inspection may examine any director or other officer or employee of a banking company on oath in relation to its business and may administer an oath accordingly (Section 35).

## Management and Control of Banking Companies.

Every banking company is managed by a Board with not less than 51 % of the directors having special knowledge or practical experience in respect of one or more of the following subjects : *(i)* accountancy; *(ii)* agriculture and rural economy; *(iii)* banking; *(iv)* co-operation; *(v)* economics; *(vi)* finance; *(vii)* law; *(viii)* small-scale industry; *(ix)* any other matter the special knowledge of, and practical experience in, which would, in the opinion of the RBI, be useful to the banking company.

Every banking company may have to hold an annual general meeting to elect its directors. The RBI can also order to call a general meeting of the shareholders of the company after giving two months time to hold elections.

An individual can occupy the position of a director in only one banking company. Section 10(A)(2-A) states that no director of a banking company other than the chairman or whole time director shall hold office continuously for more than eight years. As per Section 10(B) one of the directors of a banking company shall be the Chairman of its Board of directors who shall be entrusted with the management of the whole of the affairs of the banking company. But he shall exercise his powers subject to the superintendence, direction and control of the Board of Directors. The Chairman shall be in the whole time employment and shall hold office for a period of five years only. However, he may be eligible for re-election and re-appointment.

Section 10(B)(8) states that the RBI may permit the Chairman to undertake any part-time honorary work in the public interest if it does not interfere with his duties as such chairman.

If the RBI is of the opinion that any person who has been elected to the position of a chairman of a banking company is not a fit and proper person, it may, after giving reasonable opportunity, require the banking company to elect any other person as Chairman of the Board of Directors. In case a Chairman is removed from his office in the above manner he may, within 30 days from the date of the communication, may appeal to the Central Government. The decision of the Central Government shall be final.

The directors should neither be the proprietors of any trading, commercial or industrial concern (not being a small-scale industry) nor have substantial interest or any connection in any capacity with a firm or company, not being a company registered under Section 25 of the Indian Companies Act, 1956.

In case the office of the chairman is vacant, the RBI, if in its opinion finds that the continuation of such vacancy would affect the interest of the banking company, may appoint a person eligible under Section 10(B)(4) as Chairman of the company. As long as he holds office of the Chairman, he continues to be the director of a company. The Chairman so appointed by RBI shall be in the whole-time employment of the banking company and shall hold office for a period, not exceeding 3 years. But he is eligible for reappointment. The Chairman-so appointed will draw his pay and allowances from the banking company as determined by the RBI. He may be removed from the office only by the RBI. It is not absolutely essential for such Chairman to hold qualification shares in the banking company.

Section 35(B)(b) points out that no appointment or reappointment or termination of appointment of a chairman or Managing Director, Manager or Chief Executive Officer can be done without the approval of the RBI. As per Section 36(AA), the RBI has the power to remove managerial and other persons from the office in the public interest or for preventing the affairs of the banking company being conducted in a manner detrimental to the interest of the depositors after giving reasonable opportunity of making a representation. However, if the RBI is of the opinion that any delay would be detrimental to the interest of the banking company or its depositors, it may, pending the consideration in such representations made by them, remove them from the office of the chairman, transfer or any executive position. Any one who is removed by such an order may appeal to the Central Government within 30 days from the date of communication of such order (Section 36AA(3)). If vacancies arise in the above manner the RBI may appoint a suitable person in the place of removed personnel for a period not exceeding 3 years. They hold office during the pleasure of RBI. They do not incur any obligation or liability if they continue to execute their work in good faith.

Every chairman of a banking company should have special knowledge and practical experience of the working of a banking company or of the State Bank of India or any subsidiary bank or a financial institution or financial, economic or business administration.

As per Section 36(AB), the RBI is empowered to appoint additional directors in the interest of the banking policy or in the public interest or in the interest of the banking company or its depositors. The RBI may appoint one or more persons as additional directors of the banking company.

Section 10 prohibits the employment of certain persons to managerial and administrative positions of a banking company.

They are:

*(a)* Persons who have been adjudicated insolvents or have suspended payment or have compounded with their creditors or have been convicted by a criminal court of an offence involving moral turpitude;

*(b)* Persons who take their remuneration in the form of a commission or of share in the profits of the company;

*(c)* Managing agents;

*(d)* Persons whose remuneration is excessive in the opinion of the RBI.

According to Section 10(B), a person shall be disqualified for being a chairman of a banking company, if he :

*(i)* Is a director in any other company; or

*(ii)* Is a partner of any firm which carries on any trade, business or industry; or

*(iii)* Has substantial interest in any other company or firm;or

*(iv)* a director, manager, managing agent, partner or proprietor of any trading, commercial or industrial concern; or trading, commercial or industrial concern; or

*(v)* Is engaged in any other business or vocation.

A person is deemed to be holding substantial interest if he holds share of a company with the paid-up capital exceeding Rs. 5 lakhs or 10% paid up capital of the company whichever is less or having beneficial interest in a firm owning more than 10% of the total capital subscribed by all partners.

*Voting Rights* : Section 12(2) places restrictions on the concentration of power in the hands of few individuals. Accordingly, no individual shareholder in a banking company can exercise voting rights in excess of 1% of the total voting rights of shareholders of the banking company.

Every chairman, Managing director or chief executive officer shall Furnish to the RBI particulars relating to the extent and value of his holding of shares whether directly or indirectly in a banking company [Section 12(4)).

## INSPECTION

Section 35 empowers RBI to inspect any banking company on the directions of the Central Government. The RBI can send one or more of its officers to examine the books and accounts of the banking companies. On completion of such examination, the RBI will send a copy of its Inspection Report to the respective banking company.

The RBI, at any time, can send its officers to scrutiny the affairs of any banking company and its books and accounts. If the banking company makes a request or if any adverse action is contemplated against the banking company on the basis of the scrutiny, a copy of such scrutiny report will be sent to the banking company.

Section 35 (2) directs every director or officer of the banking company to produce all the books and documents in his custody to any RBI officer who is making such inspection. The directors or officers of the banking company should furnish any statement and information relating to the affairs of the banking company with in the time specified by the officer or officers of the RBI.

Moreover, the person making the inspection may examine on oath any director or officer of a banking company in relation to its business. If the Central Government has directed the RBI to inspect or scrutiny the accounts and documents and to inquire into the affairs of the banking company and if the scrutiny report is detrimental to the interest of the depositors, the Central Government, after giving such opportunity to the banking company to make a representation in connection with the report, can

*(a)* prohibit a banking company from receiving such fresh deposits

*(b)* direct the RBI to arrange for the winding up of the banking company under Section 38.

The Central Government may also publish the scrutiny report submitted by the RBI, after giving reasonable notice to the banking company. Finally, RBI can dispose off the application for license after considering the defects revealed in an Inspection Report under Section 35.

## Restrictions on Advances

One of the main criticisms levelled against the directors was granting of large loans to themselves or to the industries/businesses in which they were interested. In order to curb these activities and to eliminate preferential treatment, Section 20 was introduced. Accordingly, a banking company is prevented from:

*(i)* Granting any loans or advances on the security of its own shares; or

*(ii)* Entering into any agreement for granting loans and advances to or on behalf f of any of its directors, any firm in which the directors are interested in or any company (not being a subsidiary of the banking company or a company registered under Section 25 of the Indian

Companies Act, 1956 or a Government company) of which any of the directors of the banking company is a director, employee or guarantor or in which he holds substantial interest; or

*(iii)* Any individual in respect of whom any of its directors is a partner or guarantor.

RBI may also give direction to the commercial banks from time-to-time on matters relating to:

*(i)* Purposes of loans;

*(ii)* Margin to be maintained in respect of secured advances;

*(iii)* Maximum amount of loans overdraft and advances on securities or guarantees.

*(iv)* Rate of interest.

## Restriction on Payment of Dividends

In order to show an impressive picture of the company and to keep the shareholders in good humour, some of the companies were declaring exorbitant dividends without making the necessary provisions. To check such practices in the banking company the following restrictions have been imposed as per Section 15.

1. No banking company can pay any dividend on its shares unless it has completely written off all its capitalised expenses including preliminary expenses, organisation expense, share selling, commission, brokerage, amounts of losses incurred and any other item of expenditure not represented by tangible assets.

However, a banking, company may pay dividends on its shares without writing off.

*(i)* the depreciation in the value of its investments in approved securities in any case where such depreciation has not actually been capitalised or otherwise accounted for a loss;

*(ii)* the depreciation in the value of its investments in shares, debentures or bonds (other than approved securities) in any case where adequate provision of such depreciation has been made to the satisfaction of the auditor of the breaking company;

*(iii)* the bad debts, if any, in any case where adequate provision of such bad debts has been made to the satisfaction of the auditor of the banking company.

## Reserve Fund

In the normal practice every joint stock company, in order to meet the future contingencies would transfer a portion of' its profits to the Reserve Fund. A banking company is not an exception. Section 17 compels every banking company to transfer a minimum of 20% out of the balance profit of each year as disclosed in the profit and loss account before declaring dividends to the shareholders unless it is exempted by the Central Government. The Central Government, on the recommendation of the RBI, may exempt a banking company in this regard. The RBI would recommend for such exemption only when the amount in the Reserve Fund and the share premium account is equal to the paid-up capital and reserve in relation to the deposit liabilities of the banking company.

The reserve contemplated by Banking Companies Act is a separate reserve. The amount transferred to that reserve can not be utilised for business purposes. Transfer of a portion of profit of the company to its reserve should be allowed before considering the smallness or otherwise of net profit available for distribution as dividends. *(UniversalBank of India Ltd. Vs. C.I.T. 1967).* Till the reserve equals the paid-up capital, it cannot be said to be available for any other purpose. *(Indian Overseas Bank India Ltd.Vs.C.I.T).*.

## Accounts and Audit

At the end of each calendar year, every banking company should prepare a Profit and Loss Account and Balance Sheet in respect of all businesses transacted by it as on the last working day as per the Forms set out in the Third Schedule or as near thereto. These forms have been designed specially to suit banking companies.

The Balance Sheet and Profit and Loss Account should be signed:

*(i)* In the case of a banking company incorporated in India by the manager or principal officer of the company and atleast by the directors.

*(ii)* In the case of a banking company incorporated outside India by the manager or agent of the principal officer of the company.

The accounts and balance sheet referred above along with the auditor's report shall be published in the prescribed manner and three copies thereof shall be furnished as returns to the RBI within three months from the end of the period. The RBI can extend such period for another three months.

Section 30 provides for the audit of the Balance Sheet and Profit and Loss account in accordance with Section 29 by a duly qualified auditor. Every banking company should obtain prior approval from the RBI for appointing, reappointing or removing any auditor of its company. The RBI has been authorised to direct the auditor to audit the accounts of the banking company in relation to any transaction or class of transactions specified in the order.

Section 32 provides for sending three copies of such accounts ad balance sheers along with the auditors report to the registrar of companies.

According to Section 33, every banking company should display a copy of the last audited Balance Sheet and Profit and Loss account in a conspicuous place in its principal office and in every branch office in India. It should keep the copy so displayed until it is replaced by the copy of the subsequent Balance Sheet and Profit and Loss account.

### Production of Confidential Information

Banks deal with the depositors' money. In the interest of the depositors and public certain provisions have been incorporated in the Banking Regulation Act. One of such provisions is spelt out in Section 34A relating to production of documents of confidential nature. No banking company shall be compelled by any authority to make them available any information or books of accounts which according to the banking company, is confidential in nature as it would involve the disclosure of information relating to:

*(a)* Any reserves not shown as such in its published balance sheets.

*(b)* Any particulars not shown there in respect of provisions made for bad and doubtful debts and other usual or necessary provisions.

## NEW GUIDELINES FOR PRIVATE SECTOR BANKS

The RBI has announced detailed Guidelines on 22nd Jan., 1993 for setting up new private sector banks.

As per the new guidelines issued by the RBI, a private bank can be registered as a public limited company under the Companies Act, 1956 and will be issued license under the Banking Regulation Act, 1934 at an appropriate time.

While permitting new players in the banking industry it has set out the following considerations:

- They sub serve the underlying goals of financial sector reforms which are to provide competitive, efficient and low cost financial intermediation services for the society at large;
- They are to be financially viable;
- They should result in upgradation of technology in the banking sector;
- They are to avoid the shortcomings such as unfair pre-emption and concentration of credit monopolisation of economic power and cross holdings with industrial groups which beset the private sector banks prior to nationalisation;
- Freedom of entry in the banking system may have to be managed carefully and judiciously.

Based on these considerations, the RBI has formulated the following guidelines.

Such a bank shall be registered as a public limited company under the Indian Companies Act, 1956;

The RBI may, on merits, grant a license under the Banking Regulation Act, 1949 for such a bank. The bank may also be included in the second schedule of the RBI Act, 1934 at the appropriate time. The decision of the RBI in these matters shall be final.

## Minimum Capital

The bank will be governed by the provisions of the Banking Regulation Act, 1949 in regard to its authorised, subscribed and paid-up capital. The minimum paid-up capital for such a bank shall be Rs. 100 crores. The promoters' contribution for such a bank shall be determined by the RBI and will also be subject to other applicable regulations.

The shares of the bank should be listed on stock exchanges. To avoid concentration of the headquarters of few banks in metropolitan cities and other over banked areas, while granting, a license, preference may be given to those the headquarters of which are proposed to be located in a centre which does not have the headquarter of any other bank.

Voting rights of an individual shareholder shall be governed by the ceiling of ten percent of the total voting rights as stipulated by section 12(2) of the Banking Regulation Act. However, exemption from this ceiling may be granted under Section 53 of the said Act, to public financial institutions

The new bank shall not be allowed to have as a director any person who is a director of any other banking company, or of companies which among themselves are entitled to exercise voting rights in excess of 20 percent total voting rights of all the shareholders of the banking company, as laid down in the Banking Regulation Act, 1949.

The bank will be governed by the provisions of the RBI Act, 1934, the Banking Regulation Act, 1949 and other relevant statutes, in regard to its management set-up, liquidity requirements and the scope of its activities. The directives, instructions, guidelines and advices given by the RBI shall be applicable to such a bank as in the case of other banks. It would be ensured that a new bank would concentrate on core banking activities initially.

## Capital Adequacy

Such a bank shall be subject to prudential norms in respect of banking operations, accounting policies and other policies as are laid down by the RBI. The bank will have to achieve a capital adequacy of eight percent of the risk-weighted assets from the very beginning. Similarly, norms for income recognition, asset-classification and provisioning will also be applicable to i from the beginning. So will be the single borrower and group borrowers exposure limits that will be in force from time to time.

The bank shall have to observe priority sector lending targets as applicable to other domestic banks. However, in recognition of the fact that new entrants may require some time to lend to all categories of the priority sector, some modification in the composition of the priority sector lending may be considered by the RBI for an initial period of three years.

Such a bank will also have to comply with such directions of the RBI as are applicable to existing banks in the matter of export credit. As a facilitation of this it may be issued an authorised dealers license to deal in foreign exchange, when applied for.

A new bank shall not be allowed to set-up subsidiary or mutual fund for at least three years after its establishment. The holding of such a bank in the equity of other companies shall be governed by the existing provisions applicable to other banks, namely, (1) 30percent of the bank's or the investee company's capital funds, whichever is less, as set out under the Banking Regulation Act. 1949; and (2) 1.5 percent of the bank's incremental deposits during a year as per RBI guidelines. The aggregate of such investments in the subsidiaries and mutual fund (if and when set-up) and portfolio investments in other companies shall not exceed 20 per cent of the bank's own paid-up capital and reserves.

In regard to branch opening, it shall be governed by the existing policy that banks are free to open branches at various centres including urban/ metropolitan centres without the prior approval of the RBI once they satisfy the capital adequacy and prudential accounting norms. However, to avoid over-concentration of their branches in metropolitan areas and cities, new bank will required to open rural and semi-urban branches also, as may be laid down by the RBI.

Such a bank shall have to lay down its loan policy within the overall policy guidelines of the RBI. While doing, so, it shall specifically provide prudential norms covering related party transactions.

Such a bank shall make full use of modern infrastructural facilities in office equipment, computer and telecommunications in order to provide customer service. The bank should have a high-powered customer grievances cell to handle customer complaints.

Such other conditions as the RBI may prescribe from time to time.

## Narasimham Committee Report

In August 1991, the Central Government constituted a high-powered committee under the chairmanship of M. Narasimham, former Governor of RBI. The task of this committee was to examine all aspects relating to the structure, organisation and functions and procedures of the financial system and initiate financial sector reforms. The committee submitted its recommendations on 16th November 1991.

While the recommendations briefly touched upon how the Government could compensate the banks more, by reducing the SLR ratios, increasing return on SLR, reducing priority sector advances etc., its main plans were uniform accounting and better capitalisation of banks. The major recommendations of the committee are discussed under the following heads.

## Income Recognition

A Credit facility is treated as a *non-performing asset,* if the interest/ instalment remains 'part due' from a period of four quarters for the year ending March 1993, three quarters for the year ending 1994and two quarters for the year ending March 1995.

Just as plant and machinery form the bulk of the fixed assets owned by manufacturing companies, the loans and advances sanctioned by banks form their major assets. The interest income generated out of three advances minus net expenses, is credited as profit to the Profit and Loss account. But the bank shows these advances as good even when no interest is actually received. The accrued interest is credited to the Profit and Logs account, thus showing profits that never existed. Such advances for which no interest was received is termed to be Non-performing Assets.

An amount under any of the credit facilities is to be treated as past due when it has remained outstanding thirty days beyond the due date. Moreover, if one of the accounts under the new norms is an NPA, all the counts of the borrowers (other than loans with a liability of less than Rs. 23,000) will be treated as NPA'S.

All assets where the borrower's liability is more than Rs. 25,000 should be classified into four broad groups. They include loans, cash credits, overdrafts, and bill purchased/discounted.

1. *Standard Asset:* One, which does not disclose any problem. In other words, it is an advance which is not an NPA as defined earlier.
2. *Sub-standard Asset:* As asset classified as NPA for a period not exceeding two years.
3. *Doubtful Asset: NPA* which remains so far more than two years.
4. *Loss Asset:* An advance which is fully/substantially non recoverable and the security value which is negligible.

## Provisions

1. *Standard Asset*: No provision.
2. *Sub-standardAsset: 10%* of aggregate liability.
3. *Doubtful Assets:*

   *(a) First Year:* Unsecured portion + 20% of secured portion.

   *(b) Second and ThirdYear*:Unsecured portion + 30% of secured portion.

   *(c) Beyond Three Years:* Unsecured portion + 50% of secured/ portion.
4. *Loss Assets: 100%* of the total liabilities.
5. *Assets where borrower's liability is less than Rs. 25,000:* 2.5% of the aggregate liability. The RBI later granted some concessions. Accordingly, for the year ended March 1993, it is enough if the banks make a 100% provision for loss assets (Bad Debts) and not less than 30% of the total provisioning needed in respect of substandard, doubtful and small advances (i.e., with an outstanding balance of Rs. 25,000 or less). However, any gap in the provisioning for the year ended March 1993 should be covered in the next year.

## Capital Adequacy Ratio (CAR)

On the basis of Narasimham Committee recommendations all banks including the foreign banks have to maintain impaired minimum capital funds equivalent to a prescribed ratio on the aggregate of risk weighted assets and other exposure on an ongoing basis.

The RBI has stressed that Indian banks which have branches abroad have to reach a capital adequacy ratio of 8% of the risk weighted assets as early as possible and in any case by March 31, 1994, foreign banks operating in India should achieve this norm by March 31, 1993. Other banks should achieve a capital adequacy norm of 4% by March 31, 1993 and 8% by March 31,1996.

The CAR is calculated as follows :

$$\frac{\text{Total Capital Funds}}{\text{Total Weighted Risk Assets}} \times 100$$

A bank's capital funds are divided into two parts -Tier-I which is also known as core capital, should consist of paid-up capital, statutory reserves, other disclosed free reserves and capital reserves, representing surplus arising out of sale proceeds of assets. From this, investment in subsidiaries, intangible assets, losses in the current period and losses brought forward from previous periods will be deducted.

Tier II capital consist of undisclosed reserves, cumulative perpetual preference shares, revaluation reserves, (typically undervalued assets such as bank premises and marketable securities) general provisions and loss reserves, hybrid debt capital instruments and sub-ordinated debt.

Tier-I capital should not be less than 50% of total capital, the RBI has stipulated.

Most of the recommendations of the Narasimham Committee have been effected by the RBI. Thus, if a bank wishes to lend Rs. 100, it is to bring Rs. 8 as its capital.

In short, the major recommendations of the Narasimham Committee Report are listed as below :

- SLR to be brought down from 38.5% to 25% in a phased manner over a period of five years.
- Interest on SLR and CRR should be increased.
- Priority sector should be redefined and the credit target brought down from 40% to 10%.
- Banks should achieve a capital adequacy ratio of 4% by March 1993. Further banks which have an additional international presence shall achieve a capital adequacy ratio of 8% by March 1996.
- Uniform accounting practices, particularly with regard to income recognition and provisioning for loan losses, should be implemented. Sound practices with regard to valuation of investments should be adopted.

(a) No income should be recognized on NPA.

(b) Assets should be classified into four categories. Viz., standard, substandard, doubtful and loss assets for the purpose of provision in a Specific provision should be made for loss and doubtful assets and general provisions should be made for sub-standard assets.

(c) A three-year period should be allowed for achieving income recognition norms and a four-year period to, achieve provisioning norms.

(d) Provisions made by banks should be allowed as deductions for income tax purposes,

- o Special tribunals should be established to speed up the process of recoveries.
- o An asset reconstruction fund should be established to take over the bad and doubtful debts of banks at a discount.
- o Reconstruction of banks should be made in order to have three or four large banks of international character.
- o Eight to ten national banks and other local and rural banks.

- o Branch licensing, should be abolished and freedom should be given to the banks to open/close branches.
- o Foreign banks should be subjected to the requirements, which are applicable to domestic banks.
- o Greater use of computerisation should be stressed.
- o A banking Supervisory Board should be set-up under the aegis of RBI, but it should function separate from other central banking functions of the prudential norms and regulations rather than excessive control over administrative and other aspects.

## Banking Sector Reforms II

**Narasimham Committee** has made additional recommendations to improve the performance of the banks after its initial recommendations 1992.

The recommendations of the committee to increase the capital adequacy norms from 8% to 10% over a period of time. Based on this, the minimum capital risk assets ratio (CRAR) was increased to 9% from March 31, 2000.

- To bring down the NPA's to 5% and 3% by the year 2OOO and 2OO2 respectively. The banks have been advised to take effective steps for reduction of NPA's and also set up system to reduce the present level of NPA's and also to prevent re-emergence of NPAS.
- Income recognition and provisioning norms on Government guaranteed advances were brought down on par with those of other advances with effect from the financial year 2000-2001. Provisions on existing and old Government guaranteed advances which would consequently become NPAs are to be fully provided for over a period of four years beginning March 31, 1999. Further, provisioning requirements are being introduced for Standard assets with effect from financial year ending March 31, 2000. Foreign Exchange open position will carry 100% risk weight with effect from March 31, 1999. With a view to adopting prudent accounting standards and moving towards 'mark to market' valuation of the investment portfolio, with effect from the year ending March 31$^{st}$ , 2000, banks will have to classify a minimum of 75% of their securities as current investments.

* By March 31, 2001, an asset will be classified as doubtful, if it has remained in the substandard category for 18 months instead of 24 months. Banks have been permitted to achieve the new norm for additional provisioning, in phases, as under: As on March 31,2001: Provisioning of not less than 50% on the assets which have become doubtful on account of the new norm. As on March 3 1, 2002: balance of the provisions not made during the previous year, in addition to the provisions needed as on March 31, 2002.

* Banks should ensure a loan reviews mechanism for larger advances soon after its sanction and continuously monitor and identify the weaknesses in the accounts to take appropriate timely action.
* To revamp the regulatory and supervisory system to conform to Basic Committee's core principles for effective bank supervision finalized in September 1997.
* Improvement in asset quality and avoidance of asset/liability mismatch as also greater capital adequacy for the banks. Banks are advised to introduce effective risk management systems to cover various risks such as credit/market and operational risk on a priority basis. To achieve this banks have been advised by RBI to set up asset liability management practices with effect from April 01, 1999.
* To improve the transmission mechanism of monitory policy and develop further the money and debt markets. it has been decided to develop the repos market with appropriate safeguards. Further institutions like UTI, LIC, IDBI and other Non Bank participants are allowed to access short-term liquidity through monetary policies. Money Market Mutual Funds (MMF) have been allowed to offer 'cheque writing facility' to their investors. To facilitate hedging of interest rates, risks and ensuring orderly development of the derivatives market, guidelines for interest rate swaps and Forward Rate Agreements (FRAS) are being issued by RBI. Recognition of bank wise, as against industry wise, uniform approach to IIRD, technology etc. to keep phase with the economic reform process in other sectors of economy. RBI has already initiated steps to implement a number of measures as highlighted above

## MODEL QUESTIONS

**Section - A**

1. Define Banking.
2. What do you know about the supervisory board of banking companies?
3. What is the recommendations of Narasimham Committee Report-II as regard reducing of NPA?

**Section - B**

1. Explain the need for banking legislation.
2. What are the provisions related to banking in Indian Companies (Amendment) Act, 1936?
3. Explain the provisions of the Banking Regulation Act dealing with (1) Licensing of Banks and (2) Branch expansion.

4. Explain the provisions of the Banking Regulation Act that places restrictions on the payment of dividend.
5. What are the new guidelines for private sector banks as per the Banking Regulation Act?

**Section - C**

1. Explain and evaluate the Narasimham Committee recommendations.
2. Enumerate the functions of a banking company.
3. State the provisions of Banking Regulation Act relating to the Capital Requirements of Banking Company.
4. How is the Bank Balance Sheet prepared as per the audit of Banking Regulation Act?
5. Summarize the provisions in the Banking Regulation Act relating to restrictions on loans and advance.
6. Discuss the provision related to Accounts and Audit of Banking Companies.
7. Discuss in detail the control and management of Banking Companies.
8. What are the main and miscellaneous functions, which can be undertaken by the Banking Company?
9. What are the recent changes in the Banking Legislations?
10. Discuss the Narasimham Committee Report on Banking Sector Reforms II.

# 3

# ROLE OF BANKS IN ECONOMIC DEVELOPMENT

Banking system is the driving force for all economic activities. Banks through their control over the volume of money in circulation influence production, consumption, and distribution. Banks play an active role in the economic progress of a country, as they are the major instruments behind the mobilisation of resources, investment and on the operational efficiency of the various segments of the economy. The significance of the Banking System in the process of Economic Development is as follows.

- Creation and controlling the circulation money
- Promoting infrastructural facilities
- Capital Formation.
- Rural Development.
- Providing long term loans and micro credits
- Entrepreneurial development
- Balancing international trade
- Facilitating with a good medium of exchange (cheque system)
- Assistance to agriculture and SSI
- Acting as a bridge between various sectors.
- Instrument to implement monetary policy
- Catalyst to social change

- Mobilising savings
- Incentive to investment
- Controlling trade cycle

***Creation and controlling the Circulation Money :*** Bank money forms a large part of the total quantity of money supply and forms the easiest means of payment. Banks are popularly known as factories of credit, which in turn facilitates investment and thereby leads to economic progress.

***Promoting Infrastructural Facilities :*** Banks are playing a vital role in developing comprehensive infrastructural facilities including the social, educational, fiscal etc. in the country which is the lifeblood of economic development.

***Mobilising Savings and Capital Formation :*** The capital formation depends upon the mobilisation of savings. The banks nowadays have brought out novel schemes to encourage the habits of thrift. This capital mobilised by the banks is made available for productive purposes, which in turn gives lots of scope for economic development.

***Rural Development :*** India is a land of villages. Banks adopt certain measures to improve rural areas and undertake developmental activities, which in turn, will develop the whole nation.

***Provides* Long-term *Loans* and Micro *Credits* :** Industrial development, which is the indicator for the development of the economy, is made possible by the banks by giving long-term loans to industries. Banks help the small entrepreneurs especially women entrepreneurs by extending Micro Credit (small loans offered with out any collateral security). This will develop the underdeveloped areas and empower women. It is the signal for the economic development of a country.

***Entrepreneurial Development :*** Banks have special schemes for encouraging entrepreneurial skill. This helps the country in various ways like increasing employment opportunities, improving production centres etc.

***Balancing International Trade :*** Banks by helping entrepreneur increase the export surplus and thereby improve the balance of trade of the country. The Banks help the exporters by quickly obtaining money from foreign buyers and also by providing easy credit to the exporters.

***Facilitating with a Good Medium of exchange (Cheque System) :*** The cheque system provided by the banks as a medium of exchange is of great use for all sorts of transactions and helps in the promotion of trade and industry.

***Assistance to Agriculture and SSI :*** Agriculture being the backbone of the economy especially Indian economy has to be developed in all possible ways, and also the small-scale industries which provide a large percentage of employment opportunities and a sizable amount of export surplus. The Banks cater to the financial needs of important sectors of the economy and thereby help develop the nation.

***Acting as a Bridge between Various Sectors :*** Banking system acts as a bridge between various sectors (organised and unorganised) and thereby helps for overall economic development of the country.

***Instrument to Implement the Monetary Policy :*** The monetary policy of every country, which regulates the economy, is possible only with the help of a well-organised banking system.

***Catalyst to Social Change :*** Banks function as catalyst in bringing social change by extending loans to all sections of the people, i.e., weaker sections, artisans, socially backward people etc., which is bringing a balanced economic growth.

***Incentive to Investment :*** Banks encourage the people in investing in all developmental activities like housing development, industrial development, infrastructural development etc. by giving loans through various schemes, which leads to rapid economic development.

***Control the Trade Cycle :*** With the help of the effective banking system the Government can control and regulate the circulation of money and thereby controls the effect of the trade cycle to a certain level.

## MODEL QUESTIONS

**Section - A**

1. What is capital formation?
2. Mention the schemes adopted by banks for entrepreneurs.
3. Write a note on the developmental activities undertaken by banks in rural areas.
4. State the incentives given by banks to investors for developmental activities.
5. Write a note on trade cycle.
6. What is International Trade?

**Section - B**

1. What is mobilisation of capital? Also, explain the noval schemes introduced by banks.

**Section - C**

1. Discuss the significance of banking system in the process of economic development.

Or

Explain the role of banks in the economic development of the country.

4

# CENTRAL BANK

The central bank of a country is an important financial institution which is vested with certain prerogative powers by an Act of Parliament to regulate the monetary system in the country. It acts as the leader of the money market in supervising, controlling and regulating the activities of all commercial banks and other financial institutions. Central bank has become an entirely separate branch of banking, as it is distinct from the functions of other banks. It is very difficult to give an accurate definition of a central bank. Many authors have tried to define a central bank briefly; but these definitions are not widely accepted as every author has emphasised one function or the other. However, the main functions of a central bank are broadly the same all over the world; Dekock's definition of a Central Bank although it is too long, is widely accepted as he brings in all the important functions of a central bank. According to him, a central bank is a bank which constitutes the apex of the monetary and banking structure of its country and which performs, as best as it can in the national economic interest, the following functions:

(1) The regulation of currency in accordance with the requirements of business and the general public, for which purpose it is granted either the sole right of note issue or at least a partial monopoly thereof;

(2) The performance of general banking and agency services for the State;

(3) The custody of cash reserves of the commercial banks;

(4) The custody and management of the nation's reserves of international currency;

(5) The granting of accommodation in the form of rediscounts or collateral advances to commercial banks, bill brokers and dealers, or other financial institutions, and the general acceptance of the responsibility of lender of the last resort;

(6) The settlement of clearance balances between the banks and

(7) The control of credit in accordance with the needs of business and with a view to carrying out the broad monetary policy adopted by the State.

Historically, all central banks were originally started as privately owned and privately managed joint stock banks. But gradually they have become Government organisations and their main objective is to support the economic policy of Government.

## Evolution

Central banking is mostly a recent development though some central banks were established more than two centuries ago. The Risk bank in Sweden was established in the year 1668 followed by the Bank of England in 1694, which was the first bank to assume the position of a central bank, hence being known as the 'Mother of Central Banks.' The Bank of France was established in 1800 and the Bank of Netherlands in 1814 on the ruins of Old Amsterdam. The National Bank of Austria, which was reorganised as the Bank of Austria-Hungary in 1877, was established in 1817. The Bank of Norway (1817), National Bank of Denmark (I 818), National Bank of Belgium (I 850) and Bank of Spain (I 856) were also established to control the money circulation in their countries respectively.

The Federal Reserve System in America was established in 1913 while the Bank of Canada was established in 1934. In the twentieth century also, the work of establishing the central bank continued. By and large, the establishment of a central bank was encouraged in all the countries and the financial conference held at Brussels in 1920 resolved that "all those countries which had not yet established a central bank should proceed to do so as soon as possible, not only with a view to facilitating the restoration and maintenance of stability in their monetary and banking systems but also in the interest of world cooperation."

## Functions of a Central Bank

The central bank performs seven functions, as described by Dekock, in any economy. The functions as visualised by Dekock are thus:

- Bank of Issue
- Banker to Government

- Custody of cash reserves
- Custody of exchange reserves
- Lender of last resort
- Clearing house of banks
- Controller of credit

## 1. Bank of Issue

The central bank has been entrusted with the monopoly of note issue. The design, form and material of bank notes should he approved by the Central Government on the recommendations of the Central Board. There are different method of note issue which is being followed in different countries, such as the fixed fiduciary system, maximum fiduciary system, proportional reserve system and minimum reserve system. There are two departments - issue and banking, in the central bank in respect of note issue. The notes are issued by the issue department on demand by the banking department. Whenever the currency are issued to the banking department, the issue department gets cash reserves against the currency issued.

The following are the main reasons for granting the exclusive monopoly of note issue to the central bank:

*(a)* The bank can expand or contract the supply of money according to the needs of economy.

*(b)* It provides uniformity in note issue.

*(c)* The central bank can exercise control over the functions of other commercial banks as it is the supplier of cash to them.

## 2. Banker, Adviser and Agent to the Government

The second important function of the central bank is to act as a Government banker, agent and advisor. The central bank has the obligation to transact business i.e., to keep the cash balances as deposit free of interest, to receive and to make payments on behalf of the Government, both Central and State and to carry out their exchange remittances, and other banking operations. The central bank helps the Government to float new loans and to manage debt. The central bank also makes ways and means for providing advances to the Government. It makes loans and advances to the State and Local Authorities, besides acting as an advisor to the Government on all the monetary and banking matters. As an advisor, the central bank also gives advice to the Government on important matters of economic policy, like deficit financing, devaluation of currency, trade policy, foreign exchange policy etc.

The financial operations of the Government may have tremendous influence over the money market unless they are properly regulated and controlled. Therefore, there must be a closer co-ordination and co-operation between the Government and the central bank. The central bank is entrusted with the responsibility of maintaining the public debt. It issues loans on behalf of the Central and State Government. It acts as an advisor to the Government on matters pertaining to the financial markets, market conditions, terms of new loans, quantum of loans, timing of the issue of loans etc. The central bank co-ordinates the borrowing programmes of the central and state Governments to avoid any clash or unhealthy competition between them. The policy decisions are taken by the Government and the Central Government is to implement them. In order to take the right decisions, the central bank feeds the Government with necessary financial information and statistical data. The Government also consults the central bank before formulating the monetary policy. The central bank advises the Government on all monetary policies concerning allocation of funds, floatation of loans, banking legislations etc.

According to M.H. Dekock "As the Government's banker, the central bank conducts the banking accounts of Government departments, boards and enterprises; it makes temporary advances to the Government in anticipation of collection of taxes and raising of loans from public and extraordinary advances during depression, war or other emergency, and it carries the Government's transactions involving purchases and sales of foreign currencies. The central banks is also called upon to perform various services as the Government's financial agent, and it acts generally as a financial advisor to the Government."

## 3. Custodian of Cash Reserves

The commercial banks are required to maintain a certain fixed percentage of both time and demand liabilities with the central bank. The central bank, in turn, allocates transfer of funds from one bank to another for the clearance of cheques on the basis of these deposits. Thus, the central bank is not only the custodian of Government funds and wealth, but also the custodian of cash reserves of commercial banks.

The commercial banks should abide by the directives issued by the central bank; in return, they enjoy the benefits of refinance facilities. They can rediscount approved trade and commercial bills with central bank. In case of emergency, they may resort to central bank's help and the central bank will act as the lender of the last resort. If the commercial banks fail to adhere to the central bank's directions, penalties may be levied according to the provisions specified in the Banking Regulation Act including the withdrawal of certain benefits. 'I'he central bank acts not only as a custodian of cash reserves but also as controller of all banks in India. The central bank arranges for the settlement of inter-bank indebtedness through its clearing house. The clearing system reduces the expense, delay and risk involved in collection and clearing of cheques.

## 4. Custodian of Foreign Exchange Reserves

The central bank's function of maintaining the foreign exchange reserves was derived from its function as the bank of issue and custodian of cash reserves. It buys and sells gold and foreign exchange currencies from and to other countries. It also fixes the exchange rates of internal currency to that of international currency. The central bank has the responsibility to maintain the official rate of exchange. It enforces the regulation strictly in accordance with the Foreign Exchange Regulation Act and the International Monetary Fund to maintain the parity value of the rupee. The central bank has a separate "Exchange Control Programme" to supervise and control the source of foreign exchange.

## 5. Lender of Last Resort

The central bank acts as the banker's bank. Every scheduled commercial bank is required to maintain a certain percentage of its total demand and time liabilities with the central bank. This provision has two objectives. First of all, every schedule bank is expected to maintain a certain percentage of cash reserves against deposits so as to protect the interest of the depositors. Secondly, this provision helps to centralise the banking reserves of the country so as to enable the central bank to regulate and control the credit position in the country. The scheduled banks can borrow from the central bank on the basis of eligible securities or get financial accommodation in times of need or stringency by rediscounting their bills of exchange. Since commercial banks can always expect the central bank to come to their help even when all the other banks fail to do so, the central bank becomes not only banker's bank, but also the lender of last resort.

## 6. Clearing House for Transfer and Settlement of Mutual Claims

This function of clearance, settlement and transfer of mutual claims which was evolved as a method of practice, became in due course of time, an accepted normal function of the central bank. The central bank maintains clearing houses in order to set off balances between the credits, and debits of the commercial banks. As the central bank holds the deposits of the commercial banks, it transfers funds from one bank's account to the other and thereby settles the mutual claims. The transfer is made by entries to their accounts on the accounts register. The commercial banks can therefore save their time as well as the money spent on the settlement of mutual claims, through clearing house operations by the central bank.

## 7. Controller of Credit

Credit control refers to the regulation of the lending policy of commercial banks by the central bank in order to achieve integrated growth and development of all the sectors of the economy. "It is the function which embraces the most important question of central banking policy and one through which practically all other functions are united and made to serve a common purpose." (Dekock).

The financial and economic stability of a country is achieved through proper control of the power of credit creation of commercial banks by the central bank to control credit creation: the quantitative method and the qualitative or selective method. The instruments of these two methods are as below:

| Techniques of Quantitative Credit Control | Techniques of Qualitative Credit Control |
|---|---|
| Bank Rate Policy<br>Open Market Operations<br>Variable Reserve Ratio | Regulation of Margin Requirements<br>Regulation of Consumer Credit<br>Rationing of Credit<br>Direct Action<br>Moral suasion<br>Publicity |

## QUANTITATIVE TECHNIQUES

The quantitative method, as the name suggests, aims at controlling the quantity and cost of credit through various methods and on the contrary, the qualitative method aims at the control of direction and use the credit.

### 1. Bank Rate Policy

Bank rate is the official rate at which the central bank of a country is prepared to rediscount the approved bills of exchange or to lend on approved securities. The mechanism is very simple. Increase in bank rates leads to lesser demand for credit and reduced volume of credit which reduces the quantum of credit money, leading to fall in prices. Similarly, decrease in the bank rate leads to easy credit and increase in the price level. The bank rate policy will be successful only if it has decisive influence on the interest rates and credit structure in the country. The central bank changes the bank rate from time to time. In India, the bank rate has generally influenced other market rates including the lending rates of the commercial banks. Thus, a change in the bank rate policy by the central bank brings about a change in the interest rates on the loans to customers by the commercial banks and thus a chain of action and reaction begin. The central bank makes use of the bank rate either to expand or to contract the credit by the commercial banks and thus, it indirectly controls the currency flow in any economy. There are some limitations of this bank rate policy which are as follows:

*(a)* The market rate would follow the same changes in the bank rate and rate of interest by the commercial banks.

(b) The increase or decrease in the bank rate shall affect the employment, wages, prices and output.

(c) The bank rate policy would be effective only if it can influence the decisions of businessmen, the course of changes in the employment, wages etc., the market rate of interest would follow the rise or fall in the bank rate which is not possible practically.

## 2. Open Market Operations

"Open market Operations may be held to cover the purchase or sale by the central bank in the market of any kind of paper in which it deals, whether Government securities or other securities, or banker's acceptances or foreign exchange generally." (Dekock)

The technique of open market operations was evolved because of the failure of the bank rate policy to bring about the desired results in the economy. By the term open market operations, we mean the buying and selling of Government securities, bills and bonds by the central bank. Such operations are undertaken by the central bank to control the loans and advances granted by the commercial banks and through them controlling the power of credit creation by the banks and the market rates of interest.

The mechanism of open market operations is simple. The central bank, during boom conditions, sells the Government and other approved securities in the market to reduce the aggregate money supply in the economy. Buyers of these securities pay the central bank by drawing on their deposits in the banks. Hence, there is reduction in the size of member bank's deposits held with the central bank. Because of this reduction, the banks are compelled to reduce their loans. When there is slump in the economy, the central Government buys the securities in the market and pays for these securities by issuing cheque drawn on to the individual and institutional sellers of securities. The individuals deposit these cheques in their deposit accounts in the commercial banks. The commercial banks realise the proceeds of these cheques from the central bank and their reserves are increased. The banks use these additional reserves to extend more loans.

Thus, the open market operations affect the quantity of money supply in the economy. It also affects the market rates of interest indirectly. An increase in the money supply results in a decrease in the market rate of interest and *vice versa.* Hence, the changes in the quantity of money circulation, which have been brought about by the open market operations, bring about changes in the market rates of interest.

## 3. Variable Reserve Ratio

The term variable reserve ratio refers to the minimum reserves with the central bank by the commercial banks; the cash reserves may be a percentage of its time and demand deposits separately or of total deposits. The commercial banks normally have more reserves than required, the minimum reserves by law, and the excess reserves over the minimum reserves with the central bank is the basis of the credit creation of the commercial banks. If the banks are required to maintain a higher cash reserve by the central bank, then their capacity for credit creation would come down, and *vice-versa.* For example, if the reserve ratio is fixed at 20% of the 'demand and fixed deposits by the central bank, then the commercial banks are required to maintain Rs. 20 out of every hundred rupees in their deposits. If the ratio is increased, then the cash reserves by the commercial banks would also increase and *vice-versa.* The rise in the reserve ratio by the central bank means a reduction in the excess reserves with the commercial banks and hence, their leading capacity and, therefore, their power of credit creation comes down. On the other hand, a decline in the reserve ratio by the central bank means an increase in the excess reserves with the commercial banks, and hence, their lending capacity and, therefore, their power of credit creation will rise further.

## Limitations of Variable Reserve Ratio

(1) This method does not identify the changes in amounts of reserves and the places where the changes could be made more effective.

(2) It is applicable only to the banking sector and not to the non-banking, sector.

(3) In places where there is a genuine demand for credit facilities, an increase in the reserve ratio would prove to be more harmful.

## Qualitative Techniques or Selective Credit Control

The quantitative credit control affects all sections of the economy without any discrimination. It fails to influence the purposes for which the advances are made and does not affect credit in particular direction. It also fails to check undesirable expansion of credit controls in specific channels. But the qualitative credit controls are used to check the credit extended to nonessential purposes or uses with a view to control inflation in the country. The central bank has been empowered to control advances made by the commercial banks. The central bank has the right to make the necessary instruction to the commercial banks in relation to quantum of credit, the purpose of advances, margin to be maintained, the rate of interest etc.

The aims of this method are:

(1) To channelise the bank credit only to the needy sectors.

(2) The sectors which are not responsible for the disequilibrium in the economy are not to suffer.

## 1. Margin Requirements

The term "margin" refer to the difference between the loan value and the market value of the security. This method was first introduced in USA in 1934. Under this method, the Central Bank prescribes the margin to be kept by the commercial banks while lending against securities. .

The object of prescribing margin requirements is to restrict speculative dealings in stock exchanges. Higher the margin prescribed, the lesser can the speculators borrow. Higher margin also reduces the volume of credit. This method also enables the commercial banks to direct their funds to productive investments rather than speculative activities. While higher margin reduces the prospect of making speculative profits by the stock dealers lower margin expand the credit.

The tight money policy adopted by the central bank will have secondary effects on expenditure pattern in the community, leading to control over price level. This method controls the expansion of credit in those sectors of the economy which breeds inflation.

This particular method directly influences the demand for credit for speculative purposes. It can be easily administered since the credit limits are well defined.

### Limitations

(1) In practice, this method of regulation of margin requirements throws an enormous responsibility on the central bank.

(2) There are leakages of credit to finance security speculation through non-purpose" loans to speculators and to unscrupulous moneylenders.

## 2. Regulation of Consumer Credit

This is another method which is used as credit control through the regulation of consumer hire-purchase finances granted to the depositors. Consumer credit is an arrangement that enables consumers to buy goods and services at one point of time and pay for them later. The central bank would increase the down payment and decrease the instalment repayment period if a particular sector were facing inflationary conditions. The consumer would feel that it would be expensive to buy the particular product and for want of demand and sale, the prices of that product would come down. Similarly, when deflationary forces are at work, they can be encountered by easing the terms. Hence, in the case of durable goods, the credit control is effectively managed by the central bank through the hire-purchase finances.

### Limitations

(1) This method affects the middle class people only whose decisions do not make great differences in the credit pattern of the economy.

(2) This method is discriminatory in nature since it does not affect the higher income group.

(3) The problems of administration, compliance and enforcement represent a major task in this method.

## 3. Rationing of Credit

Rationing of credit is a device of credit control, which is used for the purpose of the allocation of funds among financially sound credit aspirants in accordance with a definite plan. According to DeKock, "rationing of credit and capital is a logical concomitant of the intensive and extensive planning adopted by authoritarian States."

The rationing of credit refers to the control exercised by the central bank in regulating the purposes for which the credit is granted among the various applicants. If the control aims at controlling the total credit, it may even be considered, as quantitative credit. But it becomes selective when it aims to limit only certain types of loans and advances.

The rationing of credit it of two types, viz.: (1) variable portfolio ceiling and (2) variable capital asset ratio.

Variable portfolio ceiling refers to the fixation of ceiling by the central bank on the loans and advances granted by the commercial banks; the banks cannot extend loans and advances beyond the ceiling. The term variable capital assets ratio indicates the ratio of the capital of a commercial bank to its total assets which has been fixed by the central bank. The central bank is empowered to either increase or decrease the portfolio ceiling as well as the capital assets ratio, in response to the varying economic requirements. This method has been successfully experimented with in the USSR.

This method is also not free from limitations:

*(a)* This method discriminates the bigger banks because the rationing of credit would not affect the small banks much.

*(b)* The central bank deviates from its important function of the lender of last resort by rationing of credit for selective uses.

## 4. Direct Action

Direct action may refer to all forms of restrictions imposed upon the commercial banks in general or in particular concerning lending and investment. The central bank issues directives or instructions to the commercial banks from time to time, directing them to follow certain policies, which the central bank proposes to enforce with immediate effect. These directives may be in the form of oral or written statements, appeals or warnings. This is mainly to guide the commercial banks in formulating proper lending policies so as to prohibit lending for unproductive purposes, to fix maximum limits of credit for certain purposes etc. The commercial banks are bound to comply with such directions. But sometimes, the banks under highly competitive conditions may deviate from the directives of the central bank and in those cases the central bank would impose a penal rate of interest on the borrowing bank.

### Limitations of Direct Action

(a) It is difficult to make clear-cut distinctions between essential and nonessential industries, productive and unproductive investments etc.

(b) There is difficulty in the division of responsibility between the central bank and commercial banks which may affect the soundness of the lending operations of the latter.

### Moral Suasion

Moral suasion, unlike other credit control methods, is not a statutory obligation. It is merely a persuasion or request to commercial banks not to apply for further accommodation from central bank and also not to use the accommodation already obtained for financing speculative activities. As there is no element of compulsion, the effectiveness of this method depends on the prestige enjoyed by the central bank. In USA, it was found that this method was not successful. In 1931, the Federal Reserve Bank observed: "It is impracticable to use moral suasion as an effective part of a programme designed generally to restrict or control expansion in or use of Federal Reserve Credit. It is not possible for the Federal Reserve Banks by moral suasion to prevent credit from being used for speculative purpose".

Looking back, it is seen that the central bank has sent request to commercial banks on various occasions for restricting on bank advances. By and large, the commercial banks responded favourably. With the nationalisation of the commercial banks, this method has gained much importance.

### Limitations of Moral Suasion

(1) The application and successful operation of this method depend mainly on the weightage given by commercial banks on the request, advice and suggestions of the central bank

(2) The commercial banks would not heed the persuasions under abnormal conditions like floods, droughts etc.

### 6. Publicity

The central bank employees the instrument of publicity in order to publicize the economic facts in the weekly statements of their assets and liabilities, monthly bulletins containing reviews of credit and business conditions and detailed annual reports stating their operating and activities, the state of affairs of the money market and banking system in the country. The objective is to educate public about the monetary situation in the country. Most of the central banks in the world use this method.

## Limitations

(1) It is difficult to judge the efficacy of publicity as a method of credit control.

(2) It is not useful to the fullest extent in the underdeveloped countries where people are uneducated and even those who are educated are not acquainted with the technique of banking statistics.

## MODEL QUESTIONS

**Section - A**

1. List the seven functions of Central Bank as described by Dekock.
2. What resolution was passed at the Financial Conference held at Brussels in 1920?
3. Reason out the exclusive monopoly of note issue to the central bank.
4. What do you mean by the term 'Custodian of Cash Reserve'?
5. Who is the lender of last resort? Why'?
6. What are the methods followed by Central Bank to control credit?
7. What is rationing of credit and what are the types?
8. What do you mean by margin requirement'?

**Section - B**

1. Discuss the effectiveness of bank rate policy?
2. What are the limitations of bank rate policy?
3. Explain open market operations as a method of credit control?
4. Write short notes on:

   *(a)* Margin requirements.

   *(b)* Regulation of consumer credit.

   *(c)* Direct Action.
5. What do you mean by rationing of credit and moral suasion?
6. Discuss the significance and importance of selective control?
7. Explain the functions of Central Bank as banker to the Government and Banker's Bank?
8. Distinguish between quantitative and qualitative credit controls.
9. Explain the function of central bank as custodian of cash reserves and controller of credit.
10. Write short notes on:

    *(a)* Central bank as bank of issue.

    *(b)* Central Bank as Advisor to Government.

(c) Bank rate policy

(d) Open Market Operations

**Section - C**

1. Discuss the functions of Central Bank.
2. How does a Central Bank control the volume and direction of credit?
3. Discuss the Bank Rate Policy and Open Market Operations as methods of credit control.

# 5

# RESERVE BANK OF INDIA

Reserve Bank of India is the central bank of our country which is vested with certain prerogative powers by an Act enacted in the parliament to regulate the monetary system in our country. By virtue of the powers vested with it by an Act of legislature, it occupies a central position in the monetary and banking structure in India. It acts as the leader of the money market in supervising, controlling and regulating the activities of all commercial banks, co-operative banks and other financial institutions in the country.

## Organisation and Management

Originally, the Reserve Bank of India was constituted as a shareholders' bank in 1935 with a share capital of Rs. 5 crores divided into shares of Rs. 100 each. Although started as a privately owned bank, the RBI was nationalised in 1948 in accordance with the Reserve Bank (Transfer to Public Ownership) Act, 1948. The object of nationalisation was to have a closer co-ordination between the financial policies of the Government and the monetary and credit policy of the Reserve Bank of India. The Central Government acquired all the shares of the bank from 1st Jan. 1949 by paying compensation at the rate of Rs. 118.10 per share, partly paid in cash and partly in the form of 3% pronotes.

The RBI is managed by a Central Board and by 4 Local Boards for regional areas of the country. The Constitution of the Central Board is as follows :

### Central Board Membership

| | |
|---|---|
| Governor | 1 |
| Deputy Governors | 4 |
| Directors (Nominated by each of the Local Boards) | 4 |
| Directors (from various fields) | 10 |
| Government Nominee (Ministry of Finance, Government of India | 1 |
| | 20 |

Apart from the Central Board of Directors, there are 4 Local Boards. The whole of the country is divided into 4 zones - the Western, Eastern, Northern and Southern zones, having headquarters at Mumbai, Calcutta, New Delhi and Chennai respectively. Each zone has a Local Board consisting of 5 members appointed by the Central Government for a team of 4 years. The members of the Local Board elect their Chairman from among themselves. Each Local board has representatives, in the Central Board. The role of the Local Boards is generally advisory in nature and not executive. The business of the Local Board is to advise the Central Board on such matters as may be generally or specially referred to it and to perform such duties assigned to them by the Central Board.

The Governor is the Chairman and Chief Executive authority of the RBI. The Governor is assisted by 4 Deputy Governors and 3 Executive Directors. The Executive Directors attend the Central Board meetings on invitation. The Board is required to hold six meetings in a year. The Central Board meets at least once in 3 months.

Policy decisions are taken by the Central Board. The Board has delegated some of its routine functions to the Committee of the Central Board. This committee meets frequently, generally once in a week. A sub committee is also appointed, if necessary, by the Central Board to study certain specific problem. Such *adhoc* sub-committee submits its report to the Central Board.

In order to carry on its work more efficiently and economically, the Organisation is classified into Central Office and Local Office. The Central Office is divided into various departments which are as follows :

(1) Issue Department.

(2) Banking Department.

(3) Exchange Control Department.

(4) Department of Banking Operations and Development.

(5) Department of Accounts and Expenditure.

(6) Administration and Personnel.

(7) Economic Department.

(8) Planning and Reorganisation Department.

(9) Legal Department.

(10) Agricultural Credit Department.

(11) Industrial Finance Department.

(12) Department of Non-banking Companies.

(13) Department of Statistics.

(14) Secretary's Department.

(15) The Estate Department.

(16) Reserve Bank of India Service Board

The Local offices are situated at seven important cities, each office comprising of the banking and issue departments. Wherever the RBI does not have a branch, the SBI and its subsidiaries have been authorised to act on behalf of the RBI.

## FUNCTIONS OF THE RBI

Being the leader of the money market, the RBI is entrusted with heavy responsibilities. The RBI performs 3 types of functions as that of any other central bank. They are: Banking Functions, Supervisory functions and Promotional functions. *The main function of the RBI is to regulate the monopoly* supply *in the country.* Moreover, it has been directed to take care of agriculture, industry, export promotion etc. The RBI is also responsible for the maintenance of external value of rupee. The following are the functions of Reserve Bank of India.

## BANKING FUNCTIONS

### 1. Issue of Bank Notes

As per Section 22 of the Reserve Bank Act, the RBI has been entrusted with the monopoly of note issue in India from 1st April, 1935 through its issue Department as in the Bank of England. The design, form and material of bank notes should be approved by the Central Government on the recommendations of the Central Board. It issues notes of all denominations except one-rupee notes which are issued by the Ministry of Finance, Government of India. The currency notes constitute the liability of the Issue Department. Against these liabilities, the issue Department maintains certain assets in the form of gold, gold coins, bullion or foreign exchange securities. The assets and liabilities of the Issue Department are kept separately from the Banking Department.

The RBI was following proportional reserve system of note issue till 1956. From then onwards, it follow the minimum reserve system. Under this system, the RBI is required to maintain gold and foreign exchange reserves of Rs. 200 crores, of which Rs. 1 15 crores should be in the form of gold, gold coins and bullions, whereas Rs. 85 crores could be in terms of Government and foreign securities. This is the backing against which the RBI issues currency in India. The RBI resorted to the minimum reserve system in 1957 through an amendment in the Act due to bad deterioration in the foreign exchange reserves.

The Indian money consists of bank notes, currency notes and coins. Notes issued by the RBI are called bank notes and notes issued by the Government are known as currency notes. The RBI issues notes with denominations of rupees - 2, 5, 10, 20, 50, 100, *500,* and 1,000. . There is also provision in the Act to issue notes with rupees 5,000 and 10,000 having limited circulation.

## 2. Banker to the Government

The Central and State Governments maintain their accounts with the RBI. The Government not only receives taxes but also borrows from the money market. Under Sections 20,21 and 21 A of the Act of 1938, the RBI is obliged to act as a banker to the Government by which it undertakes the responsibility of receiving money on behalf of the Government and to allow the Government to make the necessary payments through them. The RBI provides the Government with the necessary foreign exchange for making payments abroad. The RBI also carries out their exchange remittances and other banking operations. The bank is obliged to transact the Government business at free of cost. For undertaking this work, it may keep the Government cash balances at free of interest. In the absence of RBI's office, the Government's accounts are maintained with SBI and its subsidiaries who are the authorised agents of the RBI.

According to M.H. Dekock "As the Government's banker, the central bank conducts the banking accounts of government departments, boards and enterprises; it makes temporary advances to the Government in anticipation of the collection of taxes or raising of loans from public, and extraordinary advances during a depression, war or other emergency, and it carries out the Government's transactions involving purchases and sales of foreign currencies. The central bank is also called upon to perform various services as the Government's financial agent, and it acts generally as a financial adviser to the Government."

The Issue Department of the RBI maintains the currency chests at the places prescribed by the Government. The RBI is maintaining the currency chests with sufficient notes and coins. The treasury may deposit with or withdraw funds from the currency chests, depending upon the situation. The bank provides reasonable remittance facilities to the public at places where the currency chests are maintained.

The relationship between the RBI and the Government is not merely a banker-customer relationship. The RBI acts as a banker, agent and adviser to the Central Government. The relationship between the RBI and the State Government is governed by the agreements between the State Governments and the RBI.

The financial operations of the government may have tremendous influence over the money market unless they are property regulated and controlled. Therefore, there must be a closer co-ordination and co-operation between the Government, and the RBI. The RBI is entrusted with the responsibility of maintaining the public debt. It issues loans on behalf of the Central and State Governments. It acts as an adviser to the Government on matters pertaining to the financial markets, market conditions, the terms of new loans, quantum of loans, timing of the issue of loans etc. The RBI coordinates the borrowing programmes of the Central and State Governments to avoid any cash or unhealthy competition between them. The policy decisions are taken by the Government and the RBI is to implement them. In order to take the right decisions, the RBI feeds the Government with the necessary financial information and statistical data. The Government also consults the RBI before formulating the monetary policy. The RBI advises the Government on all monetary policies concerning allocation of funds, flotation of loans, banking legislations etc.

### . Banker's Bank and Lender of the Last Resort

The RBI acts as the bankers' bank. It is said about the Central Bank, "The Central Bank acts as a conductor of the banking orchestra and leader of the banking world. It is the friend, philosopher and guide to Commercial Bank." The RBI Act, 1934 and the Banking Regulation Act 1949 have given extensive powers to the RBI to control and regulate the working of the commercial banks. As per Section 42 of the RBI Act, *every scheduled bank should maintain the minimum cash reserve with the RBI It should also maintain the Statutory Liquidity Ratio (SLR)* as prescribed by the RBI. The Cash Reserve Ratio (CRR) is fixed at 4.75% of the time and demand liabilities with effect from March 2003.

The commercial banks should abide by the directives issued by the RBI. In return, they enjoy the benefits of Deposit Insurance Scheme the credit guarantee scheme and refinance facilities from development banks. They can rediscount approved commercial/trade bills with RBI. In case of emergency, they may resort to RBI's help and the RBI will act as the lender of the last resort. If the commercial banks fail to adhere to the RBI directions, penalties may be levied according to the provisions specified in the Banking Regulation Act including the withdrawal of certain benefits. The RBI acts not only as a custodian of cash reserves but also a controller of all banks in India.

The RBI arranges for the settlement of inter-bank indebtedness through its clearing house. The clearing system reduces the expense, delay and risk involved in collection and clearing of cheques.

### 4. Custodian of Foreign Exchange Reserves

The RBI is responsible for maintaining the external stability of the rupee. It enforces the regulation strictly in accordance with the Foreign Exchange Regulations Act (FERA) and the International Monetary Fund to maintain the parity value of the rupee. As the RBI is the custodian of foreign exchange reserves, the bank buys and sells foreign exchange at rates and on such terms the central government may determine from time to time. The RBI has a separate 'Exchange control programme to supervise and control the scarce foreign exchange.

### 5. Control of Currency and Credit

The preamble to RBI Act, 1934 states clearly that the RBI is to regulate the bank notes, to keep the necessary reserves with a view to securing monetary stability in India and generally to operate the currency and credit system of the country to its advantage.

*(a) Control of Currency:* The control of RBI's monetary system largely depends on the control on the constituents of the purchasing power. If there is more currency notes in circulation than it is required, the price level will be high. If the RBI intends to bring down the prices, the currency in circulation should be restricted by withdrawing the currency in circulation. If the RBI intends to follow liberal credit policy, it may increase the currency in circulation. The expansion or contraction of the currency can be exercised by the RBI as it has been given the monopoly of note-issue.

*(b) Control of Credit.* The RBI is entrusted with the responsibility of regulating the monetary system by controlling the credit prevailing in the entire financial system in the country. This is the most important function of the RBI. The stability of the money market depends largely on the careful manipulation of credit. There are two types of credit control: Qualitative credit control and Qualitative credit control.

## QUANTITAIIVE CREDIT CONTROL

The quantitative credit control may refer to the measures taken by the RBI to control the volume and direction of credit. The quantitative measures include the Bank Rate Policy, Net Liquidity Ratio System, Open Market Operations, Statutory Liquidity Ratio and Variable Cash Reserves, etc.

## 1. Bank Rate Policy

Bank Rate is the official rate at which the Central Bank of a country is prepared to rediscount the approved bills of exchange or to lend on approved securities. The mechanism is very simple. Increase in the bank rate leads to lesser demand for credit and reduced volume of credit which reduces the quantum of credit money, leading to fall in prices. Similarly, decrease in the bank rate leads to easy credit and increase in the price level. The bank rate policy will be successful only if it has decisive influence on the interest rates and credit structure in the country. The RBI changes the bank rate from time to time. In India, the bank rate has generally influenced other market rates including the lending rates of the commercial banks.

## 2. Net Liquidity Ratio System

The RBI's advances to commercial banks are regulated not only by the bank rate but also by the Net Liquidity Ratio. The net liquidity ratio is the relationship between its net liquid assets and its total demand and time liabilities.

The net liquid assets of a borrowing bank comprises of cash in hand, cash with Reserve Bank of India, balances with other banks, investment in Government and other approved securities, minus its borrowings from RBI, SBI and IDBI. Every commercial bank is expected to maintain the NLR as prescribed by the RBI from time to time. In the recent years, the NLR and the bank rate are going up to check the commercial banks from borrowing heavily from RBI.

## 3. Open Market Operations

Open Market Operation refers to the deliberate and direct buying and selling of securities and bills in the money market by the Central Bank. Purchase and sale of securities may lead to expansion and contraction of money supply in the money market. The RBI has employed this weapon mainly to assist the Government in their borrowing operations. Section 17 (8) of the RBI Act empowers the RBI to buy and sell Government securities. Immediately after the Second World War, the commercial banks experienced heavy withdrawals of deposits by the depositors due to political and other uncertainties and they were forced to sell their securities to meet their customer's demands. At this stage, the RBI was compelled to enter into the money market and bought the securities on a large-scale to maintain stability in the security prices. The purchase and sale of these securities are made through approved brokers in Chennai, Mumbai and Calcutta. Major parts of the transactions are made in Mumbai only. Although open market operations can be effectively used for maintaining price stability as in other commodities, the RBI has not used it to its full advantage. In the recent years, there has been large-scale Government borrowings for development purposes which are responsible for increase in the volume and variety of securities. The RBI can handle these securitie effectively.

## 4. Cash Reserve Ratio (CRR)

As per Section 42 of the RBI Act, 1935, all scheduled commercial banks shoul maintain certain minimum cash reserves with the RBI. The maintenance of cas deposits with RBI inspires confidence in the minds of depositors and th public about the commercial banks. Initially, the cash reserve ratio was 5% against demand deposits and 2% against time deposits. According to a amendment in the RBI Act in 1962, the RBI was empowered to vary the CR between 3-15% of the total time and demand liabilities in India. Dependin upon the monetary conditions, the RBI may either increase or decrease th CRR. An increase in the CRR will enable the commercial banks to follo stringent credit policy, as a larger amount of commercial bank's resource would be locked up with the RBI.

Over the years the CRR has been raised and at the same time the intere on cash balances has been raised to keep up the bank's profitability. Sinc payment of interest on cash balances weakens monetary control, the cas reserve had to be, raised even further. Had interest not been paid on cas balances the CRR could have been prescribed at a much lower rate achieve the same level of monetary control. With a view to curtailing th increase in reserve money, it was considered necessary to moderate th total interest payments made by the RBI to banks on their eligible cas balances under the two-tier formula.

## 5. Statutory Liquidity Ratio (SLR)

Every commercial bank, corresponding to its total time and deman liabilities, should maintain certain minimum liquid reserves as prescribe by the RBI Act, 1934 and the Banking Regulation Act, 1949. This is know as Statutory Liquidity Ratio (SLR). *The main object of prescribing a high SLR is to force the commercial banks to maintain a larger portion their assets in liquid form, leading to the commercial bank's inability grant loans and advances and to direct bank's funds in approve securities.* The liquid asset may be in the form of cash, cash with RB Cash with other banks, gold and other unencumbered approved securitie

# QUALITATIVE CREDIT CONTROL OR SELECTIVE CREDIT CONTROL

The quantitative credit control affects all sections of the economy witho any discrimination. It fails to influence the purposes for which the advanc are made and does not affect credit in a particular direction. It also fails check undesirable expansion of credit in specific channels. But th qualitative credit controls are used to check the credit extended to nonessential purposes or uses with a view to control inflation in the country. As per the Banking Regulation Act, 1949, the RBI has been empowered to control advances made by the commercial banks. The RBI has the right to make the necessary instructions to the commercial banks in relation to the quantum of credit, the purpose of advances, margin to be maintained, the rate of interest etc. The RBI has identified certain essential commodities like food grains, sugar, oilseeds and oil, cotton textiles etc. so that it could arrest such loans for speculative or hoarding purposes. Higher margin may also be prescribed if loans are obtained on these items.

The RBI introduced Prior Authorisation Scheme in 1965 under which the commercial banks have to obtain prior permission from the RBI before granting any loans exceeding Rs.1 crore to a single party. This includes a public sector undertaking also where the ceiling is fixed at Rs. 3 crores. The Prior Authorisation Scheme restricts the flow of funds to a group of industries/ persons. As per the scheme, the commercial banks must collect and furnish information about borrowing concerns to the RBI. Inter corporate lending, over-stocking, improper working capital management etc., are being scrutinised. This enables the commercial banks to grant loans on the basis of credit appraisal and actual need of the borrowers.

The commercial banks have been following the directions of the RBI in this regard and have reduced the pressure of demand rising from bank credit. The RBI encourages the commercial banks in financing export-oriented industries with an objective of restoring favourable balance of payments. The following are the different methods of selective credit controls:

(1) Rationing of credit.

(2) Prescribing margin requirements.

(3) Consumer credit regulations.

(4) Control of bank advances.

(5) Publicity.

(6) Moral suasion.

(7) Direct Action.

## 1. Rationing of Credit

The rationing of credit refers to the control exercised by the RBI in regulating the purposes for which the credit is granted among the various applicants. If the control aims at controlling the total credit, it may even be considered as quantitative credit. But it becomes selective when it aims to limit only certain types of loans and advances. It may even restrict rediscounting certain types of short-term bills. However, this technique cannot be used under normal circumstances.

## 2. Prescribing Margin Requirements

The object of prescribing margin requirements is to restrict speculative dealings in stock exchanges. Higher the margin prescribed, the lesser can the speculators borrow. Higher margin also reduces the volume of credit. This method also enables the commercial banks to direct their funds to productive investments rather than speculative activities. Higher margin reduces the prospect of making speculative profits by the stock dealers. The tight money policy adopted by the RBI will have secondary effects on expenditure pattern in the community, leading to control over price level.

## 3. Consumer Credit Regulation

With the introduction of instalment trading, the trading in non-essential consumer products like motor vehicles, electrical and electronic goods have gone up to an unprecedented level. The RBI may restrict consumer expenses on non-essential items by directing the commercial banks to fix the minimum percentage of down payment, length of period over which instalment payments may be spread etc. They may also prescribe the exemption limit for instalment purchases. By lowering the exemption cost, the instalment buying is discouraged. Similarly, the commercial banks could be restricted to allocate lesser amounts in their budgets for consumer credit.

## 4. Control of Bank Advances

The RBI has been granted powers in the statute to exercise a general control over the lending policies of commercial banks, mainly to prevent flow of credit into undesirable channels and to direct into useful channels. Immediately after the nationalization of the commercial banks, the RBI gave directions to the commercial banks to lend 40% of their loans to priority sector. Through such directives, there has been a tremendous transformation in the concept of bank advances. This Act also authorises the RBI to caution or prohibit banks generally or any bank in particular against entering into any particular transaction or class of transaction. The RBI may raise the discounting rate in respect of bills financing import trade during the periods of unfavourable balance of trade. The RBI has been adopting this technique since 1936.

## 5. Publicity

The objective is to educate the public about the monetary situation in the country. Most of the central banks in the world use this method. In India, regular weekly statements, monthly review of credit and business conditions, annual reports are published. The RBI brings out journals like RBI - monthly bulletin, Annual reports etc., which speak in volumes about the working of commercial banks and financial institutions. It is obligatory on the part of some central banks to publish such information requires by the law.

### 6. Moral Suasion

Moral suasion, unlike other credit control methods, is not a statutory obligation. It is merely a persuasion or request to commercial banks not to apply for further accommodation from RBI and also not to use the accommodation already obtained for financing speculative activities. As there is no element of compulsion, the effectiveness of this method depends on the prestige enjoyed by the central bank. In USA, it is found that this method is not successful. In 1931, the Federal Reserve Bank observed: It is impracticable to use moral suasion as an effective part of a programme

### 7. Direct Action

In case RBI finds that the credit control method employed by it does not influence the commercial banks, the RBI reports to direct action. *Direct action may refer to all forms of restrictions imposed upon the commercial banks in general or* in *particular concerning lending and investment. The* RBI's directives were successful in many cases although the commercial banks may resent as an element of force is attached therewith.

The RBI may bring direct action against any commercial bank by enforcing the restriction on credit for speculative purposes. But in many cases the commercial banks cannot be blamed as the individual or firm may borrow for one purpose and spend it for a different purpose over which the commercial bank does not have any control. However, the ultimate authority rests with the RBI.

## SUPERVISORY FUNCTIONS

Apart from the traditional functions the RBI is entrusted with the administrative functions of non-monetary nature. The RBI Act and the Banking Regulation Act have empowered the RBI with adequate powers to supervise and control the constituents of the Indian Financial System. The RBI enjoys powers pertaining to licensing and establishment of branch expansion, liquidity of their assets, advances to different sectors, management and methods of working, amalgamation, reconstruction, liquidation etc. It has the powers to collect credit information from banking companies to call the returns containing credit information. It may also depute its members of the staff to other financial institutions in which it has substantial interest. The RBI is also empowered to carry out periodical inspections on the commercial banks.

The management of the currency chests and public debt have been entrusted with the RBI. The RBI co-ordinates the borrowing programmes of the Central and State Governments efficiently to avoid any clash or unhealthy competition between them. Apart from these, the RBI has established a training college for imparting practical training to the supervisory staff of the commercial banks in the country. A large number of officers and supervisors have already undergone series of training programmes.

## PROMOTIONAL FUNCTIONS

With the nationalisation of many commercial banks, the responsibility of the RBI has indeed increased widely. With the objective of promoting rural credit, the RBI has promoted new financial agencies. A number of development banks have also been established to promote industrial and rural credit. With the main objective of eliminating the money-lenders from the rural scene, the RBI developed the co-operative credit movements. In the recent years, the Regional Rural Banks have also been set-up for developing agriculture, trade, commerce, and industry and other productive activities in the rural areas.

## MONETARY POLICY

Broadly speaking, the major objectives of economic policy in India have been growth, and social justice implying a more equitable distribution of income and price stability. Monetary policy is an arm of economic policy and in that sense, the objective of monetary policy are no different from the overall objective of economic policy.

The role of RBI as the Central Bank in Monetary policy is as follows:

### *(a)* Inflation and Monetary Targeting

At present the developing countries are faced with the problem of high inflation. The primary role of monetary policy is to control inflation as the objective of the monetary policy is to provide for economic development with reasonable price stability. At least, the rate of inflation should be gradually checked by the authorities. The monetary policy can be lauded if the Government is able to achieve zero rate of inflation. In order to achieve this, it is generally considered necessary to keep the money supply under control in tune with the national income. It would be good to have a stable monetary policy without frequent changes. The I.M.F. and World Bank advise the underdeveloped countries to set-up monetary targets. Monetary targeting makes sense only if the permissible increase in money supply is correctly distributed between the legitimate claims of the budget, the private sector and the country's need for foreign exchange reserves. However, monetary target can be under review as it would be difficult to recommend a strict monetary target. Most targets are generally kept at a range.

### *(b)* Interest Rate Policy

Interest is payable to the lenders mainly on two accounts. Primarily, the lenders should not suffer any loss on account of inflation. A lender will claim an amount plus interest calculated at the pre-determined rate of inflation, from the borrower. Apart from this, a loan is associated with the risk factor and the risk premium should also be covered. Longer the period higher will be the risk factor. The risk is also associated with the type of borrowers. Moreover, an incentive should be given for savings. The monetary authorities also administer the interest rate and control the inflationary rate in the country. They may be baffled as to how much rate of interest is to be fixed in order to provide maximum possible incentive for savings without unduly inhibiting investment. The real rate of interest should be positive and it may be regulated when there is imbalance between supply and demand for savings. In order to have the effect of the monetary policy, the interest rate will have to be very large. But unfortunately once raised, it would be difficult for the authorities to bring down interest rates in most developing countries.

### *(c)* Direct Controls

Apart from issue of currency notes and supply of money, the Central Bank of a country is empowered with the power to control credit. In order to minimise the impact of fiscal deficits, a flexible use of reserve requirement is necessary. The Central Bank uses techniques such as cash reserve ratio and statutory liquidity ratio requirements depending upon the necessity. The Central Bank can also adopt moral suasion but it can be a moderately effective measure provided that the Central Bank maintains effective personal contacts with other financial institutions. The Central Bank uses direct control techniques very sparingly.

### *(d)* Cost-Push and Wage-Push

Underdeveloped countries are often faced with the problem of wage push pressure from the trade unions. The pressure for increased wages than it is warranted is a common feature. In case the Government yields to such pressure, there is going to be a price rise due to increased wages and again there will be wage-push pressure from the same group. Such a pressure can be resisted by a non-accommodating monetary policy. Otherwise, it would be difficult to control inflation.

Even in the economic front, when there is a bad harvest, the price of certain essential commodities goes up. The monetary authorities resort to import of food grains or public procurement policy to regulate the supply. Even in the case of sudden increase in price of certain commodities, they may resort to import of such commodities. For instance, India adopted certain direct methods of import recently when the oil prices reached great heights.

### (e) Monetary and Exchange Policy

Monetary and Exchange Policy have become inseparable policies as a result of capital movements. They are highly sensitive to variation in interest rates and changes to the current climate of expectation. Most of the developing countries retain exchange control as one of the essentials of its monetary policy. They may not resort to changes in the exchange rate unless it is absolutely necessary and direct policy changes are made as the exchange rate for their currency reflect relative changes in the value of major currencies of the world. Changes in the exchange rate would affect the value of other major currencies. However, it should be understood that changes in the nominal interest or exchange rates do not bring about basic adjustment without following appropriate policy on a wide front.

### (f) Liberalization

Many of the developing countries have a mixed pattern of ownership with a heavy bias toward public control. In India, the Congress Government adopted the policy of socialism and 14 banks were nationalised as early as in 1969 with the sole objective of bringing Government control over such banks to enable them augment their finance to cater to the needs of national priorities. It has been realised that the quarter century monetary policy adopted henceforth has not borne fruits although the nationalisation of commercial banks has helped to increase branch expansion, penetration of banking into rural areas, advances to priority sector etc. Most of the public sector undertakings including a number of banks were incurring heavy losses over the years.

It is generally felt that the economic progress in developing countries have been so uneven. There has been a wide critics of the monetary policy, particularly in India that many of the financial policies have not paved the way for the economic progress in raising the living standards of the people over the last 25 years. Therefore, there is a need for rethinking in terms of "Privatisation" as in developed countries. The spirit of liberalistion will also imply that even public financial institutions, including the Central Bank, should be freed from the routine governmental intervention. According to the former RBI Governor, MT. M. Narasimhan, "Financial sector reforms would not be complete without resorting to the RBI's rightful pre-eminence and giving it full operational autonomy and control over the financial system. Profitability and survivability of Indian banks would continue to be under pressure unless the Government makes considerable changes in the financial sector. The latest trend is to abolish the present dyarchy of control over the system by the Government and R-serve Bank of India.

## What is a Bill Market?

A Bill Market is a market for purchase of short-term bills, usually of three months duration. There are two kinds of bills - *(a)* Commercial or trade bills and *(b)* Treasury bills. Commercial or Trade bills are those bills which are drawn and accepted by traders, businessmen for specific amounts which may be bought and sold in the bill market. The bill market may also be known as discount market as the commercial bills are often discounted at the bank. On the due date, the holder presents the bills to the acceptor who pays such bills. Treasury Bills are promises for specific amounts made by the government generally for large amounts. The commercial banks prefer to discount bills for the following reasons :

*(i)* The parties to the bill - the drawer, acceptor and payee are closely known to the bank.

*(ii)* There is a definite maturity date on which payment will be made.

*(iii)* The remuneration for the bank (discount) is attractive.

*(iv)* The bank need not pay the full amount of the bills. It is enough if they pay the amount less discount. Moreover, they don't have to pay cash. The amount of the discounted bill is credited to the party's account.

*(v)* In case of emergency, the trade bills can be presented with RBI for rediscounting facilities.

## Refinance Facility from Reserve Bank of India

The commercial banks meet the working capital demands of their clients by discounting their trade bills. In turn, when there is need for money to commercial banks, they approach the RBI and make use of the refinancing facility by rediscounting such trade facilities with RBI. Such facilities are available to commercial banks.

As per Sec. 17 of the Reserve Bank of India Act, 1934, the RBI can purchase, sell and rediscount bonafide commercial bills and promissory notes. For this purpose, the RBI introduced a Bill Market Scheme as early as in 1952.

## Bill Market Scheme 1952

The Reserve Bank of India introduced a Bill Market Scheme in January 1952. Although this scheme was withdrawn in November, 1971, it was a pioneer scheme in discounting bills of exchange and was useful to many industries and business houses. The RBI, not only looked into the security but also the manner in which the business was carried on. For instance, whether the bank has been overtrading during slack season. The salient features of the Bill Market Scheme 1952 are as follows:

1. The RBI granted advances to scheduled commercial banks in the form of demand loans against Bills of Exchange and Promissory Notes. The duration of such bills was not exceeding 90 days.

2. Any schedule bank desiring to avail itself of the rediscounting facility should supply detailed information of each customer whose bills or promissory notes are intended to be deposited with RBI. Other details required by the RBI are date, term, drawer, drawee, acceptor, serial number, rate of discount, net proceeds, maximum borrowings of the party, maturity date etc.
3. The amount lent by RBI on bills should not exceed the amount of loan granted to the party.
4. The application for such loan should be submitted with the local or principal office of the RBI. The RBI, may approve, reject the loan application or sanction a lower amount.
5. The RBI deals directly with the borrowing bank and not with any customer. The sanctioned loan is granted only to the borrowing bank. In case the commercial banks withdraw any bill, the commercial banks should either deposit the amount of such bills or replace it with a new bill or promissory note. The RBI would also accept early repayment of loan for the reduction of its indebtedness under this scheme.
6. A declaration was to be obtained from the customer assuring that the bill was genuine trade bill. The borrowing bank should also certify about the soundness of the party.

Although the Bill Market Scheme 1952 was promoted with much enthusiasm, it did not succeed in promoting genuine bill market in India. The Banking Commission has rightly pointed out that the Bill Market Scheme of 1952 was primarily a scheme of accommodation for banks and it did not develop a market in genuine bills.

## Bill Market Scheme 1970

The functioning of the Bill Market Scheme 1952 was reviewed. There were certain common problems amongst the business houses and the banks. The banks were meeting the short-term working capital needs of the borrowers through cash credit and overdraft facilities. The borrowers preferred to cash credit facilities, as they need not repay the amount on specified dates unlike bills of exchange which matured on a definite date. Moreover, there was a heavy stamp duty. All these made the Bill Market Scheme 1952 ineffective.

Hence, a Study Group under the Chairmanship of Mr. Narashimhan was appointed in February 1970 to review the existing Bill Market and to make their recommendations. The Study Group went into the question of enlarging the issue of bills as an instrument for providing credit and the creating of suitable bill market scheme in India. Following the recommendations of the Study Group, the RBI introduced the Bills Rediscounting Scheme with effect from 1st

November 1970. Under this scheme, the eligible bills could be rediscounted by commercial banks.

The New Bill Market Scheme was a big leap forward in the development of a bill market scheme. The Narasimhan Study Group firmly believed that the evaluation of such a Bill Market would make the bank rate variations a more effective weapon of monetary control. However, in 198 1, the RBI withdraw this Scheme and modifies it by permitting the banks to rediscount the bills with one another or with approved financial institutions.

## Modified Bill Market Scheme 1981

The salient features of the modified Bill Market Scheme 1981 are as follows:

1. All the scheduled commercial banks, urban co-operative banks selected by RBI, EXIM BANK. LIC Mutual Fund, Small Industries Development Bank SIDBI etc are eligible for rediscounting facilities under this Scheme.
2. 'I'he scheme provides for flexible limits for every eligible bank which applies to RBI. The RBI fixes the sanctioning limit for each bank for a period of 12 month ending 31$^{st}$ October, each year.
3. The bills which are to be discounted with the RBI should be of bills arising out of genuine transactions. Ordinarily, the bills should have been drawn for a period not exceeding 90 days. But in the case of 120 days bills, if 30 days have already expired, it may be taken up for rediscounting, as they will mature within 90 days from the date of rediscounting such bills.
4. The RBI will rediscount the bills provided they are duly certified by the commercial banks relating to the title of the bills, genuine trade transactions credit worthiness of the parties and signatures of the accepting bank.
5. Individual bills up to Rs. 10 lakhs on which they have obtained the rediscounting facility, can be retained by commercial banks on behalf of the discounting institutions. The RBI has granted this facility to commercial banks to avoid undue delay in the process of discounting bills.
6. As a rule, the commercial banks are expected to make payments three days before the date of the maturity of the bills with the discounting institution to enable them too obtain the redelivery of the bills. Proportionate payments can also be made and the bills can be withdrawn proportionately.

**CASH RESERVE RATIO AND INTEREST RATES : 2002-2004**
**(Per cent per annum)**

| *Item* | *Oct. 2002* | *Nov. 2002* | *Dec. 2002* | *Jan. 2003* | *Feb. 2003* | *March 2003* | *Jan. 2004* |
|---|---|---|---|---|---|---|---|
| *(a)* Cash Reserve Ratio (per cent)* | 5.00 | 4.75 | 4.75 | 4.75 | 4.75 | 4.75 | 4.50 |
| *(b)* Bank Rate | 6.50 | 6.25 | 6.25 | 6.25 | 6.25 | 6.25 | 6.00 |
| *(c)* Prime Lending Rate** | 11.00–12.00 | 10.25– 11.50 | 10.75–11.50 | 10.75–11.50 | 10.75–11.50 | 10.75–11.50 | 10.25–11.00 |
| *(d)* Deposit Rate*** | 6.50-7.50 | 6.00-6.75 | 6.00-6.75 | 5.50-6.25 | 5.50-6.25 | 5.25-6.25 | 4.00-5.50 |

*Notes* :* As applicable to Scheduled Commercial Banks (Excluding Regional Rural Banks) as on last Friday of the month.

** Prime Lending Rate (PLR) relates to five major banks.

*** Deposit rate relates to major banks for term deposits of more than one year maturity.

## MODEL QUESTIONS

**Section - A**

I. What is the primary function of RBI?
2. Classify the departments of RBI.
3. What is CRR?
4. What is NLR?
5. What is SLR?
6. State the limitations of Variable Reserve Ratio.
7. What are the aims of Selective Credit control?
8. What are the types of Rationing of credit?
9. What is Liberalisation?
10. What is a Bill Market?

**Section - B**

1. Write short notes on Statutory Liquidity Ratio.
2. What are the supervisory and promotional factions of Reserve Bank of India?
3. Write notes as rationing of credit and moral suasion.
4. Analyse the role of RBI as a banker's bank and custodian of foreign exchange.
5. Discuss how far the Reserve Bank's Control over the Indian money market is effective.
6. What are the limitations of Bank rate policy?

**Section - C**

1. Explain the various functions of Reserve Bank of India.
2. What do you mean by Selective Credit Control? Explain in detail.
3. Explain the quantitative credit control measures followed by Reserve Bank of India.
4. What are the monetary and credit control measures recently adopted by the Reserve Bank of India?

# 6

# FUNCTIONS OF COMMERCIAL BANK

Banks play an important role in the economic development of the country. They act as catalyst in commercial and industrial activities. One cannot imagine the cessation of the banking activities even for a day. There may be an economic crisis in the country if the banks stop functioning for some days.

It is often said that a banker is one who deals with other peoples' money. The term "Banking" has been understood differently by different people at different times. Even mills and industrial concerns which accepted public deposits were classified as banks between 1932-1943. According to Sir John Paget, " No person, or body corporate or otherwise can be a banker who does not - *(i)* take deposit accounts; *(ii)* take current accounts; *(iii)* issue and pay cheques and *(iv)* collect cheques, crossed and uncrossed, for his customers.But a statutory definition was introduced through the Banking Regulation Act, 1949. Accordingly, "a bank is a company which accepts deposits of money from the public, for the purpose of lending or investment, repayable on demand or otherwise." This definition excludes mere money lending. Similarly, mills and industrial concerns which merely accept deposits are excluded from the classification of the term "Banks".

The primary functions of commercial bank are the statutory functions. The commercial banks receive deposits and lend it to those who need it after making the necessary provisions for reserves as per the regulations. But the modern commercial bank does not stop with merely receiving and lending functions. They undertake innumerable functions, apart from the statutory functions.

The functions of the commercial banks are incorporated in the following chart in the next page.

The primary functions of the commercial bank are classified into receiving of deposits and lending to borrowers. The commercial bank receives deposits from the public by way of time deposits and demand deposits. When deposits are received, the bank should pay interest at the rate prescribed by the RBI. This is the borrowing rate. The commercial banks themselves cannot fix such interest rates. Similarly, when loans are granted the commercial banks charge interest on loans at the rates specified by the RBI. This rate is the 'lending rate.' The difference between the interest receivable and interest payable is the gross profit, being the main source of income for the banks.

## TIME DEPOSITS

Time Deposits may also be termed as 'Term Deposits' as the deposits arc made by the customers for a specific period. Time deposits consists of: Fixed Deposits and Recurring deposits. Term deposits are not normally withdrawn before the fixed term. Demand deposits ', as the name indicates, are those deposits which can be withdrawn by the customers at any time without giving notice to the bank. Current account and Savings Bank account fall under this category of demand deposits.

## FIXED DEPOSIT ACCOUNTS

Fixed deposits are made by the customers for a specified period, ranging from 15 days to 5 years or more. The rate of interest differs from period to period. The longer the period of deposit, higher is the rate of interest. The depositor is assured of the safety of funds, apart from higher returns. The depositor, as per the terms, agrees not to withdraw the amount earlier. In acknowledgment of the Fixed Deposit, the customer is given a receipt called Fixed Deposit Receipt, popularly known as 'FDR' in the business circle. The rules governing the fixed deposits are printed on the reverse side of the FDR.

At the end of the term, the customer may either withdraw the amount along with interest or renew the deposit for a further period at his convenience. Since the customer would withdraw the funds at the end of the period, the banker can lend the money confidently without keeping any reserve to meet the withdrawals. In case the customer needs money prior to the due date, although he may not be able to withdraw from the Fixed Deposit, he can obtain a loan from the bank on the strength of the Fixed Deposit Receipt. The banker charges interest for this loan.

Fixed Deposit account is ideal for those with high disposable income and can deposit a lump sum toward a safe investment, yielding high returns. Some banks provide for Auto Renewal Plan facility which enables automatic renewal of deposit after maturity.

## RECURRING DEPOSITS

This is a type of account which is a combination of the characters of Saving Bank account and Fixed Deposit accounts. In this account, the depositors can pay a fixed sum of money every month for various periods, say 12 to 120 months. This account is normally opened by salaried persons or individuals who get regular income. Deposits may be paid in easy instalment. The commercial banks have introduced the Recurring Deposit scheme to enable the small depositors to save for a predetermined future period. In one way it may be viewed as a compulsory savings to enable them to build up sizeable amount. The bankers allow compound rate of interest. In case the depositor needs the money even before the stipulated period he can get back the money. In such cases, the banker may pay a lesser rate of interest than it was agreed upon.

## DEMAND DEPOSITS

### *(a)* Savings Bank Account

Savings Account is an interest bearing domestic account. As the name indicates, the purpose of opening a Savings Bank Account is to save money to meet the future contingencies. A person is allowed to open a Savings Bank account provided he is properly introduced. The customer is expected to maintain a minimum balance of Rs. 500/- in his account. Nowadays, Savings Bank account holder who agrees to maintain a minimum balance of Rs. 1000/ in his account may make use of the cheque facilities. The interest is allowed at the rate of 4% on the minimum balance. In the case of pensioners who would like to have cheque facilities should maintain the minimum balance of Rs.250. The service charges for non-maintenance of minimum balance in savings bank account is Rs.10 per month. There are some restrictions relating to the number and amount of withdrawals. The number of withdrawals is generally restricted to 120 per year and the total amount of withdrawals at any time should not exceed Rs 10,000 or 10% of the balance whichever is higher. But if he wants to withdraw a large sum, he should give prior notice to the banker. However, these rules are not strictly followed.

Savings Bank Accounts are usually opened in the name of individuals. No Savings bank account is opened for a trading company or a business concern whether such a concern is a proprietary concern, partnership firm, a company or an association.

Nowadays, a banker facilitates the collection of cheques drawn in the name of the customer through the savings bank account. However, he does not collect third party cheques. A third party cheque is one which is drawn in the name of a person other than the customer. Nomination facility is also available in this account.

### *(b)* Current Account

A current account is normally opened by a businessman for the purpose of his business with a minimum balance of Rs. 2000/-. He should always maintain such minimum balance in the account. A banker should be doubly cautious to get an introduction letter from the customer at the time of opening such account. He should also see that such introductory letters are verified, due to the following reasons:

*(i)* The RBI has given a direction that the prospective customers should produce introductory letter at the time of opening the account;

*(ii)* The banker should ascertain the bonafides of the customer;

*(iii)* Since third party cheques are collected through the account, there is a chance for fraud by unscrupulous elements;

*(iv)* Since overdraft and cash credit facilities are available, the bankers should not be exploited by an unscrupulous customer.

In a current account the banker is obliged to honour the cheques drawn on him if there is sufficient balance to his credit. One of the peculiar features of the current account is that the banker does not allow any interest on the deposits whatever the balance is. However, if the customer overdraws the account he may have to pay interest to the banker-. Overdraft may be granted for a temporary period of one month or more depending upon the requirements of a customer. Cash credit facility is also available in the current account. Bankers allow certain special facilities such as free collection of outstation cheques, issue of demand drafts and mail transfers without any extra charges.

## LENDING OF FUNDS

A shrewd banker should be able to employ his funds profitably. He should lend the deposit to others, keeping in mind the principles of lending viz., safety, liquidity and profitability.

### Methods of Lending

*(i) Overdraft :* Overdraft facility is available in the current account. Businessmen make use of this facility. *Overdraft is an arrangement by which the banker allows the customer to draw up to a certain amount over and above the current account balance.* This is a temporary credit arrangement.

*(ii) Cash Credit :* Cash credit is similar to that of overdraft by which the

customer is allowed to overdraw his account. But the banker, in this case, grants the cash credit only on the basis of some security. The other difference between cash credit and overdraft is that the banker charges differential rates of interest on cash credit. For the amount actually withdrawn by the customer, he may have to pay a higher rate of interest, say, 16.5% and for the unutilised amount the customer may have to pay nominal interest, as commitment charges.

*(iii) Discounting Bills of Exchanges :* This is one of the familiar methods of granting short-term loans to businessmen. In the case of a credit sale, the buyer or his bank may accept the bill. The holder (seller) may *discount the bill before the due date.* The banker will present the bill to the acceptor on the due date and collect the amount. In case the acceptor fails to pay, the banker will debit the customer's account.

*(iv) Loans and Advances :* The banker may grant loan to the customer on the basis of certain securities. Various kinds of collateral securities are offered to a bank by its customers as cover for advances. *Loans may be granted against movable and immovable goods. Even book debts may be hypothecated by a letter of hypothecation* and loans may be obtained. In the case of an immovable property like land and buildings, the customer can *avail of the loan by mortgaging such properties.*

## AGENCY SERVICES

In order to facilitate the customers, the banks accept standing instructions from their customers either to make payments on their behalf or collect money or effect transfer of money. The relationship between the banker and customer, in this case, is that of Principal and Agent. The customer directs the banker as to what he should do. The banker acts according to his direction. In case of any loss, the customer alone will bear this as his directions are carried out by the banker. The banker will charge the customer for doing such services. Some of the agency functions are as follows :

*(a)* The banker pays rent, insurance premium, subscription etc., on behalf of the customer as per his prior instructions on the appropriate dates. The payment will be made from the customer's account.

*(b)* In the same way the bank undertakes to collect such income on behalf of the customer.

*(c)* The banker also collects cheques/bills etc., on behalf of the customer.

*(d)* In India, we do not have banks exclusively dealing in foreign exchange. The commercial banks, in addition to their normal functions, undertake the business in foreign exchange. They buy and sell foreign exchange currencies as per the regulations. They also discount the foreign exchange bills.

## FUNCTIONS OF COMMERCIAL BANKS

- **Primary Functions**
  - **Receiving of Deposits**
    - **Time Liabilities**
      1. Fixed Deposit
      2. Recurring Deposit
      3. Miscellaneous types of Deposit
    - **Demand Liabilities**
      1. Saving Bank Account
      2. Current Account
  - **Lending of Funds**
    1. Overdraft
    2. Cash Credit
    3. Discounting Bills of Exchange
    4. Loans and Advances
- **Secondary Functions**
  - **Agency Services**
    1. Payment of Rent, Insurance Premium etc.
    2. Collecting of cheques
    3. Dealing in foreign in exchange
    4. Acting as trustees
  - **General Utility Services**
    1. Safe Custody Deposits
    2. Safe Deposit Locker facilities
    3. Transfer of money.
    4. Issue to travellers' cheque, Mail Transfer etc.
    5. Acting as referees
    6. Merchant Banking
    7. Teller System
    8. Automatic Teller Machine
    9. Credit cards
    10. Gift Cheque
    11. E-Banking
    12. Miscellaneous Services

(e) The financial stability of the bank and complete confidence of the customers, dealing with it have made the bank a natural and trusted friend for undertaking executorships and trusteeship. In addition to this, an increasing reluctance of customers to trust individuals, combined with insufficient knowledge of law on their part, has led commercial banks to act as trustees/executors to their customers. As a trustee, the banker takes care of the management trust and administers the trust funds effectively. The functions undertaken under the executor/trustee services areas follows : *(i)* To handle the investments/ estates during the life time of the owner; and distribute them according to the terms of the will after his death; *(ii)* To manage the property during the owner's life time and after his death on behalf of his dependents through their life time or till such property is distributed/ applied according to the instructions of the deceased; *(iii)* To manage movables and also act as a guardian of a minor's property; *(iv)* Guide customers in filing estate duty returns and appear before Estate Duty Authorities when called upon to do so; *(v)* Administration of public trusts; *(vi)* Acting as trustees for debenture holders.

## GENERAL UTILITY SERVICES

A number of incidental functions are carried on by the commercial banks to help his customers.

### 1. Safe Custody Deposits

The commercial bank provides safe custody facilities. Under this facility, the valuables may be handed over to the banker as per the regulations. The banker verifies the value of the items deposited with him and keeps them in his locker. He gives an acknowledgement for the valuables he has received from the customer stating the description of the items and value. The bank charges depend on the period for which the valuables are kept with the bank and the value of the items kept under safe custody.

### 2. Safe Deposit Locker facilities

This is a unique method by which a customer can make use of the locker kept by the banker in the safe room. The locker can be operated only with two keys - one is with the banker and the other is with the customer. The locker can be opened only if both the keys are used. The customer is allowed to keep any kind of valuables inside the locker. The customer should pay rent periodically. Normally his bank account would be debited towards rent. The customer can use the locker at any time during the banking hours. The Banker does not have any lien on the items kept in the locker except for the outstanding rent for the locker. In case of loss of items, the banker is not directly responsible as the relationship between the banker and customer is that of lesser and lessee. This service has gained much importance now, to the extent that some firms have even opened branches exclusively for providing this service.

## 3.Transfer of Money

Money may be transferred from one place to other through the bank in the following ways.

*(a)* ***Purchase of Bank Draft :*** The customer may purchase a bank draft drawn in favour of the payee. The procedure for purchasing a draft from the bank is a simple one. A form for obtaining a draft should be filled in by entering the required particulars. The amount payable to the payee along with the commission should be paid into the bank account. The banker will issue a bank draft in the name of the payee. A bank draft is nothing but a cheque issued by one banker ordering the other branch of his bank to pay the specified sum of money to the payee mentioned therein. The customer can send this by registered post to the payee who can collect the draft through his account or collect cash if it is not crossed in the respective branch. While sending a draft to the payee, it is recommended to cross the draft and send it by registered post.

*(b)* ***Mail Transfer and Telegraphic Transfer :*** The customer can transfer funds from one place to another through Mail Transfer (MT) or Telegraphic Transfer (TT). Mail Transfer is a method by which the customer requests his banker to transfer a portion of the balance in his account to the payee's account, kept in a different place in the same bank for a nominal commission. After receiving the customer's instruction the banker arranges to send an advice to the concerned bank manager, through mail, asking him to credit the account of the payee with certain amount as instructed by his customer.

In the case of Telegraphic Transfer, the banker in one place advises the other bank manager by a telegram to credit the account of a specified customer on the other end with the necessary funds. Hence, the transfer is made and such telegraphic transfer enables the payee to make use of such funds within a short time.

*(c)* ***Traveller's Cheque :*** A traveller's cheque is a printed cheque of a particular denomination. A banker may issue traveller's cheque at the request of the customer after obtaining the customer's signature. When he travels either within the country or out of the country, he may pay by traveller's cheque. The traveller's cheques are accepted in banks, restaurants, and hotels and in certain other places. Before receiving the traveller's cheques, the customer is expected to sign on the traveller's cheque, which is to be countersigned by the banker. At the time of payment, the customer is expected to sign in the presence of the person who accepts the traveller's cheque. The signature should tally with the signature already affixed at the time of issue.

### 4. Acting as Referees

When a seller intends to sell his goods to an unknown buyer, he may do so only after knowing the financial standing of the buyer. In this case, the buyer would request his bank to reveal his financial standing when an enquiry is made by the seller. The bank may respond to such an enquiry only with the customer's consent.

### 5. Merchant Banking

Some commercial banks have also started Merchant Banking Division in order to assist new industries to obtain various types of information and plan out their promotional activities. The banks assist the promoters to obtain technical data relating to feasibility, market demand and other relevant information. Banks also underwrite shares and debentures of companies.

### 6. Teller System

The reputation of the bank depends on its ability to satisfy the customers at the counter. Acceptance of cash and payment of cheques are the two important services at the counter. The customer feels irritated if he is made to wait for a long time either at the time of deposit or withdrawal of cash. Some banks have even put up a notice at the bank assuring their customers that the cheques could be encashed within a specified time. However, it is often felt that the waiting time at the counter is longer and should be reduced. In order to minimise the waiting time of the customers, the teller System has been introduced. *Under this system, the teller examines the cheques presented to him and pays the cheques up to certain limit to the holders on identification. In case of doubt, he may refer to the records.* Some banks allot codes on cheque forms based on the creditworthiness of the accountholders. In case of doubt about the balance in the customer's account, the teller may direct the presenter to the accounts counter where the cheque will be dealt with.

The teller combines himself the twin functions of passing the cheque and paying the cash. Many banks have fixed a ceiling on the amount of the cheque paid by the bank.

### 7. Automatic Teller Machines (ATM)

In the last few years, the ATMs have revolutionised the banking system in the country. Some Foreign Banks have introduced Automatic Teller Machines (ATMs) to facilitate their customers to withdraw and deposit cash without any waiting time. The credit cardholders can also withdraw emergency cash from the ATMs at various centres in the country at any time -day and night. The ATMs work like a computer. The customers could save considerable waiting time while depositing and withdrawing cash.

## 8. Credit Cards

Many commercial banks in India, particularly the foreign banks, have introduced credit cards among their customers and non-customers. The credit card acts as an instrument of credit. The credit cardholders need not carry cash. They may purchase goods from many authorised dealers, using the credit cards. The credit cards can also be used to settle accounts with the merchants as the cards offer the power and flexibility to plan payments in easy instalments. The customer may have to pay certain service charges to the bank when he makes use of this card, apart from paying interest on the outstanding balances.

Some banks offer their cardholders certain unique benefits like personal accident insurance and limited liability on lost credit cards. The cardholders may have a feeling of security and peace of mind.

## 9. Gift Cheques

The gift cheques are issued by the commercial banks in different denominations to facilitate their customers to make presents to their relatives and friends on important occasions like marriage, birthdays, religious and other festival days, etc.

## 10. E-Banking

With the introduction of Computers in Indian Banks and with arrangements of shared payment network system services are provided across the Banks. Customers need not visit the banks to do the banking transactions when their Banker provides them, electronic banking, Tele banking or remote banking facilities.

## 11. Debit Card

Debit Cards are generally used by customers for withdrawal of cash from ATMs. Debit Card differs from the conventional credit cards in the-sense the debit cardholder's -account gets instantaneously debited unlike in the case of credit cards whereas the cardholders are given a credit for fixed period.

## 12. Electronic Fund Transfer System (EFT)

Electronic Fund Transfer System uses computer and electronic technology as the substitute cheques and other paper transactions. Funds are transfered instantly among various branches at various locations in the country through the network, using latest communication technology.

## 13. Any Time Banking

Any Time Banking have helped the customers to overcome the time limitations of four hours of customer service. The customers are given a host of Banking Services including Deposits, Withdrawal, requisitions and transfers.

### 14. Anywhere Banking

With the introduction of tele- banking and networking of all branches through communication network, customer becomes the customer of entire bank rather, than a branch as all the branches are connected by a satellite. Inter-station connectivity of ATMs has facilitated withdrawal from other stations a service useful for frequent travelers. Financial details can be accessed from remote locations and basic transactions can be effected from outside the bank.

### 15. Electronic Pass Book

An Electronic Pass Book adapted to Indian conditions has been introduced as part of the "Anywhere Banking Programme".

### 16. Tele Banking

Tele Banking is yet another innovation, which carries the concept of 24 hour banking to the customer's home or business place. Tele banking services function based on the voice processing facility available with bank computers. The customer will be able to call the bank any time and enquire balances or transaction history, transfer funds between accounts, between branches, request for draft, cheque books, information on new scheme, maturity of deposits details of interest rates and give instructions for stop payment.

### 17. Banking through the Internet

Banks have started disseminating information about the products and services through their websites. Many Indian Banks have set their own websites with interactive features like account opening forms can be printed from the sites and used for opening accounts under the different schemes. Banks like ICICI use their websites for their public issues by making the application forms and details of the issues over the net. Customers can connect to the banks through website over the internet, logging to the internet banking service and access their account, view statement of account, conduct financial transaction and much more.

### 18. Corporate Banking

Remote banking has become very popular among corporate customers especially big business industrial houses, which are already automated. More and more banks are providing customer terminals right in the customer's office, which will facilitate the customers to operate the account without physically coming to the bank.

At present by utilising remote banking facility, corporate customers will be able to get the following services:

- Getting their current balance or getting their statement of accounts for any predefined period.

- Ordering Cheque books.
- Ordering Intra-bank and Inter bank Fund transfers.
- Instructing stop payments of cheques.
- International remittances.
- Opening letter of credits.

By obtaining a special SWIFT (Society for worldwide Inter Bank Financial Telecommunication), authentication facility in arrangement with their bankers, customers will be able to directly prepare messages in the SWIFT format by sitting in their office, transfer the particulars in the respective templates to their bankers. The Bankers will directly authenticate the transaction.

## 19. Miscellaneous Services offered by Banks

- Specialised services in foreign exchange management to NRI's and other customers.
- Personal tax and financial planning.
- Broad based merchant banking related services.
- Stocks and bonds brokerage services (i.e., buying and selling of equity shares, debentures, bonds, etc., at the branches. Including dealing with brokers, registration, settlement, payment, receipts).
- Safe keeping of securities.
- Anticipation and collection of corporate benefits such as dividends, interest consolidation etc.
- Maintaining of client's accounts of securities.
- Hybrid products/Services related to insurance and banking.
- Securities dealing and underwriting.
- Property and real estate management/brokerage.
- Pension and trust management.
- Travel related service.
- Innovative leasing products/service.
- Factoring.
- Mortgage loans.
- Bank management training/consultancy.
- Buying and renting real estates.
- Non-life insurance services.
- Travel and entertainment cards.
- Technical consultancy.

# PROCEDURE FOR OPENING A BANK ACCOUNT

In recent times, commercial banks compete with one another and resort to attractive advertisements informing the public about the facilities available in their banks, rates of interest, their services, location of ATM centers etc. These advertisements are legally considered as *'Invitation to offer'. Only* when a proposed customer submits an application for opening an account in a prescribed form, it is a real offer. In other words, *a customer makes an offer by submitting an application.* It is for the banker to accept it or reject *it. When he accepts the offer, a contract is formed between a banker and customer and the contract is complete once the banker accepts the initial deposit.* Thus he opens an account in the name of the customer. The commercial banks follow uniform procedure in opening an account.

Any one who intends to open a Savings Bank account should submit an application in a particular format with the bank. The application is available to the customer at free of cost. Normally, the application contains the following particulars:

1. Name of the applicant
2. Age and Date of Birth
3. Father/Husband's name
4. Profession
5. Address : Office and Residence (with Tel.No.)
6. Name and Signature of the referee
7. Specimen Signatures

# INTRODUCTION

A banker follows an established practice of obtaining an introduction for their new customers before opening an account with them. The application contains a column for the name and address or account number of the referee. Usually, bankers would accept the introduction given by an account-holder of the same branch. In certain cases, the officials can also introduce the applicants. For instance, an employer can introduce his employees or a Warden of a hostel can introduce his wards. These references are normally accepted. However, it is the duty of the banker to verify or crosscheck the genuineness of the introducer.

## Risks in Opening Accounts without Reference

If a banker opens an account without reference or introduction, he may have to face the following risks:

1. ***Risk of Conversion :*** As commercial banks accept cheques for collection through Savings Bank Account and Current Account, it is absolutely

necessary to know the genuineness of the parties opening accounts. Otherwise, an unscrupulous person may open an account in some one else name, steal his cheques and deposit them in this account for collection. Even though a banker might act in the course of his business and in good faith, he will be held liable for negligence and conversion. Hence the banker should take adequate care while opening accounts for new customers. The following cases explain the risks faced by the bank :

(a) *In Ladbroke Vs. Todd.:* A thief opened an account with a stolen cheque after forging the endorsement of the payee. The bank collected the cheque. The thief withdrew the amount. The bank lost the statutory protection because no introduction was obtained while opening the account.

(b) The banker should also enquire and record the name and the nature of profession or business and other particulars of the employer of a customer while opening the account as he may be held negligent if he collects for him cheques payable to his employer *(Savory & Co. Vs. Lloyds Bank Ltd., 1932).*

Two clerks working in Savory & Co. stole bearer cheques belonging to the company. They drew cheques payable to third parties. One clerk was having an account in his own name and the other in his wife's name. The stolen cheques were deposited in these accounts. Savory & Co. charged the bank for conversion on the following grounds that the bank did not make proper enquiry about (i) the customer's employment particulars and (ii) the customer's husband's name and employer's name at the time of opening the account.

(c) *In Guardians of St. John's Hampstead Vs. Barclay's Bank Ltd. (1923),* a customer opened a fictitious account, giving his real name as the referee. He gave an impressive introduction. When the problem about the conversion arose, the banker lost the statutory protection due to his failure to follow-up the reference given by the applicant.

(d) A banker cannot defend himself even though there is inadequate staff. In Cruplin Vs. London Joint Stock Bank, Justice Pick ford said: "It is no defense for a banker to say that they were so busy and had such a small staff that they could not make enquires. If they could not make enquires when necessary, they must take the consequences".

2. ***Reserve Bank of India Directions :*** The RBI has given directions to all the commercial banks, through a circular, directing them to get introduction while opening new accounts to check the black money in operation. In the absence of getting introduction, persons may open many accounts in different names. In case banks grant personal loans with out security, recovery may also be difficult.

3. ***Risks of Issuing Bogus Cheques :*** When an account is opened in the name of an unscrupulous person, cheques issued to him may be misused. After having purchased goods from different shops, he may issue cheques indiscriminately against the interest of the public. Then, the banker will be in trouble.

4. ***Risk in the case of Undischarged Insolvent :*** Having opened an account in the name of undischarged insolvent, the customer may persuade the bank to grant him overdraft, cash credit or loans. Later on, the banker may not be able to recover the funds.

5. ***Risk in the case of Minor's Account :*** When an account is opened in the name of a minor, the account should be operated by his guardian. In the absence of getting introduction about the guardian, the banker faces serious risks.

## Processing the Application

Once the application along with the specimen signatures and two copies of recent passport size photographs are given to the bank, the banker processes the application. Every detail of the application is examined by the banker, particularly the introduction and age of the applicant. If the applicant is a minor, the account should be operated by the guardian. In some cases, savings bank accounts are opened in the name of minors provided they are able to understand the banking operations. In these cases, extra care should be taken by a banker while operating his account. The banker faces serious risks because the bank will have to face all the consequences for the mistake committed by a minor.

If a banker is satisfied with the particulars given in the application, he allows the applicant to make the initial deposit (not less than the minimum balance prescribed to the account) after filling the pay-in-slip. Of the two copies of the customer's photograph, one is affixed in the specimen signature file and the other is affixed in the customer's Pass Book.

***Pay-in-slip*** is a printed slip with perforated counterfoils available at the bank. This slip is filled up showing the amount of coins, notes, bills, cheques which are paid into the credit of the customer's account. This slip contains information relating to the party depositing the money, nature of account, date and signature of the depositor. This slip is signed by the cashier and the counter-foil is returned to the depositor. The depositor can retain this as a proof for deposit.

***Pass Book :*** After having deposited the money in the new account, the customer can wait for opening an account in his name. Once an account is opened in his name, the amount is credited to his ledger. Then a Pass Book in the name of the customer is prepared and handed over to the customer.

A Pass Book is a diary-like book in which the banker records the transactions related to his customer's account for the latter's use. This diary like book is called Pass Book because it passes frequently between a banker and customer. It enables the customer to verify the entries therein with his ledger account. A businessman prepares a Bank Reconciliation Statement with the help of Pass Book. In case of any discrepancy, the customer should bring it to the notice of the banker and the banker alone can make entries in the Pass Book.

***Statement of Accounts :*** Nowadays many banks do not issue Pass Books. They send the statement of account to their customers periodically. Statement of Account is nothing but a copy of the customer's account maintained by the banker. In case customer is to know the recent transactions with the banks, the ATMs give a Mini-statement. Currently, the Pass Book is replaced by Statement of Affairs and the Pass Book has become an obsolete document.

## Law Relating to Pass Book

After having opened an account with the bank, the customer starts operating his account by depositing further sums of money into his account and withdrawing money from the account whenever needed. One of the special features of banking business is that each and every transaction with the bank is supported by a document. In case of deposit, the pay-in-slip and the Pass Book and in the case of withdrawal, the withdrawal slip or cheque leaf and the Pass Book stand as supporting documents. If certain wrong entries are made in the Pass Book, the balance in the Pass Book/Statement of Affairs may be favourable either to the banker or customer. Now the question arises whether the entries in the Pass Book or Statement of Accounts are finally binding the customer or not. Different opinions were expressed by many authors.

According to Sir John Paget, "The proper function which the pass book ought to fulfill is to constitute a conclusive an unquestionable record of transactions between the banker and the customer and it should be recognised as such. After giving full opportunity of examination on the part of the customer, all entries, at least to his debit, ought to be final and not liable to be subsequently reopened, at any rate to detriment of the banker".

Sir John Paget's definition was based on the fact that there were instructions for the customers printed in the Pass Book as *"Please tender the pass book at frequent intervals for being written up. Accumulation of entries for longer periods may mean delay in returning the pass book. Unless the constituent brings to the notice of the Bank any discrepancy/errors/omission/ unauthorised debits immediately, the entries in such pass books shall be deemed as correct and shall bind the constituent for all purposes and intents"*.

In the case of *Devaynes Vs. Noble (1816),* the same view was expressed. It was decided in this case that the Pass Book is returned to the customer for verification and if there appears any errors or omission, he should have brought it back to the bank for rectification; if not, his silence is regarded as admission of correct entries.

However, in several cases thereafter, the decision on this point has been reversed.

*In 'Keptigalle Rubber Estates Co. Vs. National Bank of India Ltd.',* Justice Bray refuted the proposition that a pass book constitutes a settled account and is binding on both banker and the customer. He remarked, "It would be absurd to hold that the taking of a pass book and its return constitutes a settled account". Similarly in *'Canara Bank Vs. Canara Sales Corporation and others',* it was held, "An implied contract as to the settlement of accounts does not arise between a customer and his banker merely by reason of the banker sending a pass book to a customer and the customer failing to point out any irregularities therein".

Another case which favoured them was Chatterton Vs. London and County Bank where in it was said, "The customer is not bound to examine the entries in his Pass Book; and that the banker, upon receipt of the pass book returned by his customer without objection from time to time, is not entitled to infer that the latter has accepted the entries as correct".

Any one may make a mistake and a banker is not an exception. If entries are made correctly in the Pass Book, no dispute arises. The problem arises only when the Pass Book contains wrong entries which may be favourable either to the customer or banker.

## Effect of Entries favourable to the Customer

The Pass Book may show a favourable balance for the customer because of duplication of credit entry, entering a higher amount for such entries or omission of a debit entry or entering a lower amount for a debit entry. In *Akrokerri (Atlantic) Mine Ltd. Vs. Economic Bank (1904),* it was held, "The Pass Book belongs to the customer and the entries made in it by the bank are statements on which the customer is entitled to act".

Relying on the higher balance shown by the Pass Book, when a customer issues a cheque, the banker is not entitled to dishonour it. If he dishonours such cheque, he will be held liable for damages. *(Holland Vs. Manchester and Liverpool District Banking Co.).* However, this does not mean that a customer can hold the banker liable for dishonouring cheques issued before he received the passbook written up with erroneous entries *(Smith Vs. Cox & Co.).*

The customer has to prove that he has acted in good faith in taking advantage of the wrong entry favourable to him. It would be difficult for businessmen to prove their innocence. As they are maintaining their regular books of accounts, they would be expected to know their receipts and payments.

But the position would be different in the case of non-traders. In the case of *'Skyring Vs. Greenwood (1825),* the decision was in favour of an army officer who received a higher amount by mistake. Trusting this balance, he was issuing cheques to different suppliers. It was held that he has spent the money overpaid while performing his duty.

In the above case, the customer has altered his position. If the customer has not altered his position by relying upon a wrong entry, then the banker will not be held liable. In the case of *'United Overseas Bank Vs. Mr.Jiwani* (1977)', the banker has credited Jiwani's account twice for $1 1,000 which facilitated him to buy a hotel with out borrowing money from elsewhere. He had issued 2 cheques for $3 1,000. On discovering the mistake, the plaintiff bank brought an action against Mr.Jiwani for the recovery of the money paid by mistake. It was held that although the banker had given him inaccurate information, Mr.Jiwani had not acted differently and Mr.Jiwani would have still purchased the hotel by borrowing extra money. Moreover, it was not fully proved that he was not aware of the wrong entry so the banker was not liable.

*In Canara Bank Vs. Canara Sales Corporation and others,* the Chief Accounts Officer of the Corporation forged the signature of the Managing Director of the Corporation on many cheques between 1957 and 1961 for more than Rs. 1,26,000. When it was discovered by the Corporation in March, 196 1, the Corporate sued the bank. But the bank replied that the Corporation did not raise any objection at the appropriate time even though the monthly statements were supplied to them regularly. It was held that the bank was liable because there was no binding on the part of the customer to examine his passbook and report the discrepancies to the bank.

## Effect of entries favourable to the Banker

The Pass Book may show a favourable balance for a banker because of duplication of debit entries, entering higher amounts for such entries; omission of credit entries or entering lower amounts on credit side of the passbook. In this case, it is difficult to define with accuracy to what extent they bind the customer. A passbook is written by the banker or his agent; hence a customer cannot be made to accept this against himself. However, when a customer has acted in a manner so as to render the entries a settled one, then, he is guilty of negligence in regard to them. However, it is still doubtful as to what acts or omission on the part of the customer are tantamount to settlement of an account or to negligence in regard thereto.

*In Balakrishnan Pramanink Vs. Bhowanipore Banking Corporation Ltd.,* the bank used to charge compound interest for the customer and was recording them in his pass book also. The customer used to scrutinise entries in the pass book and call for explanations whenever needed. Subsequently, the customer realised that he has been charged with compound interest. It was held that the customer, by his conduct, had rendered the entries as settled ones and so later on, he could not complain about the compound interest debited to his account.

In Chatterton Vs. London and County Bank, it was held that the return of the pass book by the customer to the banker did not constitute a binding acknowledgement of the accuracy of the entries even when he had placed tick marks against them. However, a signed acknowledgement of the accuracy of the entries might operate against the customer.

From the above cases it is quite clear that the banker should be careful to make entries in the pass book. If a customer, by himself takes up the duty of examining his pass book and if he is negligent of verifying those entries unfavourable to him- he is said to be negligent. Those entries constitute a settled matter and cannot be reversed after undue delay. If a particular customer has been asked to check the entries in his Pass Book, he is under obligation to examine and report any discrepancy to the bank. If he is silent, he is presumed to have accepted the entries in the pass book.

In India, the position is not well defined as in U.S. where the situation is favou'rable to a banker. In U.S. pass book/statement of account is an authentic record and one of the duties of the customer is to examine his pass book. Whenever the pass book/statement of affairs is sent to him, he should examine it carefully. Discrepancy, if any, should be brought to the notice of the bank authorities with out reasonable delay, failing which it is presumed that he has admitted the entries as correct.

Most of the commercial banks send the Statement of Accounts to their customers and ask them to verify and report any discrepancy.

## CREATION OF CREDIT

A banker is a businessman who deals with other people's money. Deposits are made by the public through Saving Bank account, Current account, Fixed Deposit account, Recurring Deposit account and miscellaneous types of accounts. In the case of term deposits (Fixed deposits, Recurring deposits and miscellaneous deposits), the banker knows the term of deposit and the time of withdrawal of such deposits. Hence, such deposits can be lent for such periods even without keeping any reserve. However, statutory reserves may have to be maintained. In the case of other deposits, although the customer can withdraw at any time, the bankers, by their experience, know that the customers may not withdraw their deposits immediately. Even if they withdraw, all customers will not withdraw at the same time.

Some account-holders, after depositing large amounts, do not operate the account at all for some time. The bankers, taking full advantage of the customer's behaviour, lend these amounts to the persons who are in need of money. Even when a banker sanctions a loan to a customer, he does not pay in cash. The customer is asked to open an account with the bank and the loan amount is placed to the credit of the borrower.

## Primary and Derivative Deposits

Primary deposits are made by the depositors in the banks with various objectives. Some of them deposit their money in the bank for safety; some others deposit such funds to meet certain unforeseen contingencies in the future while others for receiving interest on such deposits. When such deposits are made in the bank, the banker is a debtor and the customer is a creditor. The banker is obliged to repay the amount to the customer whenever demanded by him as per the terms. For instance, the customer can withdraw his money from his current account without giving notice to the bank. However, the customer cannot withdraw the amount on the same terms from fixed deposit account. The depositors will decide as to how much they should deposit and how much they would withdraw at any time. These deposits are known as Primary Deposits.

In short, Primary Deposits are those deposits through which cash flows into the firm. Primary deposits are determined by the customers.

Derivate deposits are those deposits which are derived from Primary deposits. While granting loans and advances to the customers using primary deposits, the banks do not normally pay cash to borrowers. They allow them to open an account in the bank and credit their accounts. There is no physical transfer of cash. Thus, a borrower acquires a claim against his credit balance in the bank account just as a depositor has a claim against his (primary) deposit. Derivative deposits are basically multiplied primary deposits. They are determined by the bank.

## Multiplicity of Credit Creation

Commercial banks attract various types of deposits from the public. The banker's business is to lend the same after keeping the necessary reserves as per the law. By virtue of experience, the banker knows that the deposits made with the bank may not be withdrawn for some time. Even if it is withdrawn, all depositors do not withdraw at the same time. Moreover, time deposits are not withdrawn immediately. Hence, the bank can safely lend the same to others, keeping a minimum margin for withdrawal. There are various methods of creation of credit:

### 1. Money at Call and short notice

Commercial banks fully realise the fact that the unused cash in their lockers is a loss, as they have to pay interest to the depositors. Hence, they fully make use of their resources. They lend money even for short periods ranging from 24 hours to 3 days to stockbrokers, speculators and certain businessmen who are to take delivery of their consignment immediately. The bank has a safe method of opening an account in the name of the borrower and allow him to operate the account or withdraw the amount making use of cheques supplied by the bank. Banks, with their experience, know that cash is not withdrawn immediately. The brokers/speculators issue cheques to the parties in settlement of their accounts. The parties who receive the cheques do not come to the bank for direct encashment of such cheques. In the mean time, some cheques may also be in circulation for some time by endorsement. However, ultimately, when cheques are received by the bank for clearance, the bank may not have to pay cash in most of the cases. The presenter's account (the holder) may be credited and the customer's account is debited, facilitating creation of credit. In this case, there is no physical transfer of cash. Hence, the money at call and short-notice increases the deposit of bank.

### 2. Discounting Bill of Exchange

Discounting Bill of exchange is one of the familiar methods of granting short-term loans to businessmen. In case of a credit sale, the buyer may accept the bill and the seller may discount it with a bank. The bank will discount only commercial bills for a term not exceeding 90 days. As per the practice, the banker credits the customer's account who is empowered to withdraw it by cheques. When the holder of the cheque presents it, the necessary adjustments are made. Thus, credit creation takes place.

### 3. Loans and Advances

A bank employs most of its funds through loans and advances by providing credit facilities to businessmen and others. There are three methods of lending. They are overdraft, cash credit, and loans and advances. Overdraft facility is available in current account. Overdraft is an arrangement by which the banks allow the customer to draw over and above the current balance on any day. This is a temporary credit arrangement. Cash credit is also similar to overdraft, by which the customer is allowed to overdraw his account. But the banker, in this case, grants cash credit only on the basis of some security. Loans and advances are also allowed by the bank after receiving some security.

In all the three methods of lending, the banker does not part with cash immediately but credits the customer's account. The customers are allowed to make use of the cheque facilities without paying cash. Hence, credit is multiplied.

### 4. Investments

In a few cases the commercial bank invests in long term securities such as government bonds, shares, debentures etc. The bank may issue a cheque drawn in the name of the seller who will again deposit the same into bank for collection, facilitating credit creation.

The question arises as to whether a bank can lend money more than what it has. There may be divergent views on this issue. Some are optimistic in saying that a bank can lend more than what it has whereas some others wonder as to how it would be possible for a long time.

## Mechanism of Credit Creation

The optimists argue that bank deposits are promises on the part of the bank that they would repay their deposits as and when demanded by them. As bankers lend loans and advances to the borrowers without physical transfer of money, the credit creation takes place. Such created money adds to the total money supply of the bank in the country as a whole. Thus, we have a concept of real money and credit money. Bank credit refers to multiplication of loans and advances. Thus, banks acquire assets in the form of cash, securities, bonds, other fixed assets and created deposits. Sayers remarks, "Banks are not merely purveyors of money but also, in an important sense, manufacturers of money." The following is the formula.

$$k = \frac{1}{r}$$

where, k=deposit multiplier

r = ratio of cash reserves to deposits.

For instance, if the bank receives a deposit of Rs. 1,000 from a customer and the cash reserve ratio being 20%, the deposit multiplier will be calculated as follows :

Cash received from the depositors Rs. 1,000. Leaving 20% as reserve for withdrawal by the depositor, the bank can lend Rs. 800. When the bank lends this amount, the borrower's account is credited with Rs. 800. The Total Multiplier at this stage will be (1,000+800) Rs. 1,800.The final sum arrived at will be :

1,000 + 800 + 640 + 512 + 409 + 328 + 262..... 5,000.

Using the formula :

$$k = \frac{1}{r}$$

$$k = \frac{1}{.2}$$

= 5 times of the deposit

Total credit = 5 × 1000 = 5,000.

The creation of credit depends on the ratio of cash reserves to deposits (r), which is determined by the bank. It also depends on the number of times the loan is multiplied. In case a banker lends from the deposit only one time, then the multiplier will be only Rs. 1,800. (Cash deposit Rs. 1,000 and Loan granted to the borrower Rs. 800).

Hence, lower the cash reserve ratio, higher will be deposit multiplier; higher the number of times multiplied, higher will be the multiplier.

Some bankers are ventureous and keep only a small percentage for the withdrawal of depositors and lend the balance to the persons who are in need of loans. They also try to maximise their lending. In case of conservative lenders, the quantum of credit creation will be lesser as they are risk avoiders. Persons like Edwin Cannon, Walter and Leaf do not agree with the idea of creation of credit.

## Limitation of Creation of Credit:

It may appear that the banks can create unlimited credit. But it is highly dangerous to create credit beyond certain level. As long as the depositors do not demand for money, the banker has no problem. But for some reason or other, when they begin to withdraw, the bank may not be able to meet their demands, finally leading to liquidation of the bank. The following are the limitations of credit creation:

### 1. Quantum of Money in the Bank

The limiting factor for credit creation is the quantum of cash that a bank has in its vaults. Banks may obtain cash through primary deposits, owned capital and borrowed funds. If the bank has larger cash, large credit can be raised. According to Crowther, "The bank's cash is the lever with which the whole gigantic system is manipulated." Higher the percentage of cash reserve ratio, the smaller will be the volume of credit creation.

### 2. Ratio of Cash Reserves

The customers continue to deposit and withdraw money every day. As long as the deposits match with the withdrawals, theoretically, the banker does not have to keep any reserve. However, on some days, the withdrawals may exceed deposits. In order to meet the customers' needs, banks always keep with them a portion of deposits as reserve to meet the demands of the customers. Even the RBI Act has given direction to the commercial banks to maintain reserves. According to Section 42 of the RBI Act, 1934, every scheduled bank should keep a minimum cash reserve known as statutory reserve with the RBI. The statutory reserve may vary between 3% and 15% of the time and demand liabilities. The RBI will notify the cash reserve ratio, from time to time, in the official Gazette of India. In case the RBI increases the cash reserve ratio, the amount available for lending is reduced. If the cash reserve is less, the amount available for lending is more, leading to multiplication of more credit.

### 3. Confidence of the Public

The entire exercise of credit creation depends on the confidence enjoyed by the public. A slightest suspicion about the reputation of the bank will force the customers withdraw all their funds, bringing disaster to the bank. Alternatively, tremendous confidence in the bank will ease the situation and enable the bank to lend all their funds without keeping even reasonable reserves. The success of the bank depends on its ability to meet the demand of the depositors.

### 4. Business Conditions

The nature of business conditions would determine the volume of credit creation. The trade cycle consists of different stages such as boom period, stagnation period and recession/depression periods. During boom periods, the industries flourish and there is optimism all over. The entrepreneurs who would look for more opportunities resort the help of the banks for advances. They influence the banks to multiply credit. However, during times of depression, the economic activities lie low, making the entrepreneurs to adopt more cautious approach. This leads to lesser demand for cash and lesser credit creation.

### 5. Desire to hold Cash

The public deposit their savings in the commercial banks. In case of adverse economic conditions, the prices are very high and the people need more money and withdraw their deposits leading to depleted funds in the banks. This would restrict the ability of the bank to create more credit.

### 6. Banking Practices

The banking practices play a significant role in expanding the credit. Only when cheques are widely accepted, the bank can multiply their credit by providing cheque facilities to all their clients. Cheque currency acts as a substitute for cash. But in a country like India, cheques are not popularly accepted even by businessmen for variety of reasons.

### 7. Availability of Honest and Sound Borrowers

There may be different types of borrowers. Some of them borrow without any security and want immediate cash. Some others provide adequate security for obtaining loans. The banks can take loans on the strength of such securities and lend to other customers. According to Sayers, "The banks put this newly created money into the hands, not of everybody at once, but of those individuals who can offer to the bank the kind of asset which the bank think attractive."

## MODEL QUESTIONS

**Section - A**

1. What are the primary functions of Commercial banks?

2. What is the main source of income for a commercial bank?
3. What are Time Deposits?
4. Write a note on "Recurring Deposit".
5. List out the miscellaneous types of deposits.
6. What are Demand Deposits?
7. Give reasons for verifying the introductory letter at the time of opening a Current Account.
8. What are the principles of lending?
9. List out the methods of lending.
10. Distinguish between cash credit and overdraft.
11. Write a note on Credit Card.
12. Write a note on Primary Deposits.
13. Write a note on Derivative Deposits.
14. List out the various methods of creation of credit.
15. List out the general utility services rendered by Commercial Banks.
16. What is Electronic Banking?
17. What is a debit card?
18. What is Electronic Fund Transfer system?
19. What do you mean by Any Time Banking?
20. Explain Anywhere Banking.
21. What is Tele banking?
22. Explaining Banking through Internet.
23. What is SWIFT?
24. Can an advertisement by a bank inviting customers to open an account be considered as an offer?
25. Distinguish between a withdrawal slip and a cheque.
26. Write a note on pay-in-slip.
27. Who is a survivor?
28. What are the contents of a pass book?
29. Write a note on statement of accounts.
30. What are the advantages for a banker in preparing statement of accounts?
31. Distinguish between statement of affairs and a pass book.

**Section - B**

1. Write short notes on (1) Teller System and (2) ATM.
2. What are the risks faced by the banker in opening the savings or current account in the name of a customer without introduction?

3. Explain the effect of entries in the pass book favourable to the banker.
4. Explain the effect of entries in the pass book favourable to the customer.
5. Are entries in the pass book is a conclusive proof of the record of transactions anker and the customer?
6. Describe briefly the agency services rendered by the banks in order to facilitate the customers.
7. Explain the various general utility services rendered by the Commercial Banks.
8. Briefly explain the different Time Deposit accounts.
9. Explain the different types of Demand Deposit accounts.
10. Write short notes on (1) Mail Transfer (2) Telegraphic transfer and (3) Traveller's Cheques.
11. What are different methods of lending adopted by Commercial Banks.
12. Write short notes on Banker's service as the Referee and as Trustee and Executor.
13. What are the limitations of Credit Creation?
14. What are the miscellaneous services offered by banks?
15. Explain the risks in opening of a bank account without reference.
16. What are the laws relating to pass book?

**Section - C**

1. Define Banking as per Banking Regulation Act. Discuss the functions of commercial Banks.
2. Bring out clearly various types of deposits.
3. "Loans create deposits". Discuss the statement.
4. Explain in details the mechanism of credit creation.
5. Explain the procedure adopted by a bank in opening a deposit account.

# 7

# ELECTRONIC BANKING

The revolution of information technology has made a tremendous impact in the banking industry. The manual process is being converted into computers for doing the transaction processing. The basic accounting registers have been changed into and storage into of floppies digital audiotapes and compact disc. The very outlook of the banking hall is changing from a clumpsy look with counters, books, registers overflowing cupboards, to neat counters with just PC for an operator, and well decorated banking hall. The trade is undergoing just drastic changes in the payment systems through the medium of point of sales terminals and Electronic Fund Transfer Point of Sales (EFTPOS) through cards. The communication within/between the branches of the banks are replacing a typed letter on paper to electronic media through e-mail. The banking industry is trying to take advantage of the revolution in the information technology towards reducing the cost of operation, to improve its efficiency to provide better customer services and to meet the competition inside and outside the industry. Some of the technology adopted by the banking industry will be dealt in detail.

## ANY TIME BANKING

Any Time Banking refers to banking service available 24 hours a day and 365 days a year. Such a facility is made available to the customers through AUTOMATED TELLER MACHINES (ATMs). In the present day of severe competition banking services are driven by technology which is more oriented towards better services to the customers. The very fundamental concepts of banking especially relating to the place of banking, banking hours, remittance business have started to loose their meaning.

## AUTOMATED TELLER MACHINE (ATM)

ATM is a machine in the nature of a computer in general sense, but it is dedicated to do certain type of specific jobs only. It is a very user-friendly system and the customer does not require any training to use it. It is totally menu driven which displays instructions to the customers step by step as to how to operate the ATM. The hardware and software used in the ATMs are proprietary that is, the software used in one machine cannot be used in another machine. Further in the manufacture of ATMs, there are no specific standards and each of the vendors follows his own specifications. So each model is different. However, the functionality aspects of the ATMs are uniform.

### History of ATM

The first ATM was developed in the year 1965 and introduced by Barclays Bank, London. This was a primitive model in which the customers were expected to go to the teller, get a voucher passed and then go to the machine insert the voucher into the machine to obtain cash payment. This was not that useful as the only utility was to replace some of the work carried out by the cashier/ teller. The first model of the ATM was introduced by Chemical Bank in the year 1969.

### Types of ATM

ATMs are of two types :

1. Cash Dispensers
2. Full Function ATMs.

The full-fledged functions performed by ATM's are

1. Deposit of cheques or cash
2. Sale of stamps
3. Account balance enquiry
4. Update pass book
5. Generate statement of accounts
6. Utility payment like payment of telephone bills or electricity bills.
7. Request for a chequebook.

The cash dispensers will have limited functions when compared to the full function ATMs. Cash dispensers can be networked and can be made on- line with branch systems.

The limitations of cash dispensers are

1. Accept cash
2. Cannot dispense non currency instruments like issue of cheque books, gift cheques or travèler's cheque

## Models of ATM

Basically, there are three models of ATM

*(a)* WALL TYPE
*(b)* LOBBY TYPE
*(c)* DRIVE–IN TYPE

In the wall type the facial of the ATM is located in the closed lobby. Access to the lobby is restricted. The customer has to insert the card in the slot kept near the door kept outside. An independent card reader will check the validity. Video Surveillance is kept outside to take the picture of the customer involved in the transaction. In USA installation of Video Surveillance is mandatory.

The lobby type ATM is placed in a secure place but the facial opens into the lobby of banking hall, hotel, airport lounge etc., this will be located in busy places. A shutter protects this type. After the insertion of card in the slot, the machine will be automated for transaction.

The purpose of drive-in-type is the customer should be able to operate the ATM without getting out of his car. Continuous monitoring and cleaning of this type is necessary, as it will be exposed to pollution.

## Advantages of ATMs

1. Customer can choose his transaction according to his convenience.
2. The banking hours are effectively increased from a minimum of 4 hours to the maximum of 24 hours.
3. As it is menu driven, the customer knows how to operate the ATM in a simple manner.
4. The indifferent behaviour of employees because of inexperience, job stress and ignorance could be avoided, as there is no personal contact between the banker and the customer.

## Limitations of ATM

1. Cash withdrawals for large amount are not permitted.
2. Other banking activities like for credit limits and locker facilities, the customer has to contact the banker in person.
3. Cash dispensation is restricted to certain denominations only.

## CREDIT CARD

A credit card system is a type of retail transaction settlement and credit system, named after the small plastic card issued to users of the system.

- A plastic card that can be used by the holder to make purchases or obtain cash advances available by the card issuing financial institutions
- Some of the world wide accepted credit cards are American Express, Diners club, Euro card/Master card, Visa etc.,

### Classification of Credit Cards

Credit cards can also be classified as general purpose and proprietary cards. General-purpose cards are those which are accepted by merchants in addition to accepting Master card and Visa cards. On the other hand, proprietary cards are those, which are tied to the retailer. These cards can be used in the retail store.

Credit cards are now available with low- value cards, high – value cards, gold cards with different limits and additional facilities attached to it like group insurance, specific concessions on specific use.e.g. Air travel and hotel accommodation.

## FACILITIES OFFERED UNDER CREDIT CARD

### Cash Advance Facilities.

Most of the credit cards provide for cash withdrawal through ATMs. However, this is a chargeable service. Banks will impose maximum and minimum amount and multiple amounts. Banks may impose a withdrawal limit of say 10,000 during a calendar month. Usually, the service charges imposed by banks may range from 1.5to 2 %of the withdrawal amount with a minimum say 20Rs. To 25 Rs. Per withdrawal. Thus, the cardholder will have to pay within the next billing cycle.

### Special Travel Service

Some of the banks have arrangement with hotels and airlines, wherein special discounts are allowed for the cardholder ranging from 10% - 20%.

### Supplementary Cards

Family/spouse can make use of these cards. The banks for the issue of such cards give age restrictions. When the card holder is away from the family, say on business tour, the nominated member can make use of these cards The bank may or may not charge extra for the issue of such cards.

### Teledrafts

If the cardholder needs a draft or a pay order the customer need not come into the bank. He can call up the bank and give the necessary details of the draft to be issued and indicate the card number. The bank will take up the responsibility of sending the draft to the customer for a nominal fee.

### Personal Accident Insurance Cover

This is an additional facility adopted by most of the banks to the cardholder. The insurance cover may vary from 2 lacs to 8 lacs. The amount may vary depending upon the type of the card. This coverage may be applicable for spouse also.

### Flexible Repayment Options

Under this facility, the cardholder need not pay full amount of the purchase made and demand raised. Depending upon the terms of the issue, the cardholder may pay 5% to 10% of the amount and roll over the amount to the next billing cycle. The roll over amount is treated as advance by the banks and the amount carried over will be charged 2.5% as interest.

Other facilities may include things like free supply of magazines, Payments at Petrol bunks and holiday packages etc.,

## PERSONAL IDENTIFICATION NUMBER -ATM TRANSACTION SECURITY

The cardholder operates the ATM by inserting the card into a slot and then by keying in the PIN. Recognition of the cardholder by the ATM will be made only through PIN. The cardholder should maintain the secrecy of the PIN digits. He should not keep both the card and the PIN number together. In case the card is lost, it is the PIN number which will come for the cardholder's rescue.

Access lock and video surveillance system are other form of security for the ATM's from vandalism.

Data Encryption—Decryption is a process by which sensitive data such as PIN can be rendered unintelligible for storage in a database or when being transmitted over any communication lines and then subsequently returned to its original form when necessary, Data Encryption Standards (DES) is approved by International Organisation of Standards (ISO) for use with ISO standards related to PIN security and message authentication.

A key is a sequence of numbers used as one of the variable input into the DES algorithm and plays an important role in encryption-decryption process. The security of the DES encryption and decryption is dependent upon on the encryption key confidential. To ensure total secrecy of the keys it is generally split into two parts, with each part know only to one person. Thus, at any point of time any one person knows the entire key.

Crime prevention through environment design is another strategy for safety of the system as well as its users.

- Access lock should be on the lobby door to restrict trespassing.
- Set-up a real view mirror in the ATM lobby
- ATM should not be installed to Crime Prone area.
- Providing hidden cameras or video surveillance system in the lobby for tracing or identifying the culprit.

## DEBIT CARD

The debit cad is a plastic card used at the point of sales to make payments for generally small amounts and also for withdrawing cash. A debit card is basically a better way of carrying cash or Chequebook. It is an electronic card that one can use as a convenient payment mechanism. The card is generally issued by the bank and connected through ATM.

The major differences between credit and debit cards are

| **Credit Card** | **Debit Card** |
|---|---|
| **1. Accesibility** | |
| Customer uses his line of credit | customer access to his deposit accounts |
| **2. Transaction process** | |
| Borrowing funds from bank to payment | drawing funds from his deposit to make payment. |

Debit card allows the holder to spend only what is in his account and purchases should be kept track of just as if one is writing a cheque. Debit card usually offers some protection against loss, theft or unauthorized use, which the stored value card does not.

There are two types of debit card. They are direct debit card and deferred debit card.

Direct debit cards allow only "on-line" transactions, also called point of sale. It is an immediate electronic transfer of money from your bank account to the merchants' account. The system will check whether one has necessary funds in his account for the purchase.

A deferred debit card looks similar to the credit card bearing a Visa or Master card logo, and can be used whenever your cards name is displayed; it is not a credit card. Rather, this card allows "off-line" transactions as well as on line. The merchant's terminal reads your card and creates a debit against your account. However, instead of debiting your account immediately, the transaction is stored for processing later- usually within two or three days.

### Benefits of Debit cards

1. Obtaining a debit card is very easy. If you open a bank account, you can get a debit card.
2. Debit cards are more readily accepted than Cheques.
3. It frees you from carrying Cheques book or cash.
4. When using debit card one dos not have to show identification papers or give out personal information during the course of transaction.
5. This is of great use to international travelers from having to stock up on travelers cheques or cash during their journeys.

### Drawbacks of Debit Card

Unlike credit card debit card will not give you any grace period. They are immediate pay now deal. You have to keep record of your transactions.The debit card is very costly especially when using an ATM that is not affiliated with your bank.

## SMART CARDS

Smart cards are plastic cards like credit cards just the size of the visiting card with an implanted computer chip on them, which is responsible for storing sensitive data and processing them. Today in western countries a person carries a variety of cards like library card, video rental card, insurance card, frequent flyer card etc. The first smart card came into existence in 1977.

Some major developments in smart card field in India are.

- The Indian postal department brought out smart cards way back in 1995
- IIT Mumbai has given smart cards for students for the use of canteen, library and general stores.
- Bharath Petroleum launched India's first retail and loyalty card for petroleum. Consumers can pay for fuel and other purchases through this card.
- Prepaid phone card, Internet banking, Internet shopping, transportation, health care are some of the areas of application for smart cards.

### Working of Smart Cards

The smart card has to be inserted into smart card reader, which in turn reads the information stored in the card. Then after appropriate action has been taken, the reader updates the information on the card.

The smart cards have built insecurity keys such as PIN that authenticates the user. Secondly, tampering with a smart card is difficult, as this would destroy the microchip inside. Thirdly, manual entering of access code is eliminated. It is an intrinsically secure device.

The future of the smart card depends on the amount of the data that can be stored on them and also the type of the data that can be stored.

## ELECTRONIC FUND TRANSFER

The transfer of funds in India is practically done through Telegraphic transfers, Mail transfer and Drafts. However, the courier services changed the situation but it is restricted to certain areas like, cities and metros.

Normally, the TT credit to be credited to the beneficiary account after 2 to 4 days. With the improved technology in communication coupled with the privatization of banks necessitated the Government to feel the importance of Electronic Fund Transfer. Government constituted Saraf Committee to draw up blue print for the phased improvement in this system.

1. The standard procedure for sending a TT electronically is as follows.
2. Application should be obtained according to the standard procedure.
3. Transmission of data will take place after inputting the data into the system
4. Interpreting the message at the receiving end.
5. Downloading the data into the system for processing.

The advantage that one can get out of EFT is once the data is fed into the system, no manual intervention takes place. However, for this the adoption of technology should be of very high level.

### BANKNET and RBI Net

RBI has come out successfully in the implementation of EFT (RBIEFT), which will be available to all the banks for transfer of funds. The carrier will be known as BANKNET. The software used for this RBIEFT will be RBInet.

The communication between the offices of the RBI will be on the BANKnet

### IDBRT VSAT Network

The Institute for Development and Research in Banking Technology (IDRBT) Hyderabad has planned to set-up a Nation-wide WAN using the VSAT technology to provide communication infrastructure services to the Indian Banking Industry. This will enable the banking sector in meeting their communication requirements to increase efficiency, improve the quality of present services and provide new services to the customers. The network is intended to enable the following applications.

- Database queries
- Transacted oriented applications
- File transfer
- Any-Where banking
- Automated Teller Machine
- Credit/Debit card applications
- EFT at point of sales
- Inter branch Reconciliation
- Government securities transaction settlement
- Currency chest accounting
- Corporate Web Sites

The actual design of the network will be as follows:

- CENTRAL HUB
- REMOTE (VSAT)

### Central Hub

The Hub, which will be located at IDRBT, Hyderabad is the center of all the network activities. The equipment, hardware and software located at Hub will control, monitor and manage the entire network. This Hub configuration will be able to take of about 1000 VSAT supporting banking applications. All the components are configured in such a way that the failure of any part of the component does not affect the normal operations. This will ensure continuous service since the application is time sensitive.

### VSAT

VSAT (Very Small Aperture Terminal) is the equipment, which is installed at the end user premises. It provides the end user an access to the entire network the two types of VSAT which are used in the IDRBT network

Type 1 VSAT is used for applications, which require less bandwidth and low speed.

Type 11 VSAT provides high bandwidth and faster response from the network. This is required for applications such as video conferencing, voice and to transfer large databases.

## ELECTRONIC FUND TRANSFER FROM POINT OF SALES (EFTPOS)

This relates to credit card/debit card/smart cards, when these are used for purchase of an item or for payment of a service, the card are inserted into a terminal kept at the merchant's store. As soon as the card is inserted, the terminal shows the details of the card. The genuiness of the card is verified for effecting the necessary transaction. The equipments for the terminals are purchased or leased to the merchants. The POS terminals have proved to be very effective in combating fraudulent transaction by on-line verification of the cards.

On the larger issue of electronically initiated funds transfer, issues like authentication of payments instructions, the responsibility of the customer for secrecy of the security procedure would also need to be addressed

## ONLINE TAX ACCOUNTING SYSTEM (OLTAS)

The Income Tax Department has set up a National Tax Information Network (TIN) to act as repository of all related information, including payment and refund of taxes. It would enable assesses to pay taxes and get refunds electronically, besides providing the Income Tax Department with information for accounting in a scientific and accurate manner. Under the OLTAS a network of about 11,000 branches of various branches of various banks authorized for collection of tax receipts has been established. The Reserve Bank and the Tax Information Repository and National Securities Depository Ltd. (NSDL) are also a part of OLTAS. Data are captured from the challans submitted by tax payers tendered at the designated bank branches and transmitted electronically to the repository. The OLTAS works in a fully secured environment, with data being transmitted through encryption facilities and digital signatures for enhanced security.

## ON LINE BANKING

This would mean any banking service delivered to the customer by means of a computer-controlled system that does not directly involve the usual bank's branch. In essence in virtual banking the traditional paradigm of customer's integration is replaced by an electronic paradigm, which is very innovative. In the changing environment adaptation to market realities as well as technology is causing the virtual banking revolution. Thus, online banking is the result of customer-pull and bank-push. The customer can access the bank round the clock from their homes, offices, while on the move, or from any other place where the connectivity could be established. For customers, Internet banks provide 24 hours access to an account, allowing them to pay the bills, to categories their income and expenses, to produce cash flow reports and to print budgets whenever they please.

The reasons for the rapid development of on-line banking are :

1. The routine banking transaction is becoming cumbersome, costly and time consuming.
2. The introduction of ATM imparted flexibility to bank customers and gave further fillip to virtual banking
3. The use of computers as accounting tool and also as a tool to expand and improve customer service.
4. The introduction of credit cards and debit cards helped both the consumers and retailers to be free from cash handling.

## Benefits to the Banks

*(i)* Lower operating costs

*(ii)* Possibilities of attracting new customers

*(iii)* Greater operational/customer base

*(iv)* Reduce overall risk to the institution handling transactions

*(v)* Greater opportunities to sell across

*(vi)* Saving on cost of developing system through sharing of network

## Benefits to Customer

1. More convenience
2. Wider range of products and services available to the customers
3. At lower cost they can access for banking services
4. They can be more aware of the stage of their accounts.

The banks should ensure the following service standards :

*(i)* The service should be error free

*(ii)* Attitudinal change should be there by the banks to take of the marketing of their products which should be consumer centered

*(iii)* It should be used for routine transactions. The services could be used for selling more profitable products such as loans and investment products.

The popularity which virtual banking have won among customers, owing to speed and convenience, is likely to have more demand in the future. While most of the electronic banking have built-in security features such as encryption, prescriptions, maximum monetary limits and authorizations. The system operators have to be extremely vigilant and provide clear-cut guidelines.

## UPDATION FACILITIES

From the conventional banking where the services are provided manually across the table, it has come to a stage where the customer is not required to visit the bank for routine transactions. Some of them are dealt as follows :

## TELE BANKING

In this, the customer is required to open the account with the bank initially by visiting the bank. The customer is given the additional facility of using the telephone line for certain type of routine transactions. The bank generally provides telephone-banking services over the telephone on a special number. The number at the bank is connected to a terminal in the bank, which is either handled manually or is automated by connecting the same to the computer network.

The services that are available provided under tele banking can be classified under groups :

### 1. Public enquiry

This refers to routing enquiry by the customers as well as non-customer for information like interest rates, facilities offered.

### 2. Private Enquiry

The other enquiries are specific to account, which are confidential in nature and will be revealed to the account holder. The Following

- Balance in the account will be verified after giving the code and the account number
- The customer can find out the status of the cheques issued by him or cheque deposit for credit of his account.
- The customer can also request for issue of cheques for his account.
- Request for the statement of accounts
- Requesting the bank through the identification code conveyed over phone can make cash withdrawal. Later, the bank arranges to deliver the cash through staff or courier the same. Issue of draft is also possible by adopting the same procedure as that of cash withdrawal.

## HOME BANKING

In addition to the following facilities available in tele-banking, the following are the facilities available in home banking.

- Browse through his account
- Down load statement of account
- User remittances or payment of bills.

However, for providing such facilities the banks impose their own restrictions of maintaining the minimum balance to cover technology overheads costs to some extent.

## CORPORATE BANKING

Providing terminal to customers generally to the corporate offices (REMOTE TERMINAL -RT) could be one of the business strategies for the banks. In this case instead of permitting the customers to log in from his home/office or even while on move, the corporate clients are provided the terminal in their office to enable them to access their account for certain limited purposes. Since RT is for specific functions these could be done by specific software, which could be menu, driven. Through this terminal the customer could do the followings

- Balance enquiry
- Status enquiry of cheque payment or collections
- Down load statement of account
- Pass on instructions to the bank for payment of salaries/due to the staff
- Opening of letter of credit/guarantees
- Receive intimation/advises from the bank

## MODEL QUESTIONS

**Section - A**

1. What do you mean by the term electronic banking?
2. List the various reasons why there is a necessity for the hanks to change from their traditional type of working?
3. What do you mean by ATM?
4. State the different models of ATM.
5. What is PIN?
6. What do you mean by an e-mail?
7. Define an on-line banking.
8. What do you mean by an EFT?
9. Name some of the software used in the networking of banks.
10. List some of the facilities of the credit card holder.
11. What will be he future of the smart card in India?
12. What is a debit card?
13. What do you mean by tele banking?
14. What is home banking?

15. What is Corporate banking?
16. What is OLTAS?

**Section - B**

1. Explain the advantages of ATM.
2. What are facilities offered under HUB?
3. Distinguish credit card from debit card.
4. Bring out some of the developments of Smart card in India.
5. Explain the process involved in OLTAS.
6. State the advantages of on- line banking.
7. Bring out the importance of EFT

**Section - C**

1. Discuss the importance of Personal Identification Number in the electronic security transaction.
2. Bring out a detailed essay on the ATM cards.
3. Elaborate the various facilities offered to the credit card holders.
4. Discuss the methodology adopted by the Banks in EFT.
5. Bring out the importance of online banking and substantiate your views.
6. Explain the various updation facilities of the banking industry in detail.
7. Write an essay of the future developments of the banking industry with respect to electronic banking.

# 8

# ELECTRONIC CLEARING SYSTEM

Historically in most of the developing countries where banking facilities were not well developed, the system of payment by cheques was not quite common and the demand for cash was high. But in recent years the use of cheque system has become popular in our economy. This has led to the establishment of an efficient clearing system.

A clearing house may be described as an Organisations get-up by banks operating at a particular place, for facilitating settlement of their claims against each other as represented by cheques, drafts and other instruments drawn on various banks.

The clearing system makes available to banks (which are members of the clearing house) a simple and efficient means of exchanging and obtaining payment for cheques drawn on other member banks. Each member bank sends to the clearing house, daily a clerk, who delivers the cheques etc., to representatives of the banks on which they are drawn. The cheques delivered by a bank constitute its "inward clearing." Assuming that all cheques are paid, a bank has to pay or receive the net difference between its outward and inward clearings for the day. Cheques which are returned unpaid become the "outward clearing" of that bank and correspondingly, they become the inward clearing for the bank which has initially delivered them. An outward clearing for bank represents amounts receivable and an inward clearing means amounts payable. The settlement of the day's clearing or, in other words, receipts and payments of the balances receivable and payable are effected through the member banks' accounts with RBI or the State Bank of India. This is the broad mechanism of the working of a clearing house.

Membership of a clearing house is usually open to a scheduled bank though a non-scheduled bank may be admitted as member if the rules of the clearing house so provide. The clearing houses are autonomous bodies and frame their rules and regulations, which, *inter alia,* may lay down the conditions which a bank must fulfil for being admitted as a member, e.g., it should be a scheduled bank or should have cleared through another member bank, a certain minimum number of cheques. The rules also provide for clearing hours, arrangements for return of unpaid cheques, etc. Although, the RBI has not framed any "regulations" for management of clearing houses, it has provided the required assistance and guidance to the clearing houses for framing their rules and regulations. Wherever the RBI has an office, the clearing house at that centre is managed by the Bank; at other places they are managed by the SBI or its subsidiaries.

All the labour, delay, risk and expenditure are substantially reduced, by the representative of all the banks meeting at a specified place at a stipulated time, for exchanging the instruments and arriving at the net position regarding receipts and payments. The place where the banks meet and settle their dues is called the 'clearing house'. The banks who are members of the clearing house maintain accounts with the supervising bank. The settlement of dues is done by the supervising bank by debiting or crediting, as the case may be, the accounts of the respective banks. The clearing house arrangement exists in most of the towns. The supervising bank of the clearing house is the RBI at places where it has a banking department. In other centres, SBI, a subsidiary of SBI or a scheduled bank conducts the clearing house.

In the clearing house, the representatives of banks meet on every working day, at a stipulated time and present all the instruments. Specific rules have been formulated regarding the working of the clearing house. According to these rules, the instruments that can be presented include ' besides cheques, demand drafts, dividend warrants, pay orders, Indian Postal Orders and bills accepted payable at a member bank and due on the date of clearing. Each instrument should bear a clearing house stamp with the name of the bank sending it and the date and hour of clearing through which it is passed. Each member bank sending the instrument to the clearing house, should be careful to see that the instruments are *prima-facie* in order, so that as few as possible may have to be returned unpaid for technical reasons.

Each instrument returned unpaid should have a written answer attached to it, stating the cause of dishonour; moreover, the instrument should be returned through the clearing house before a stipulated time. All instruments, except those which are returned unpaid within the stipulated time, are deemed to have been paid by the drawee bank. However, if the drawee bank wishes to return an instrument after the stipulated time it may do so, by sending the instrument to the presenting bank at the counter, with a request to accept the instrument as a special case. Such a return is a matter of mutual courtesy between banks and cannot be claimed as a matter of right by the drawee bank.

When it is necessary to return a cheque, the reason for the return should be clearly stated on a separate memo, usually called a return memo, so as not to cast, as far as possible, any aspersion on the drawer's credit.

## CLEARING SYSTEM

Bank functions involve among other things, transfer of deposit from one person to another. The transfer of Mr. A in Mumbai to the account of Mr. B. in Kanpur branch of the same Bank is simple enough; the entire transaction is internal to the Bank concerned. But when the debtor and creditor i.e. the drawer and the payee of the cheque, bank with Central Bank of India writes a cheque in favour of Mr. B who banks with Canara Bank, how is the deposit actually transferred from one to the other? It would seem that the Canara Bank will send its representative to the branch of the Central Bank of India and obtain payment and put it into the account of the customer.

This will not be a feasible proposition because everyday individuals all over the country are sending cheques drawn on their accounts at one bank to people who bank with other banks. There will be a continual stream into each bank, of cheque drawn on each of the other banks. Such exchange of cheques therefore takes place in the Clearing House.

Clearing is an arrangement through which a bank exchanges cheques drawn on other banks for those drawn on it. In the absence of such an arrangement, each bank would have to present cheques to each of the other banks for receiving payment of cheques over which they have a claim. Not that it is not done anywhere (-at small centres with say two bank branches and limited transactions, across the counter bilateral settlement is still being done-), but the volume of transactions and the number of bank branches at many centres will render the above process impracticable.

The Representatives of all banks in a city meet at stipulated times at the Clearing House and exchange cheques. Getting back to their respective banks, they put through the cheques in the concerned accounts. Instruments which are unpaid and so dishonoured are returned to the banks which presented them, when they meet again during the day, or on the next day. This also known as 'Special Clearing'.

### Settlement

Let us see how the settlement takes place actually.

The Central Bank of India presents cheques drawn on other banks which were paid in by its customers. The instruments are grouped by the Central Bank of India bank-wise and the amount due from each bank-wise and the amount due from each bank is shown therein. The aggregate of these amounts represents the total amount to be received by Central Bank of India from all other banks. The instruments are presented to the respective banks along with a memo. Likewise, Central Bank of India also receives cheques presented by other banks. The aggregate of the totals of such instruments delivered by other banks represents the total amount of cheques drawn on Central Bank of India and payable by it. The difference between the two amounts is the net debit or credit to Central Bank of India, i.e. the net amount payable or receivable by it as the case may be. The Central Bank of India as well as other member banks keep an account with the presiding bank-branch (Which manages the clearing house), through which these debits/credits are passed.

## Clearing House

The primary object of the Clearing House in a town is to make arrangements for the speedy and economic collection of cheques, bills and other documents payable or deliverable through offices of the members and sub-members of the House situated in that town by a system or systems of clearing.

Whenever Reserve Bank of India (RBI) is willing to undertake the management of the Clearing House, or the State Bank of India (SEBI) or one of its associates (as may be specified by the SEBI) in the event of RBI not undertaking the management, and in the absence of either, one of the public sector banks in that centre which may be specified by the RBI, shall be bank managing the Clearing House. The manager of the branch of the bank managing the Clearing House shall be the ex-officio President of the Banker's Clearing House at the centre. The President shall be the ultimate authority in managing the Clearing House. The President is assisted by a Standing Committee.

Clearing houses are established in most of the cities, where the volume of cheques is large. Some centres have more than one clearing per day. This arrangement results in considerable saving of time and costs.

Clearing houses are autonomous institutions having informal regulations and rules regarding the conduct of operations. Reserve Bank of India for this purpose has published "Uniform Regulations and Rules for Bank's Clearing Houses". These are related to, among other subjects, admission of members, entrance fee, minimum daily balance in the house, cessation of membership, jurisdiction of clearing, hours of clearing, return discipline, and other relative matters.

Some important rules for the conduct of Bankers' Clearing House are furnished below.

Rule 14. All cheques and other documents passed through the clearing shall bear a Clearing House stamp affixed by the collecting member bank with its name and the name of the branch presenting the documents and indicating the date of clearing and delivery through which these are passed.

*Note:* For the purpose of these rules, documents will include, besides cheques, bankers' demand drafts, dividend warrants, pay orders, Indian postal orders and bills accepted payable at a member bank and due on date of clearing but will not include coupons and bankers' fixed deposit receipts.

Rule 15. The members agree that the Clearing House stamp of a member affixed on a document shall denote and mean.

*(i)* When the document is drawn payable to the member or to a sub member sponsored by such member on account of a named, e.g. ABC Bank A/c XYZ, a discharge by endorsement by such member, and a certificate by it to the effect that the document has been or will be credited to the account of such person.

*(ii)* In the case of any other document payable to or endorsed in favour of a member or such sub-member a discharge by endorsement by endorsement by such member or as the case may be by such sub-member.

Rule 16. All documents to be cleared must be properly endorsed or otherwise discharged before being sent to the Clearing House. The supervisor of the Clearing House shall assume that the documents being exchanged are in all respects complete.

Special crossing stamps standardised by RBI must be branded on the face of each clearing instrument.

*Size :* Two parallel lines of length 2 inches at a distance of 1/4th inch between them. The names of the bank and the branch are to be incorporated in between the lines.

*Placement :* At the top left hand corner with a slanting of 60 degrees to the base and should be affixed in such a manner that it does not deface the crossings etc. if any made by the customer.

## Electronic Clearing System

The introduction of MICR clearing in the four Metropolitan Cities has paved the way for Credit Clearing, Debit Clearing and Floppy Input Clearing Systems in the Banking industry. The pre-requisite for a true Electronic Fund Transfer (EFT) system is the full automation of the clearing house, the Central Settlement institutions as well the use of electronic media for message transmission. Some progress has been made with the introduction of ECS and EFT systems in India.

RBI has introduced a special variant of Electronic Funds Transfer System in the form of an Electronic Clearing System (ECS). This is an up gradation to the paper based payment system and involves both the credit transfers and the debit transfers. However, it is not a true EFT system, as the processing is not entirely based on the principles of EFT in the absence of proper infrastructure.

## Electronic Credit Clearing

This has been launched by the RBI in April 1995 and initially introduced in the four metropolitan cities. This scheme is to provide an alternative method of effecting bulk payment transactions passing through the clearing houses. Around 23% of the cheques passing through clearing at the four metropolitan cities, represent interest/ dividend warrants/refund orders issued by the Companies and Government Departments. The significant attribute of these payments is that they represent low value payments which are not repetitive in nature.

The cheques are generally issued by the corporate body that makes the payment to the same set of beneficiaries on a periodical basis. This kind of transaction involves a single debit but multiple credits. The corporate body gives an authorisation to debit the account and credit the beneficiaries. The details of the payments are furnished on a magnetic tape or a floppy. The corporate body has to pay service charges through their sponsor banks, to the bank maintaining the accounts of the beneficiaries. The bank does not recover any additional charges from the beneficiaries.

At present this clearing service is not only in automated environment. The details of the payments which is the input of the clearing houses is on magnetic tape or a floppy but the banks of the beneficiaries are provided with printed details for posting of payments. However, the banks of the beneficiaries have an option to receive the details on electronic media that is supplied duly in an encrypted form. The outer limit for individual credit has been fixed at Rs. 1,00,000.

## Electronic Debit Clearing

This clearing service has been introduced in Mumbai and Chennai for collection of Telephone Bills. This service is operated on the principle of authorised debit. This system involves multiple debits and a single credit. The customers who would like to utilise this service give a mandate to debit their accounts on receipt of debit, clearing advice from the Debit Clearing System. The consumer has an option to indicate a maximum limit for each debit entry. The Telephone Department submits the details on magnetic media. The inter-bank funds settlement is effected by debiting various banks and crediting the accounts of the Telephone Department.

The RBI has introduced the Electronic Clearing Service-RAPID (Receipt and Payment of Instruments/document) in February 1997, for payment of Electricity Bills of M/s. BSES Ltd., at Mumbai. This scheme enables the

Customers to pay their bills either in cash at any bank or to debit their bank account towards their payment of bills.

A MICR Reader captures the payment details from the specially designed bill and the schedules are prepared on a floppy. These schedules are combined together for an onward submission to the clearing house. On settlement, the clearing house debits the individual presenting banks of the consumers and credits the sponsor bank of the utility company. The credit details are also furnished to the utility company on floppy.

## Floppy Input Clearing

The RBI has introduced another mode of electronic clearing in 1995 at all the clearing houses managed by it. The participating banks have equipped their service branches with PCs. The participating banks submit their inter bank claim statements in floppies to the clearing houses which consolidates and the settlement statements are prepared. This enables for more accurate and fast settlement process.

## MODEL QUESTIONS

**Section - A**

1. What is a clearing House?
2. What is an Electronic Clearing System?
3. What is Floppy Input Clearing?

**Section - B**

1. How does a clearing house operate?

**Section - C**

1. Explain various set of reasons approved by the Clearing House in clearing a cheque.
2. Explain clearing system in detail.
3. Discuss the Electronic Credit and Debit System in detail.

9

# SPECIAL TYPES OF BANK CUSTOMERS

Banks deal with accounts of large number of customers in the course of their business. There are certain types of customers' accounts which require special care. When an account is opened, a contract arises between the banker and customer. The contract is valid only when both the parties are competent to enter into contract. Hence, the banker has to be very careful about the character, capacity and competency of his customers at the time of opening and operation of their accounts. The banker should deal with them differently according to the situation . The following are the Special Types of Customers :

1. Minors
2. Lunatics
3. Illiterate Persons
4. Married Women
5. Agent
6. Bankrupts
7. JointHinduFamily
8. Drunkard
9. Partnership Firm
10. Joint Stock Company
11. Local Authorities

12. Executors and administrators
13. Trustees
14. Joint Account
15. Non-trading Organisations

## 1. Minors

A minor is a person who has not attained the age of majority. According to Sec.3 of the Indian Majority Act, 1875, a minor is a person who has not completed the age of 18 years; and in the case of guardian of his person or property is by court, it is extended to 21 years. Sec. 11 of the Indian Contract Act, 1872, declares a minor as incompetent to enter into any contract. Therefore, a contract with a minor is void and unenforceable. The banker should be very careful with minors as money lent to a minor can not be recovered even if he had falsely representing himself as a major. The following are certain special privileges enjoyed by a Minor:

1. A contract entered into by a Minor is void and is not enforceable.
2. A minor cannot be compelled to repay the loan unless it is for the necessaries of his life.
3. Money lent to a minor cannot be recovered even if he had falsely representing himself as major at the time of obtaining such loan.
4. A banker cannot recover the money due from the minor and even from his guarantor as it was decided in the case of "*Coutts & Co. Vs. Browne Lecky and others*", it was also added that in the absence of any liability of the principal debtor , surety cannot be held liable, the liability of the surety being secondary and co-extensive with that of principal debtor.
5. Even without repaying the loan, the minor has the right to get back the securities pledged with the bank.
6. A minor can never be appointed as Trustee but he can sign as witness in a contract provided he is able to understand the contract.
7. A guarantee given by a minor is invalid.
8. According to Sec.26 of the Negotiable Instruments Act, 1881, a minor is allowed to draw and endorse any cheque, bill or promissory note. But it will be valid against all parties except a minor.
9. An adult who had accepted a bill during his minority can be dishonoured by him. The creditor cannot recover this from the adult.
10. A minor can be a partner in a partnership firm and enjoy the benefit of partnership firm. But he is not liable for the debts of the firm.

Minors are privileged children in law. Some one has humorously remarked about the treatment given to the minors when matters relating to minors go to the court of law :

"The law protects the infants; excuses their lashes; guides them in their legal proceedings; the judges are their counselors and the juries are their servants".

Taking into consideration the risk involved with the minor, the banker should take the following precautions while opening an account:

1. A banker should open a minor's account in the name of his guardian. Many may feel that the banker does not face any problem with the minor as long as his account shows credit balance. But there may also be chances of allowing inadvertent overdraft to a minor. Hence, it is better to open an account in the name of his guardian.
2. Since guarantor is not liable for the money lent to the minor, the banker should include the guarantor also as principal debtor.
3. Where minor acts as agent of another major, all his actions are valid and bind the principal.
4. A minor can be held liable for the loans given to him for his necessaries of life. Hence, it is recoverable from his properties.

## 2. Lunatics

Lunatics are persons of unsound mind. According to Sec.12 of the Indian Contract Act, 1872, persons of unsound mind are disqualified from entering to a valid contract. However, his disqualification does not apply to contracts entered into by lunatics during the period of sanity or contracts which are ratified during such periods. A banker should take the following precautions while opening an account in the name of lunatics:

*(a)* First of all, the banker should confirm whether the applicant is a lunatic or not. He should not be carried away by rumours or gossip or hearsay information.

*(b)* Once the banker comes to know of such defect in a person, it would be good for the bank to avoid such customer.

*(c)* An existing customer may become insane; in such a case the banker should be doubly cautious. He cannot presume that a customer is insane. The banker should get an official proof of his insanity. Once he gets the official confirmation, the banker should immediately stop paying his orders.

*(d)* In the case of an existing account-holder, the banker can act in the usual manner so long as he has no knowledge about of his insanity.

*(e)* When the banker comes to know of such problem in a customer, the

banker should not act in haste. He can make all attempts to check about the situation tactfully with their close relatives. However, he must get the official proof.

(f) If he is recovered from his mental illness, the banker must obtain a certificate from two medical officers certifying his mental soundness before resuming operations on the account.

## 3. Illiterate Persons

An illiterate person is one who cannot sign his name. Such person cannot read or write or understand the text. He may not be able to operate the bank account by his own. Such person should come to the bank with his Pass Book for withdrawal of money from his account. He, can not be given cheque books. While opening an account in the name of such illiterate person, a banker should get his left-hand thumb impression in the *presence of two persons known to the bank for identification* in the application. The banker should explain to the illiterate person about the nature of the account he intends to open, the implications and conditions for operation of the account to the account-holder clearly.

The banker should note two identification marks in the bank record for future reference. Two copies of recent photograph attested by a first class magistrate should be obtained. One should be kept with the specimen signature file and the other should be affixed in his Pass Book. The banker should also obtain a good introduction.

It would be good if the banker allows him to open Savings Bank account only and not current account. In case he opens a joint account with another literate person, cheque book facility may be- provided but should allow only the literate person to operate the account.

## 4. Married Women

A married woman can open an account in her name. She can enter into contract and bind her separate estate. In the case of an overdraft, granted to a married woman, the banker has no remedy unless she has separate estate. Even her husband cannot be made liable unless the banker has obtained his personal guarantee or the amount has been drawn for this purpose of her necessities of life.

## 5. Agents

An agent is a person who acts on behalf of another person. He can open an account and this account should be considered as the personal account of an agent. He can enjoy all privileges meant for any other person unless he is guilty of breach of trust. If a person is authorised to act on behalf of the principal, by a power of attorney, the banker should carefully examine whether the documents the powers have been conferred on the agent. On receiving notice of the principal's death, insanity or bankruptcy, the banker must suspend all operations of the account.

## 6. Bankrupt

A banker should not open an account in the name of an undischarged bankrupt. If a banker comes to know of an existing customer becoming bankrupt, he is expected to stop all operations of the account and inform the Official Assignee appointed by the court.

## 7. Joint Hindu Family

Joint Hindu Family consists of all persons lineally descended from a common ancestor and includes their wives. All the male members are coparceners of the Joint Hindu Family. Every male member acquires interest in the joint property by birth. The affairs of the family are contributed by the senior most male member called 'The Karta'. The banker is expected to take the following precautions while operating an account of a Joint Hindu Family.

1. The banker should obtain the signatures of all adult members while opening the account.
2. The Karta is alone entitled to operate the account. He can create charges over the ancestral property only in the interest of the family in general and ancestral business.
3. In case of borrowings, the banker must take absolute precautions whether it is borrowed for the benefit of the family.
4. In case of lending the banker should insist on obtaining the signatures of all adult male members.

## 8. Drunkard

A drunkard is an intoxicated person who is not capable of understanding the implications of his actions. He is not in a position to form a rational judgement till his drunkardness lasts. Hence the contract entered with the drunkard is void. If the banker finds the applicant under the influence of liquor, he should refuse to open an account.

Just because he consumes liquor, he is not to be treated as drunkard. Only when he loses his mental balance, the banker should be careful. When such a person presents a cheque for payment, to be on the safer side, payment can be made in the presence of a witness.

## 9. Partnership Firm

A partnership is established by an agreement amongst the partners. While opening an account, in the name of a Partnership firm, a banker should take the following precautions :

*(i) **Number of Partners :*** He should carefully examine the partnership deed to see that the number of partners does not exceed the statutory limit (10 for banking business and 20 for any other business). In case a minor is admitted into the partnership, the banker should note the date on which he will attain majority and obtain a fresh letter signed by him and other persons on that date.

*(ii) **Title of Firm's Account :*** The banker should ensure that the firm's account is opened only in the name of the firm and not in the names of individual partners.

*(iii) **Right of Applicants to open an Account :*** To open an account, the banker should insist that all partners sign the application together. He should obtain their specimen signatures for purpose of control.

*(iv) **Partnership Letter :*** Banker should honour cheques signed by all authorised partners and hence should maintain a record of names and addresses of partners and nature of business of the firm.

*(v) **Revocation of authority to operate the Account :*** Authority given to a partner to operate the firm's account may be revoked by any of the partners. In these circumstances, the banker should stop payment of cheques signed by such partner.

*(vi) **Delegation of Authority :*** A partner may delegate his authority in operate the firm's account only on obtaining written consent from all others.

*(vii) **Endorsement :*** A banker should honour a cheque payable to the firm, endorsed by the partner in his own favour, only after enquiring with other partners.

## Implied authority of a Partner

A partner, for purposes of business, binds the firm by his acts and deeds. He is also liable both individually and jointly with other partners for acts of the firm.

For example, an amount borrowed by a partner on behalf of the firm is binding on the firm and members of the firm. Similarly, when a promissory note is executed on a firm by its partner and money is used for the firm, every partner is liable for debt incurred (Gurren Subbaravude & Others Vs. Moto Potula Narasimham & Others).

If a partner does something which is not related to the kind of business carried on by the firm, other partners and the firm will not be liable for the same.

## Borrowing power of a Partner

A partner has the implied authority to borrow money on behalf of the firm, for the purpose of carrying on the firm's business and such debt is binding on the firm. This will not hold good in case the partner is not a managing partner or the partnership deed expressly limits his powers.

A partner does not enjoy implied authority in the following cases:

1. to submit a dispute relating to the business of the firm to arbitration;
2. to open a bank account for the firm in his name;
3. to compromise or relinquish any claim by the firm;
4. to admit a liability or withdraw a suit on behalf of the firm;
5. to acquire or transfer immovable property on behalf of the firm;
6. to enter into partnership on behalf of the firm.

However, a partner may do any of these acts with express authority of other partners.

## Liability of the Partners in respect of firm's debts

The liability of the partners of a firm is unlimited and every partner is liable to pay the debts of the firm to an unlimited extent. But if debts are due from the firm and the partners on dissolution of the firm, then Sec.49 of the Indian Partnership Act shall apply, i.e., Debts of the firm shall be settled out of the property of the firm and the surplus if any, shall be available for private debts of the partners. Personal assets of the partners shall be applied first to meet claims of their individual creditors and the surplus if any, shall be available for debts of the firm.

But if the partners sign the loan documents individually as well as jointly, then the creditors of the firm can recover their debt simultaneously from the assets of the firm and the partners. The banker, at the time of opening the account should therefore insist that the partners of a firm sign the documents individually as well as jointly.

## Death of a Partner

If a partner dies, the firm stands automatically dissolved, unless specifically stated in the Partnership Deed. If the firm stands dissolved the banker should close the firm's account immediately. This is important because if the firm's account shows a debit balance the deceased partner's estate is liable to pay the debts incurred by the firm before his death. If under the circumstances, the banker does not close the firm's account the rule in Clayton's case will apply.

If the firm does not stand dissolved, it is reconstituted and the banker should open a new account in the name of the reconstituted firm. Cheques issued by the deceased partner should not be honoured by the banker without confirmation from the surviving partners. On the opening of a new account after the death of a partner, a fresh mandate should be taken by the banker from the existing partners.

### Retirement of a Partner

When a partner retires his liability towards the banker ceases in respect of all transactions undertaken subsequent to the date of his retirement. He should however inform the banker promptly of his retirement. If at that time the bank account of the firm shows a debit balance, the banker may close the firm's account to retain his right to claim money from the retiring partner. If under the circumstances, the banker does not close the firm's account the rule in Clayton's case will apply. Cheques issued by the retiring partner should not be honoured by the banker without confirmation from the other partners. On the opening of a new account or continuance of existing account after the retirement of a partner, a fresh mandate should be taken by the banker from the existing partners.

### Insolvency of a Partner

When a partner is declared insolvent, the partnership comes to an end unless there is an agreement to the contrary. The insolvent partner ceases to be a partner from that date and his liability ceases in respect of all transactions undertaken subsequent to the date of his insolvency. The insolvent partner is not competent to operate the firm's account. Cheques issued by the insolvent partner before his adjudication should not be honoured by the banker without confirmation from the other partners. The banker closes the firm's account and opens a new account in the name of the reconstituted firm to determine the liability of the insolvent partner. Otherwise the rule in Clayton's case will apply.

## 10. Joint Stock Company

A joint stock company is an artificial person with perpetual succession under the provisions of the Companies Act. A company is a legal entity separate from that of its members. Therefore, it can own properties in its own name, carry on lawful business and incur liabilities in its name. While opening a bank account in the name of the company, a banker should carefully examine the Certificate of Incorporation and the Certificate of commencement of business in case of public limited company and Certificate of Incorporation in case of private limited company. These documents prove that a company is duly registered and incorporated.

In addition, the banker should examine the Memorandum of Association which is the Charter of the company to note the objectives for which the company is incorporated. For, any contract entered into by the company outside the scope of its objectives is *ultra vires* and unenforceable at law. The banker should also examine the Articles of Association of the company, to know the powers of the Directors, procedure for borrowing, limits on borrowing, procedure and authority to draw and endorse cheques on behalf of the company. Further, he should obtain certified copies of the Memorandum and Articles of Association for his own record.

Along with the application to open a bank account in the company's name, the banker must be given a certified copy of the Resolution passed by the Board of Directors of the company, appointing the bank concerned as the banker of the company, and the names of the persons authorised to operate the account. The banker must also be given the names of the persons who are authorised to execute documents, enter into a mortgage and advance payments on behalf of the company.

## Borrowing powers of the Company

Board of Directors of the company shall borrow money otherwise than on debentures only buy a resolution passed at a meeting of the Board. This resolution should mention the arrangement to be made by the company with its bankers for borrowing by way of cash credit or overdraft or otherwise and not the, actual day-to-day operation of these accounts, by means of which the arrangement so made is actually to be availed of.

The banker should ensure that the total borrowings of the company do not exceed the aggregate of the paid up capital of the company and its free reserves. Temporary loans in the ordinary course of business do not form part of total borrowings.

It is to be noted that arty borrowing by the company may be ultra vires the directors but not ultra vires the company, i.e., when the Directors borrow without express authority and the company benefits from it, money can be recovered from the company.

## Registration of Charges

While granting a loan on the basis of a fixed or floating charge over the assets of a company the banker should be careful about the fixed or floating charge over the same assets. He should also ensure that the charge over the assets of the company created in his favour is duly registered with the Registrar of Companies within the prescribed period. Further he should inspect the 'Register of mortgages and charges' maintained at the office of the Registrar of Joint Stock Companies.

## Directors' Personal Accounts

If the director authorised to operate the company's, account has a personal account with the same branch of the bank, and deposits cheques drawn in favour of the company to be credited to his personal account, the banker should make a thorough enquiry before doing so.

### Additional precautions in case of Private Limited Companies

The banker should be very careful in advancing loans to a private limited company which has recently been incorporated by conversion of business of a sole trader, as sometimes such conversions are made with a view to defraud their creditors. The banker should, therefore, make necessary enquiries to avoid such a situation.

## 11. Local Authorities

Local Bodies or Authorities are trustees for the public funds under their control. Hence, the banker has to take maximum care in the dealings of local authorities.

In case of local bodies the name of the bank may be specified in the Act itself. If the Statute does not mention any such name, the banker should insist on a resolution being passed by the governing board and a true copy of such resolution signed by the Chairman, President or Chief Executive Officer should be produced while opening an account. The officials who are authorised to sign the cheque also should be provided either in the Statute or resolution. The banker is expected to be aware of the borrowing powers of the authorities and the limit up to which they can borrow as per the Statute.

## 12. Executors and Administrators

Executors are those persons who are appointed to conduct the affairs of a person after his death. He is named in the will and if he refuses to act, then, the court will appoint another person called 'Administrator'. 'Executors and Administrators' are allowed to open account with the bank. The following precautions should be taken by the banker while opening the account in the name of Executors and Administrators.

*(a)* The banker should keep in mind that the executors account is nothing but the deceased estate account.

*(b)* The executor/administrator should be permitted to operate the account only after he has obtains the probate (official confirmation of the will) from the court.

*(c)* The banker should thoroughly examine and understand the text of the probate (official copy of the will together with the certificate of the court) or letter of administration or trust deed as the case may be.

*(d)* More than one person can be appointed as executors in such cases, the banker should be very careful, He should get clear instructions about the nature and power delegated to each of them. In the absence of such information, the banker should take a mandate signed by all the executors as to how cheques and bills are to be signed and endorsed, holding all the executors jointly and severally liable to any

overdraft. Even if the executor wants all the executors to sign the cheques, the banker should honour his word.

*(e)* If an executor becomes insolvent, the banker need not stop the bank account, as insolvency of an executor does not terminate his appointment. However, when he becomes insane, the banker must immediately stop his operations.

## 13. Trustees

A trustee is a person in whose care the control of an estate is placed under a Trust Deed. The person for whose benefit the trust is formed is called the 'beneficiary'. Sometimes, two or more persons may be appointed as trustees. When a bank account is opened in the name of a trustee, the banker has a duty to the real owner to see that no trust funds are frequently transferred by the trustee to his personal account. The banker should take the following precautions.

1. The banker should thoroughly examine the Trust Deed appointing the applicants as trustees.
2. He should ascertain their powers and functions.
3. In the case of two or more trustees, the banker should find out as to who would operate the bank account. In the absence of this information, he should see that all of them should sign the documents, bill, cheques, etc.
4. The banker should check whether the trustees have power to borrow money and if so, on what conditions.
5. In case of death of the trustee or trustees, the banker should act according to the directions given in the trust deed. In the absence of such information, the banker should resort to the help of the court. However, if there is a provision for appointment of new trustee, he must adhere the clauses mentioned in the trust deed.
6. The insolvency of a trustee does not affect the trust property belongs to the beneficiaries. But it would not be safe for the banker to assume that the continuing trustees posses full powers to deal with the property.
7. A married women can be appointed as an executive. But her husband cannot be held liable for her act as trustee unless he interferes in her duties in the capacity of the executrix.

Finally, a banker should clearly distinguish between a trust property and the personal account of a Trustee. At any point of time, both should not be mixed. He should be very careful to protect the interest of the beneficiaries. When he comes to know that the funds are misapplied, a banker will be justified in dishonoring a cheque drawn by a trustee. Similarly, when trust money is deposited in the personal account of the trustee, the banker should question the reasons for it. Similarly, a cheque payable to the trust account should not be collected and credited to his personal account.

## 14. Joint Accounts

A Joint account is one, which is opened in the bank in the name of two or more persons. While opening a joint account, the banker should take the following precautions:

1. The banker should get clear instructions from the parties intending to open a Joint account.
2. The instructions obtained from the parties should relate to:
   *(a)* Names of the persons intending to open the Joint Account.
   *(b)* Their Age, Profession, addresses.
   *(c)* Name/Names of the persons operating the Joint account.
   *(d)* Nature of the Joint Account (either or survivor/former or survivor/ (All to sign without the right of survivorship).
3. The banker should ascertain whether the person/persons authorised to operate the account should also be empowered to overdraw the account.
4. If one of the joint account holders becomes insolvent or insane, the banker should suspend the operation of the account. He should act according to the instructions given by the solvent/ insane account holders along with the official receiver appointed by the court. The rule of survivorship does not apply in this case.
5. Ordinarily, on the death of one of the joint account holders, the survivor is entitled to all the amount and the survivor is answerable to the representatives of the deceased person. The legal representatives of the deceased may claim the money. In order to avoid this, the banker should see that the mandate given b y the joint account holders contains an express provision to the effect that the survivors are entitled to get the balance on the death of any of them. If a joint account with the provision of either or survivor is opened, this problem can be avoided.

### Joint Account in the names of Husband and Wife

In the case of joint account of husband and wife, difficulty arises when one of them dies. The question arises whether his wife is the entire beneficiary for the balance in the joint account. In the case of Guran Dutta Vs. Ram Dutta, a Hindu husband deposited a sum of Rs. 1 lakh in the joint names of himself and his wife payable to either or survivor. The husband died leaving his wife and three sons. The wife withdrew the balance in the account through one of her sons. Others filed a suit objecting to this withdrawal. The court held in their favour saying, although it was a deposit in joint names, it did not constitute a gift by the husband to his wife.,

On the death of any one of the joint account holders, if a dispute arises over the balance amount in the joint account, the banker should not decide by himself. He should direct the parties to go to the court and get a direction. If the intention is to provide protection to his wife, then money should be paid to the wife (Foley Vs. Foley). But if the intention is only for convenience, then, the rule of survivorship does not arise as it was held in Marshall Vs. Crutwell.

## 15. Non Trading Organisation

### Clubs, Societies and Charitable Institution

The clubs, societies and charitable organisations are non-trading organisations and are registered under Societies Registration Act.

The banks have to be extra careful in dealing with such organisations.

*(a)* While opening an account the bank should verify whether a resolution is passed by the governing body, appointing the bank to act as a banker to the club or society in question. The names of the person or persons who are entitled to operate the account should be mentioned in the resolution without any ambiguity.

*(b)* The borrowing powers of the club mentioned in the Charter and the limit mentioned in it should also be verified by the banker when the club requests the banker for a loan.

*(c)* In case of death or resignation of a person in charge of operating the account, the banker should stop operation of the account until fresh nomination is made by the club or association.

*(d)* While transfers are made to the personal accounts of the officers who are operating the accounts of the societies, clubs or associations, the banker should exercise maximum care.

In dealing with the following the banks should observe the following precautions:

1. The society must have be incorporated as per the Society Registeration Act. Then only it gets legal recognition and is empowered to enter into valid contracts.
2. A registered society is governed by provisions of the Act under which it is registered. A copy of the same should be furnished with the banker. He should ensure that the persons observe these rules responsible for managing the society.

3. To open a bank account, the banker must be given the copy of the resolution passed by the Managing Committee of the Society stating appointment of the banker and the names of the persons authorised to operate the account. The banker must also be given the copy of the resolution passed by the Managing Committee of the Society regarding, purpose for which borrowing is permissible and the powers of the Managing Committee to create a charge over the assets of the Society.
4. In case of death or resignation of the, person authorised to operate the account the banker should stop the operation of the society's account till another person is nominated by the society.
5. If the person authorised to operate the society's account has a personal account with the same branch of the bank, the banker should ensure that the funds of the society are not being credited to such personal account.

## MODEL QUESTIONS

**Section - A**

1. State the risks of a banker while opening a Savings Bank Account in the name of an illiterate person.
2. Can an illiterate person open a bank account?
3. Write short notes on opening of a bank account by married women.
4. Write any two precautions the banker has to take while operating the account of a Joint Hindu Family.

**Section - B**

1. What are the precautions taken by the banker while opening the account in the name of a minor?
2. An adult opens an account falsely representing himself as a minor. In case of a secured loan granted by a bank is there any risk for the banker?
3. Can a cheque drawn in favour of a firm be credited to a partner's personal account?
4. How far is an advance granted to a minor safe for a banker?
5. Discuss the banker's role in relation to non-trading organisations.
6. What are the precautions to be taken by the banker while opening an account in the name of Executors and Administrators?
7. Explain the procedure for opening of an account by the trustee.
8. Is there any risk in opening and maintaining a current account in the name of the survivor in the case of the joint account?
9. Write notes on *(a)* Banker with local authorities
   *(b)* Agents.

10. Explain the position of a banker in case of account of lunatic's and insolvents.
11. What precautions should a banker take in opening accounts in the names of married women and charitable trust?

**Section - C**

1. What are the precautions taken by the banker while opening the accounts in the names of *(a)* Partnership Firm and *(b)* Joint Stock Company?
2. Discuss in detail the special types of bank customers.

10

# BANKER AND CUSTOMER

## Definition of the term " Banker "

In order to understand the term 'Banker' and "Customer", it is essential to know the definition and meaning of these terms. Many authors, at different point of times, have attempted to define the term 'Banker'. But there was no satisfactory definition until the passing of the Indian Companies Amendment Act of 1936. The main reason for such confused state being the changing nature of banking business. Some do feel that even the definition given in the Banking Regulation Act, 1949 may become obsolete in the years to come.

According to Section 3 of the Negotiable Act 1881, the term 'banker' includes "*Any person or a corporation or a company acting as a banker*". This is not at all a helpful definition. This is only a needless repetition. The English Law that was a model for enacting the Indian Law in most cases has failed to provide any satisfactory definition. Some have considered a banker as one who deals with other peoples' money. Even mills and industrial concerns, which accepted public deposits, were classified as banks between 1932-1943.

According to the Japanese Bank Act. 1927, Banks are defined as *Institutions, which carry on operations of giving as well as receiving credits.* "

Dr. H.L. Hart defines a banker as, "one who, in the ordinary course of his business, honours cheques drawn upon him by persons from and for whom he receives money on current accounts". This definition is based on the judgment given in many cases at that point of time. According to Sir John

Paget, *"No person or body corporate otherwise, can be a banker who does not (i) take deposit accounts, (ii) take current accounts; (iii) issue and pay cheques and (iv) collect cheques, crossed and uncrossed, for his customers"*.

As there were many interpretations for the word 'Banker' and 'Banking', it was necessary for a statutory definition. Hence, a statutory definition was introduced through the Banking Regulation Act, 1949. Accordingly, "A *bank is a company which accepts deposits of money from the public, for the purpose of lending or investment, repayable on demand or otherwise, and withdraw by cheque, draft, order or otherwise"*. This definition excludes mere money lending from the banking business. Hence, mills and industrial concerns, which accept deposits, were excluded from the classification of the term "Banks".

## Definition of the term 'Customer'

The term 'Customer' of a bank has not been defined either in English Law or Indian Law. According to Sir John Paget, *"To constitute a customer, there must be some recognisable course* or *habit of dealing in the nature of regular banking business"*. This definition clearly points out two basic requirements for being a customer of a bank:

1. To be a customer, the person should have some sort of an account with the bank.
2. He should also have had a few transactions with the bank (The number of such transactions, i.e., deposits/withdrawals, were not clearly stated by Sir John Paget).

This definition intends that the purchaser of a bank draft does not become a customer of a bank. Even a person who has just opened a bank account does not entail himself to be a customer unless he waits for some time for completing a few transactions and be familiar with the banker. Usually, businessmen distinguish between a regular customer and a casual purchaser.

## Duration Theory

As Sir John Paget was emphasizing duration and the subsequent transactions after opening a bank account, this definition was popularly known as Sir John Paget's 'Duration Theory'.

This duration theory was exploded when Justice Baihache pronounced his famous judgment in the case of 'Ladbroke Vs. Todd'. According to his judgement, the relationship between banker and customer begins as soon as the first cheque is paid in and accepted for collection. This view was confirmed in another English case 'Commissioner of Taxation Vs. English, Scottish and Australian Bank'.

In an Indian case, the Kerala High Court discarded the duration theory based on Dr.H.L.Hart's definition. According to H.L.Hart, "A *customer is one who has an account with a banker or for whom a banker habitually undertakes to act as such*".

The Kerala High Court, in the case of 'Central Bank of India Ltd. Vs. Gopinath Nair' the Judge observed: *"Broadly speaking, a customer is a person who has the habit of resorting to the same place or person to do business. So far as banking transactions are concerned, he is a person whose money has been accepted on the footing that the banker will honour up to the amount standing to his credit, irrespective of his connection being short or longstanding"*.

The duration theory of Sir John Paget has now become obsolete and the above judgement made the meaning of 'Customer' very clear:

1. To constitute a customer, one should
   *(a)* Open an account with a bank - be it a Savings Bank account, Current account, Fixed deposit account or Recurring deposit account.
   *(b)* The dealing between a banker and customer must be of banking nature.
2. A customer may be an individual, partnership firm or any body corporate.
3. A person who does not have a deposit account in his name but avails of the services of the bank (purchase of draft/ encashing a cheque/ using ATM) cannot be considered as a customer of a bank.

## General Relationship between Banker and Customer

In addition to the primary functions, a banker undertakes to do certain agency services. In some cases, he may act as a bailee or lessee. In all these cases, there is a contractual relationship between banker and customer. The relationship between a banker and customer, primarily, is that of debtor and creditor.

### 1. Debtors and Creditor Relationship

The primary functions of the commercial banks are to receive deposits from the public and lend the same to the borrowers at higher rates of interest. When the banker receives deposits from a customer, the banker is a debtor and the customer is a creditor. The customer continues to be a creditor so long as his account shows a credit balance. Once, his account shows debit balance, the customer becomes a debtor. Once money is deposited with the bank, it becomes the banker's property and he can use it as he likes. Although the customer is a legal creditor possessing the right to claim the same as per the agreement, he has no right to claim the same identical currency notes. It is enough if the banker pays him in legal tender. In the case of 'Official Liquidator, Hanuman Bank Ltd. Vs. K.P.T.Nadar and others', it was held: *"The mere fact that a banker invites deposits and is prepared to pay interest thereon, is proof enough of his intention to make use of it as he likes and earn interest there from, so as not only to enable him to pay interest to his depositor but also to earn profit for himself. But even if the bank pays no interest on the money deposited, he is his customer's debtor and not a bailee because he undertakes to repay on demand a sum, equivalent to the amount deposited with him and the customer has no right whatsoever to claim the same identical coins or notes deposited by him with his banker"*.

A banker is a privileged debtor as he need not give any security for receiving the deposit from his customers. A customer is an unsecured creditor and does not get any charge over the assets of the bank even when the bank goes into liquidation. However, the Deposit Insurance Credit Guarantee Corporation (DICGC) minimises the risk of the depositor to the extent of Rs.1, 00,000.

A bank debt differs from an ordinary debt in the following ways:

*(a)* In the case of an ordinary commercial debt, it is commonly understood that the debtor should go to his creditor and settle his debt as per the terms of agreement. But in the case of bank debt, the Creditor (customer) should go to the bank and demand payment as per the bank procedures.

*(b)* The Customer, as a creditor, should demand payment at proper place and time. He should go to the bank during the working hours and demand payment either by issuing, a cheque or using a withdrawal slip.

*(c)* In the case of ordinary commercial debt, the debt becomes time barred after three years as per the Limitation Act, 1963. However, in the case of a bank deposit, the time for filing a suit for the recovery of money deposited with the banker, if refused by the bank, is three years from the date of demand. Normally, a banker will pay the money on Fixed Deposits after the expiry of the term provided the Fixed Deposit Receipt (FDR) is duly discharged. However, if the demand for money is made after unreasonably long period, there may be some practical difficulties to return the amount as the commercial banks would have returned such unclaimed deposits to Reserve Bank of India if they are not operated for 10 years.

## Right to Combine Accounts

It has been, proved beyond doubt in several cases that a customer cannot combine his accounts while issuing a cheque for payment. For the purpose of computation of balance in his account, the customer cannot expect the banker to adjust from any other account maintained by him either in the same branch or in any other branch. For instance, a customer has Rs.2, 000 into his credit in the savings bank account and Rs. 10,000 in another account. While making payment the customer cannot issue a cheque exceeding Rs. 2,000 in one S.B account and Rs.10, 000 in another account anticipating that the banker would take into consideration the totals of both accounts. If he does so, his cheque will be rightly dishonoured by the bank.

In the case of *State Bank of India Vs. Vathi Samba Murthy (1988),* it was decided that the customer cannot combine account for the purpose of withdrawal. It was clearly indicated that cheque relating to one account cannot be used in respect of another account even though the same person may be having two accounts.

However, the situation on the banker's side is different. The banker can combine several accounts for the purpose of collecting his dues from his customer. If there is an overdraft in one account, the banker can collect the dues from another account showing a credit balance after fulfilling the following two conditions as was decided in *'Halesowen Presswork and Assemblies Ltd. Vs. Westminister Bank Ltd.*

1. The banker should give notice to his customer of his intention to combine accounts and
2. There should not have been any arrangement at the time of opening accounts to keep the accounts separately.

Although the banks have a right to combine accounts, a banker cannot combine a customer's personal account with a joint account of the customer and another person *(Radha Raman Vs. Chota Nagpur Banking Association* Ltd.). Moreover, the bank can combine the accounts only for an existing debt and not a contingent debt.

## 2. Trustee and Beneficiary

A Trustee is one who holds the money or assets of the beneficiary and performs certain functions in the interest of the beneficiary. A banker does not act as a trustee while receiving deposits. The customer is only a debtor and cannot have any lien over the assets of the bank. He is only a general creditor of the bank.

Money deposited with the bank for special purpose: But if the customer has deposited the money for meeting certain specific tasks (example: for purchasing a draft) or deposited certain valuable for safe custody, then, the position is different. In this case, the banker acts as a *trustee* and the customer is the *beneficiary* as the ownership continues to stay with the customer. The customer can claim the amount as a preferential creditor in case of liquidation of the bank as it was decided in "Veji Lekhamsey & Co. Vs. Dr.Banjaji (1955). The Bombay High Court held: *"In the case of a mere debtor and creditor relationship, the customer can claim the amount due to him from the bank as an ordinary creditor. But if the relation is that of Trustee and Beneficiary, then, the customer is entitled to claim the amount as a preferential creditor".* However, the position of the banker as a Trustee or Debtor is determined taking into consideration the circumstances in each case.

When a cheque is sent for collection, the banker acts as a trustee till the cheque is collected. Once it is collected and the customer's account is credited, the relationship between the banker and customer changes. The banker becomes the debtor and the customer becomes the creditor. Before the receipt of the actual proceeds from the collecting banker, if the collecting bank goes into liquidation, the money thus collected belongs to the customer and it will not be available for distribution to the general creditors.

In certain cases, the relationship between a banker and customer is that of bailor and bailee. It is customary to deposit in the bank certain items of value, example: sealed envelopes, documents of title; packets and parcels, locked boxes; etc. The position of the banker in such a case is that of a bailee/ trustee.

### 3. Lessor and Lessee

In the case of safe deposit locker facilities offered by banks, the relation between a banker and customer is that of lesser and Lessee. In this case, the banker is the Lesser and the customer is the Lessee. The banker lets out his premises (locker) for the use of his customers. In case of loss of assets kept in the locker, the banker is not directly responsible. The banker has no lien over the assets kept in the locker as long as the rent is paid regularly to the bank.

### 4. Principal and Agent

The commercial banks also undertake the agency services like purchase and sale of securities, collection of cheques etc. on behalf of the customers. Due to stiff competition, the commercial banks compete with one another to undertake wide-range of agency services.

In order to facilitate the customers, the banks accept standing instructions from their customers either to make payments on their behalf or collect money or effect transfer of money. The relationship between the banker and customer, in this case, is that of Principal and Agent. The customer directs the banker as to what he should do. The banker acts according to his direction. In case of any loss, the customer alone will bear this as his directions are carried out by the banker. The banker will charge the customer for doing such services.

The financial stability of the bank and complete confidence of the customers dealing with it have made the bank a natural and trusted friend for undertaking executorships and trusteeship. In addition to this, an increasing reluctance of customers to trust individuals, combined with insufficient knowledge of law on their part has led commercial banks to act as trustees

## Special Features of Relationship between a Banker and Customer

The contract between the banker and customer paves the way for certain duties and rights for the banker.

### Duties

1. The banker should receive the customer's money and credit his account.
2. He should receive cheques and bills sent by his customer for collection and the credit his customer's account without delay.
3. He should return the deposit as per the contract; He should honour customers' cheques to the extent of his balance in the account. He should use reasonable care in paying cheques drawn upon him by his customers, to refrain from any action likely to damage his customer's reputation.
4. He should maintain the secrecy of his customer's account.
5. He should observe the customer's instruction as mentioned in the mandate.
6. He should give reasonable notice before combing the accounts of his customer or closing his account.

### Rights

- Right to charge reasonable interest on loans and reasonable commission for the services rendered by him.
- Have a general lien over his customer's securities coming into his hands in the ordinary course of business.
- Right of set-off like any other debtor.
- Right to appropriate payment.
- Right of not seeking the creditor for payment. The ordinary rule is that the debtor should seek his creditor and pay his debts. Contrary to this, demand is necessary in the case of bank debt. The creditor (Customer) should make a demand for payment by drawing cheques on the banker.

## 1. Statutory Obligation to Honour Customer's Cheques

The contract between banker and customer impose certain obligations on the part of the banker and customer. One of the obligations on the part of the banker is to honour the customers' cheques. The obligation to honour customer's cheques is imposed on the banker by the Negotiable Instruments Act, 1881. According to Sec.31 of the Act, *"The drawee of a cheque having sufficient funds of the drawer in his hands properly applicable to the payment of such cheque must pay the cheque when duly required so to do, and, in default of such payment, must compensate the drawer for any loss or damage caused by such default'*.

According to this Section, the banker should honour his customer's cheques failing which he may have to pay compensation to his customer for any loss or damage. Hence, the banker must deal with the cheque carefully. The words mentioned in the section *'having sufficient funds'* will mean that the balance available in the account should be at least equal to the amount of the cheque. For the purpose of computation of balance, the customer cannot expect a banker to adjust from any other account maintained by the customer either in the same branch or in any other branch. Cheques are payable at the branch where the account of the customer is kept and each branch is kept as separate identity. Even the Halbury's Laws of England says, *"A balance in one branch of a bank does not entail a customer to draw on another branch where he has no account or had overdrawn, for different branches of a bank are, for the purpose of separate entities, though the bank may apply funds which it holds at one branch to meet an overdraft of the customer at another'*. However, the minimum balance maintained in a current account or savings bank account, as the case may be, can be used for payment of cheque. The banker cannot simply dishonour a cheque just for want of minimum balance. If there is no minimum balance in the customer's account, the banker is empowered to charge the customer with incidental charges.

The banker should also see whether he had already agreed for an overdraft or cash credit to enable him to pay the cheque. There is no need for a written agreement for allowing overdraft to the customer. If an overdraft or cash credit has been agreed upon the current account balance would have been increased to that extent. If there had been practice of allowing overdraft for a customer when there is no sufficient fund, the bank should follow the same practice in the subsequent cases (Indian Overseas Bank, Madras Vs. Naranprasad Govindlal Patel, Ahamedabad, 1980). It was held in this case that although overdraft is a temporary arrangement between a banker and customer, it is a contract and it cannot be terminated by the bank unilaterally. If the bank decides to stop this practice in the case of a customer, he should give notice to the customer. If the bank dishonours the cheque without adequate notice, then, the bank is presumed to have dishonoured the cheque wrongly although it could be honoured within the limits of the overdraft. In this case, overdraft is not a grace shown by the banker to the customer.

In a few cases, the customer would have asked the banker to apportion certain amount in his account for certain specific purpose. When a cheque is received by the bank for payment, he will be justified in computing the balance in the customer's account after deducting such amount.

When a cheque is deposited into bank for collection, the customer should check with the bank whether the cheque has been collected and credited to his account to compute the balance in his account. If cheques are issued in anticipation of collection, such cheques may be dishonoured if cheques/bills sent for collection are not collected. There may be many reasons for the delay in the collection of cheques such as holidays for the bank, outstation cheques, strike in the banks, clearing house problem etc. The customer can compute the actual balance as on date in his account can be computed only after checking with the banker whether the proceeds have been collected or not.

The payees of the cheque may be allowed to deposit in the bank the deficit, i.e., the difference between the balance in the customer's account and the amount of the cheque to enable the banker to honour such cheque. However, the banker should be careful to see that he, at any cost, should not reveal the balance in the customer's account to any one other than the customer himself.

The words,' when *duly required to do* so contains number of conditions attached to the cheque. The cheque should have been properly drawn and it should be complete in all respects. The cheque should have been properly written and signed by the drawer. The obligation to honour the cheque is extinguished when he receives a garnishee order from the court against the customer. A garnishee order is an order issued by the Court directing the banker to stop payment from a particular customer's account. The issuance of a garnishee order prevents the banker from paying away a balance up to the total amount for which it is made unless the claim of the judgement creditor has been satisfied.

## Consequences of Wrongful Dishonour

A banker must deal with the payment of cheques carefully. His position is like that of sitting between the devil and the deep sea. If he honours a cheque by mistake, the money is lost and at the same time, if he dishonours the cheque with out sufficient reasons, he is to compensate the drawer for the loss suffered by him.

Payment of customers cheques is one of the statutory functions of a commercial bank. If the banker dishonours a cheque either by mistake or by negligence, it is said to be wrongful dishonour and the banker is liable to compensate the loss suffered by his customer. The following are some of the reasons for wrongful dishonour of cheques.

*(a)* Negligence on the part of the banker.

*(b)* Faulty computation of the balance in the customer's account.

*(c)* Failure to credit deposits made by the customer.

*(d)* Failure to send the cheques/bills for collection.

*(e)* Posting the wrong amount/posting the correct amount in the wrong account.

(f) Wrong debit in the customer's account.

(g) Payment made against the countermanding order.

Section 31 of the Negotiable Instruments Act, 1881 deals with the statutory obligation on the part of the bank to honour a cheque issued by a customer and the compensation payable in case of wrongful dishonour of the cheque. The *'loss or damage'* stated in section 31 of the Act would mean two kinds of losses:

(a) Monetary loss.

(b) Defamation to the customer, i.e., loss of reputation in the public.

## Monetary Loss

Some times, the monetary loss may be heavy. In case of a contract work for Rs. 10 lakhs, the customer would have paid an earnest money deposit of Rs.5,000 by cheque. In case this cheque is dishonoured by mistake, the customer would lose the contract worth of Rs. 10 lakhs where in his profit may be 15%. Hence, the customer may claim a monetary loss of Rs.1.5 lakhs although the cheque dishonoured in question was only for Rs.5,000.

## Loss of Reputation

A trader or a reputed person in the society may claim compensation not only for his financial loss but also for loss of reputation. It is difficult to assess the loss of reputation. The quantum of loss may vary from person to person depending upon his trade and status. In case a cheque issued by a reputed person for a smaller amount is dishonoured by the bank by mistake, the compensation will be heavy, i.e., smaller the amount of the cheque, higher will be the compensation for affected tradesman. It is normally presumed that credit or reputation is the essence for any businessman. When it is lost, every thing is lost and it would be very difficult to retrieve it. Hence, courts award higher compensation to the customers, if their cheques are dishonoured by mistake or by negligence, leading to loss of reputation. It is not necessary for the customer to prove his special damage. If it is proved, it would be easier to determine the compensation payable to the customer.

In the case of *'Davidson Vs. Barclay's Bank Ltd.'*, the customer issued a cheque for $2.15s.8d. This cheque was dishonoured by mistake. The plaintiff was awarded $250 compensation, as he was a trader.

In another interesting case, 'Sterling Vs. Barclays Bank Ltd.', a cheque issued by Mrs. Sterling was wrongly dishonoured. But she was not entitled to substantial compensation as her earlier two cheques were dishonoured and no claim was made earlier.

In the case of a non-trader, the compensation may be meager as in the case of 'Mrs. Gibbons Vs. Westminster Bank Ltd.'. Although a cheque for $9.16.0

drawn in favour of her landlord towards the payment of rent was dishonoured wrongly, Mrs. Gibbons was awarded only nominal damages, as she was a non-trader. In her case, she was to prove her damage.

When a non-trader proved the substantial damages suffered by him, heavy compensation was payable to him. In the case of Canara Bank ltd. Vs. Rajagopal', the customer, Mr.Rajagopal, issued a cheque for Rs.294 from his personal account with Canara Bank to his company being the collection made by him as representative of a company where he was employed. The company endorsed his cheque in favour of the Telephone Department. When the cheque was dishonoured by mistake, the telephone department disconnected the company telephone, leading to the dismissal of Mr.Rajagopal from the company where he was working. When the matter was taken to the court, the High Court upheld the damages to the extent of Rs. 14,000 for the loss of reputation and mental agony.

## II. Obligation to maintain Secrecy of Customer's Account

After opening an account with a bank, the customer continues his financial dealings with the bank. As the bank is maintaining the customer's account, the banker is fully aware of the financial dealings of the customer. The financial dealings between a banker and his customer is confidential. Revealing the facts of the customer's account to others may lead to financial loss as well as loss of reputation to the customers. If the customer suffers any loss on account of unwarranted disclosure of his account, the banker will be compelled to compensate for the loss suffered by the customer. Hence, a banker should not disclose his customer's financial position, nature and details of his account to any other person.

Maintaining the secrecy of his customer's account is a legal one arising out of an implied contract. As early as in 1868, in the case of *'Hardy Vs. Veasy'*, it was decided that a banker should not reveal the secrecy of his customer's account to third parties. In another case, *'Tournier Vs. National Provincial and Union Bank of England Ltd.'*, it was said that there was a qualified contractual duty, which was acquired by the bank in the character of banker not to disclose information concerning the customer. Hence, the banker was held liable to compensate for the loss suffered by the customer.

Moreover, Sec. 13 of the Banking Companies (Acquisition and Transfer of Undertakings) Act, 1970 states, "The banker should observe, except as otherwise required by law, the practices and usages customary among the bankers and in particular not to divulge any information relating to the affairs of the constituents except in circumstances in which they are, in accordance with the law or practices and usages customary among bankers, necessary or appropriate for them to divulge such information".

Sir John Paget goes to the extent of saying that a banker should maintain secrecy of his customer's account even after the account is closed and even after the death of the customer. It is immaterial whether the account is in debit or credit. This duty of secrecy goes beyond the state of account. It extends to all transactions that go through the account.

Judge Bankay is also of the opinion that the duty to maintain the secrecy of the customer's account is a legal one arising out of contract and the duty is not absolute but qualified. He classified the qualifications under four heads where :

*(a)* Disclosure is under compulsion by law;

*(b)* There is a duty to the public to disclose;

*(c)* The interest of the bank requires such disclosure; and

*(d)* The disclosure is made by the express or implied consent of the customer.

## A. DISCLOSURE UNDER COMPULSION OF LAW

Although a banker is to maintain secrecy of his customers account he is obliged to disclose the information relating to his customer's account when the law specifically requires him to do so. His duty to the law of the country is more than the duty towards his customer. There are various provisions in the law compelling the banker to disclose information relating to his customer's account. The following are some of the important statutes enforcing the banker to reveal the details relating to customer's account:

### 1. Under Income Tax Act, 1961

Income tax should be payable by every individual or any body corporate to the Central Government according to the Income Tax Act, 1961. The Income Tax authorities are responsible for collecting income tax. According to Sec.131, the income tax authorities have the powers for enforcing the attendance of any person including any officer of a banking company and examining on oath and compelling the production of books of accounts and other documents and issuing commissions.

Sec. 133 empowers the officers of the income tax authorities

*(a)* To call for necessary information from any bank for the purpose of assessment of the bank's customers and

*(b)* Compel a bank or any officer of the bank to furnish information or statement useful to the tax authorities.

Sec.285 of the Act requires the banks to advise the income tax officer the names and address of those who have earned Rs.and above as interest on deposit in any financial year. Moreover, the income tax officers have free access to the books of accounts kept by the banks.

### 2. Under Sec.4 of the Banker's Book Evidence Act, 1891

A banker may be asked to produce a certified copy of his customer's account in the ledger. This certified copy is admitted as evidence of the matters, transactions and accounts related to customer's account.

### 3. Under the Indian Companies Act, 1956

When there is a dispute in a company, the Central Government appoints an Inspector to investigate the affairs of any joint stock company. In such cases, the company should

Produce all books and papers to the inspector and to give the inspector all assistance in connection with the investigation.

### 4. Under the Reserve Bank of India Act, 1934

The RBI is empowered to collect credit information from banking companies. The Act also provides that the credit information supplied by the Reserve Bank to the banking companies should be kept confidential.

### 5. Under the Banking Regulation Act, 1949

Every bank is compelled to submit an annual return of deposits which remain unclaimed for 10 years.

### 6. Under Sec.3 of the Gift Tax Act

The Gift tax Officer can examine the banker on oath and compel him to produce the books of accounts.

### 7. Under the Exchange Control Act, 1947

The Government has the power to gather information about the financial position of a customer who is suspected of violating the provisions of the Exchange Control Act, 1947.

### 8. Under Criminal Procedure Code

Sec.94 (3) compels a banker to produce the account books before the Police while conducting an investigation about the customer. However, a court order is essential in this case.

### 9. Under Foreign Exchange Regulation Act

Most of the commercial banks in India are dealing with foreign exchange transactions as they are authorised by the Reserve Bank of India. The Directorate of Enforcement and the RBI are empowered to inspect the books and accounts and other documents of any authorised dealer and also examine on oath such dealer or its director or officials in relation to business.

### 10. Garnishee Order

When a Garnishee Order nisi is received, the banker must disclose the nature of the account of a customer to the court.

## B. DISCLOSURE IN THE INTEREST OF THE PUBLIC

A bank may have large number and variety of customers. A few accounts may attract deposits from anti-social elements. At the time of opening an account, although an introduction is obtained about the customer, the banker may come to know of the actual dealings and links at a later date. It is not easy to identify such accounts. But when the banker has a proof, he can reveal this to the respective authorities. Following are some of the situations when the banker reveals the secrecy of customer's account.

*(a)* Disclosure of the account of an enemy in times of war.

*(b)* Disclosure of an account of a revolutionary body or terrorist Organisation to avert danger to the State.

*(c)* Disclosure of an account where money is kept for extreme political purpose.

*(d)* Disclosure of an account for an unlawful association.

*(e)* Disclosure of an account where the bank's books reveal that the customer is contravening the provisions of any law.

*(f)* Disclosure of an account where sizable funds are credited.

## C. DISCLOSURE IN THE INTEREST OF THE BANK

1. When the banker finds it difficult to collect the loan from his customer, he may take the matter to the court for settlement. In this connection, he may have to reveal this to his guarantor also.

2. It is a common practice among the bankers to exchange information about the customers. When an enquiry of this type comes to a banker, for the sake of common courtesy, he should respond to his fellow banker, as he may also be useful in this way in future. The banker will disclose his opinion based on the financial records with him without taking into consideration the rumours about the customer.

3. As a defense of past action, the banker may disclose the customer's account as was in 'Sunderland Vs. Barclays Bank Ltd.'. In this case, a cheque issued by Mrs. Sunderland drawn in favour of a tailor was dishonoured. When her husband inquired this, Mrs. Sunderland asked the bank to give proper reason for the dishonour of the cheque to her husband. To defend himself, the banker had to reveal the parties to whom the cheques were issued, some of them in favour of bookmakers. Mrs. Sunderland was annoyed over this and filed a case against the bank for revealing the secrecy of her account to her

husband. It was held that the banker was not liable, as Mrs. Sunderland had wanted the bank to explain to her husband why that cheque was dishonoured.

## D. DISCLOSURE AT THE EXPRESS OR IMPLIED CONSENT OF THE CUSTOMER

With the willingness of the customer, the banker can reveal the accounts of the customer in the following cases:

1. The customer himself may come forward to give the bank's name as referee when he deals with credit purchases. When the supplier inquires about the customer's creditworthiness, the banker normally gives a reference. The banker is justified in giving information or opinion based on the financial records available with him.
2. The banker should also answer the enquires made by the proposed surety regarding the account of the customer as the guarantor would be anxious to know the financial position of the customer for whom he intends to give guarantee. The banker is expected to reveal the exact position - neither more nor less. It would be good if the banker gives his general opinion about the customer's account without mentioning the figures.
3. For the purpose of getting visa to go to a foreign country, the customer may ask the banker to furnish the financial statements. In this case also, the banker can give the exact details about cash balance as on date and other relevant financial information as available on the record.

### General Precautions

In short, the banker should be careful in revealing the secrecy of his customers' account. If he is negligent, he will be liable to pay compensation for unwarranted disclosure. Apart from the points stated above, the banker should follow certain general precautions while disclosing customer's account:

1. The banker should give his opinion or statement based on the records available with him, ignoring the rumours about the financial conditions of the customer.
2. The banker should give his general opinion about the customer's account without mentioning the actual figures.
3. At any cost, the banker should not be negligent in giving the information.
4. Information should be given only after getting the express consent of the customer in writing.
5. The banker should furnish only the required information neither more nor less.

6. Information should not be conveyed over the telephone.
7. The banker should give the information honestly and without any bias.
8. The banker should be in the habit of adding the words *'Opinion given without any responsibility'* while replying to any trade enquiry.
9. While sending information to the customer through an agent, it should be put in a closed cover, preferably sealed.

## Risks of Unwarranted Disclosure

In case of wrong disclosure of the customer's account, the banker would be held liable to his customers and third parties as follows:

*(a)* ***Liability to the Customer :*** When the banker gives wrong information, which adversely affects the customer, the customer will file a suit against the bank claiming substantial damages from the bank.

*(b)* ***Liability to the Third Parties :*** When trade enquires are made, the banker should have given correct information. If the bank has given a rosy picture of an account of a customer intentionally, although it is not true, the supplier of goods may suffer a loss. In such case, the creditor who has acted on the banker's word may claim damages from the bank.

## III. Banker's Rights

*(a)* ***Banker's Right of Lien :*** Lien means the right to retain goods belonging to others until the debt due to him is fully repaid. There are two kinds of lien-Particular Lien and General Lien. It would be good to know the distinction between a particular lien and general lien for proper understanding of the Banker's lien.

## Distinction between Particular Lien and General Lien

Particular Lien is related to a craftsman who has spent time, labour and money in completing a specific task. For example, a piece of cloth is given to a tailor for stitching a shirt. If the tailoring charge is not paid, the tailor can retain the shirt until the charge is paid to him. Assuming that another piece of cloth is given to the same tailor for stitching pants, and if the tailoring charge for the shirt is not paid, the tailor cannot retain both the pants and the shirt for payment of tailoring charge for the shirt. The tailor cannot exercise the right to retain both because he has only a particular lien. If the customer pays charges for the pants, the pants should be returned to him. But the banker's position is different. A banker enjoys a general lien. It gives him the right to retain goods not only in respect of a particular debt but also in respect of a general balance due to him.

A particular lien arises from a specific transaction and attaches only to the property connected with that transaction whereas a general lien arises out of the general dealing between two parties and covers any property that one party may be holding for the other.

Section 171 of the Indian Contract Act, 1872 confers the right of general lien on the banker. Accordingly, *"Bankers may, in the absence of a contract to the contrary, retain as a security for a general balance of account, any goods bailed to them"*.

## Banker's Lien as an Implied Pledge

The banker's general lien conferred upon him the right to retain the borrower's property until the loan is repaid with interest. It is clearly revealed in various cases that banker's lien is described as an implied pledge. Implied pledge gives the banker not only the right to retain the property but also the right to sell after giving reasonable notice to the borrower when he does not take any steps to repay the bank's loan.

Even Lord Campbell is of the opinion that banker's lien is an implied pledge. According to him, "A *banker's lien is regarded some thing more than an ordinary lien and it is an implied pledge. This gives the right to sell* the *goods. He can sell the goods on default if the time is fixed for repayment of the loan. If time is not fixed, he can sell after requesting the customer to pay the loan and giving a reasonable notice of his intention* to *sell"*.

In another case, *'Deverges Vs. Sandeman'*, the Judge was of the opinion that one-month notice was a reasonable one.

## Conditions for Exercising Lien

The banker can exercise general lien under the following circumstances:

1. There should not be any agreement between banker and customer inconsistent with the lien.
2. The property should have come into the hands of the banker in the capacity as a Banker.
3. The property should not have been entrusted with the banker for any specific purpose.
4. The possession should be lawfully obtained in the capacity as a banker. The customer should not have left it inadvertently with the banker. The banker should not have used force, coercion or misrepresentation for obtaining the property.

## Circumstances in which the banker can exercise his Lien

*(a)* Bills, cheques, notes etc. and goods that come into the hands of banker.

(*b*) Bonds, coupons deposited for collection.

(*c*) Goods and securities standing in the name of the borrower.

(*d*) Securities not taken back after the repayment of the loan/loans.

## Exceptions to the Right of Lien

1. ***Safe Custody Deposits :*** Bankers receive valuables such as sealed boxes, parcels, documents, jewels and other valuables to be kept with them for safe custody. The relationship between banker and customer is that of bailor and bailee. A banker cannot exercise lien over the safe custody deposits.

2. ***Documents deposited with the banker for special purpose :*** When documents are deposited with the bank for special purpose, the banker becomes a trustee. Hence, the banker cannot exercise general lien.

3. ***Money deposited for specific purpose :*** If money has been deposited for specific purpose, the banker cannot exercise any lien over it. Even in the case of ordinary deposit, the expert opinion is that the banker can not have a lien on it although the banker can exercise his right of set-off as in the case of *'Brahammaya Vs. K.P.Thangavel Nadar (1956)'*. It was held, "The lien under Sec. 171 can be exercised only over property of some one else and not own property. Thus when goods are deposited with or securities are placed in the custody of the bank, it would be correct to speak of rights of the bank over the security or the goods as a lien because the ownership of the goods or securities would continue to remain with the customer. But when moneys are deposited with the bank as a fixed deposit, the ownership of the money passes on to the bank and the right of the bank over the money lodged with it would not be really a lien at all. It would be more correct to speak of it as a right of set-off or adjustment'.

4. ***Securities for Future Loan :*** Securities lodged with the bank for getting a loan before such loan is actually granted to the customer. A banker cannot exercise his right of lien on the securities laodged with. However, It should be noted that the banker's right of lien is not barred by Law of Limitation.

## (*b*) Banker's Right of Set-off

Right of set-off is a legal right which entitles a debtor to take into account the sum immediately owing to him by a creditor when determining the net sum due to the creditor. For example, a banker has allowed an overdraft to Mr. X amounting to Rs.25,000 and Mr. X's Savings Bank account shows a credit balance of Rs.10,000. In case X fails to pay the overdraft, the banker can exercise his right of set-off by combining both accounts by which the banker can claim the net difference of Rs.15,000 from his customer. The mutual adjustment of debit and credit balances is called Set-off . The banker can exercise the right of Set-off like any other debtor.

**Conditions for exercising the right of set-off :**

1. The debts must be a certain sum. The banker can not exercise his right of set-off against the guarantor if the liability of the guarantor is not determined. The exact liability of the guarantor can be determined only when the principal debtor fails.
2. The accounts must be in the same name and in the same right. For instance, an individual account cannot be combined with a Joint account wherein there is another party.
3. The right can be exercised in respect of debts due and not in respect of future debts.
4. There should not be any agreement contrary to the right of setoff.

A banker has the automatic right of set-off in the following cases :

*(a)* On the death, insolvency and insanity of the customer.

*(b)* On insolvency of a firm or winding up of a company.

*(c)* On receiving a notice of assignment of a customer's credit balance.

*(d)* On the receipt of a garnishee order from the court.

*(e)* On receipt of notice of a second charge over securities mortgaged.

As a general rule, a banker can exercise his right of set-off. He can also exercise it at his discretion. But if the credit balance is on current account, he must give the customer reasonable notice of his intention to exercise the right of set-off.

## *(c)* Right of appropriation

A customer may open one or more accounts with a bank. Similarly, he may also take one or more loans from the bank. When money is deposited with the bank, as a general rule, the debtor who makes payment to his creditor shall have the right to say for which account he is making the payment. This right is provided to the debtor according to Sec.59-61 of the Indian Contract Act, 1872.

A debtor can appropriate the payment by an express intimation or under circumstances implying that the payment is made for a particular debt. For instance, when the customer has accepted a bill for Rs. 1,000 falling due on 15th February 2004. This bill was discounted with the bank. The customer has also taken a loan from the bank for Rs.5, 000. When the customer (debtor) pays Rs. 1,000 on 15th February 2004 without any instruction to the bank, it should be presumed that the customer's intention is to pay the bill only and not the loan.

In case a debtor has not indicated the account to which the amount sent is to be adjusted or there is no circumstances to believe to which debt the amount is to be applied, then, the creditor can decide as to which debt it should be applied. If neither of them indicated the appropriation, then the payment shall be applied in the order of time.

### *(d)* Right to claim Incidental Charges

The practice of charging incidental charges on unremunerative accounts is common amongst the bankers, particularly among the foreign banks in India. However, the nationalised banks are not very strict with their valued customers, although they have the right to claim incidental charges.

Banks use different terms like 'Processing charges', 'Service charges', 'Appraisal charges', 'Penal charges' etc., depending upon the services tendered to their customers. The incidental charges are levied under the following circumstances:

1. When a customer's account shows a balance less than the minimum balance prescribed by the bank.
2. While collecting an outstation cheque or foreign cheque.
3. When part of the Cash Credit is not utilised by the customer.
4. When the customer opts to close the account with the bank within a very short period.
5. When the banker spends some money while doing agency services for the customer, for example: Postal charges, Telephone charges, clerical charges etc.

### *(e)* Right to charge Compound Interest

A banker lends to his customers in the form of Cash Credit, Overdraft, Loans and Advances or discounting bills of exchange. In all these cases, the banker charges interest on loans as per the agreement. The agreement between the banker and customer may specify the rate of interest and the type of interest (compound rate).

Although compound rate of interest is strictly prohibited in the ordinary debt, bankers are exempted from. Usually, banks charge interest on loans at the end of every quarter. The practice of charging interest may vary amongst the bankers. Some foreign banks in India were charging interest at the end of every month. For this purpose, a clause is included in the agreement at the time of opening the account. The customer need not pay the interest in cash. Once the interest is debited to the customer's account, the total becomes a debt due from the customer.

## LAW OF LIMITATION

Bankers, businessmen and even common men and women are dealing with loans and advances. As per the provisions of the Limitation Act, 1963, a debt will become a bad debt after the expiry of 3 years from the date of the debt. The implication is that the debtor need not legally pay the debt once 3 years are over provided there was no contact between the debtor and creditor. But the banker is exempted from the Limitation Act. According to Article 22 of the Part 11 of the schedule to the Limitation Act, 1963, the period of limitation for the refund of bank deposits is 3 years with effect from the date of a customer making a demand for his money. Sec.26 of the Banking Regulation Act, 1949 has prescribed a period of 10 years to consider a banking debt as bad debt. In the case of Fixed Deposit, a period of 10 years will be calculated from the date of expiry of such fixed deposit. This is an advantage to the customer. However, in the case of overdraft, the period of 3 years will commence from the date on which it is made use of by the customer. In the case of safe custody deposit, the law of limitation period commences from the date of demand.

## Importance of Customer Relations

To survive in today's highly competitive financial services market,banks must realize the full potential of every customer relationship. A very important aspect of bank marketing is 'relationship management' which is a philosophy of doing business, a strategic orientation, that focuses on keeping and improving current customers, rather than on acquiring new customers. Relationship management implies attracting, maintaining and enhancing customer relationships. Servicing and selling to existing customers is viewed to be just as important as acquiring new customers. The primary goal of relationship banking is to build and maintain a base of committed customers who are profitable for the organization.

## Benefits to Bank :

Following are the benefits to a bank for maintaining and developing a loyal customer base.

### Increasing Purchases :

As customers get to know a bank and are satisfied with the quality of its services relative to that of its competitors, they will tend to give more business to the bank.

### Lower costs :

There are many start up costs associated with attracting new customers. They include advertising and other promotion costs, operating costs of setting up accounts and systems and time costs of getting to know the customer.Even ongoing relationship maintenance costs are likely to drop over a period of time. For example, early in a relationship, a customer is likely to have questions and to encounter problems as he or she learns to use the service. Once learning has taken place the customer will have fewer questions ( assuming the quality of service is maintained at a high level ) and the bank will incur fewer costs in serving the customer.

### Free Advertising through the word of mouth :

When a product is complex and difficult to evaluate and there is risk involved in the decision to buy - as in the case of many services, consumers often look to others advice on which bankers to consider. Satisfied and loyal customers are likely to provide a bank with strong word of mouth endorsements. This form of advertising can be more effective than any paid advertising the bank might use and has the added benefit of reducing the costs of attracting new customers. Further , customers that came up based on a reference turn out to be better—quality customers ( in terms of profitability and likelihood of loyalty) than customers who are attracted by price promotions or a new advertising campaign.

### Benefits to Customers :

There are certain benefits for the customers also :

Customers are more likely to stay in a relationship when quality, satisfaction and specific benefits exceed the monetary and non-monetary costs. When bank can consistently deliver service value from the customer's point of view, clearly the customer benefits and has an incentive to stay in the relationship. Customers also benefit in other ways from long term associations with a bank. Sometimes, it is these relationship benefits that keep customers loyal to a bank more than the attributes of the core service.

### Customer Relationship Management :

Customer Relationship Management ( CRM ) plays an important role in relationship banking which will help in attracting customer segments that have the potential to sustain a long-term relationship with the bank. CRM basically aims at redesigning the organization around customer's requirement.

### Meaning of Customer Relationship Management :

Customer Relationship Management is an enterprise approach to understanding and influencing customer behaviour through meaningful communications in order to improve customer acquisition, customer retention, customer loyalty and customer profitability.

### Definition of Customer Relationship Management :

Customer Relationship Management is defined as " a comprehensive strategy and process of acquiring, retaining and partnering with selective customers to create superior value for the company and the customer".

## Importance of Customer Relationship Management :

Developing close and co-operative relationship with customers is more important in the current era of intense competition than it has ever been before.Customer Relationship Management starts with in-depth knowledge of customers, their habits, desires and their needs, by analyzing their cognitive, effective behaviour and attributes. CRM applies this knowledge to develop and design marketing strategies, to develop a relationship with the customer. Customer knowledge and customer interaction on the basis of this knowledge are the two pillars on which any CRM design and its successful implementation rests. CRM is an iterative process that turns customer information into positive customer relationships. Two important processes of CRM include proactive customer business development and building partnering relationship with most important customers. These lead to superior mutual value creation.

## Customer Relationship Management in Banks :

One of the determinants of the success of the relationship marketing strategies of a bank is how the customers understand the resulting service quality. In India, with the onset of financial deregulation, banks are functioning increasingly under competitive pressures. In this arena, in order to prosper, it will be imperative for banks to focus on developing long-term relationships with their customers.

With the initiation of financial sector reforms, banks have been given a great degree of freedom in determining their rate structure for deposits and advances, as well as their product range. The freedom of choice which the bank customers did not have earlier because of standardized products and regimented interest rates has now been given to the customers. Therefore, the focus of banks should be to shift their orientation from transaction marketing to the cultivation of relationship marketing with the increasing competitive pressures emanating from within the banking system, from non-banking institutions as well as from the domestic and international capital markets.

## Customer Grievances :

In these days of fierce competition, in order to survive, Commercial banks have to seek business by aggressively marketing their products. Product differentiation is often employed as a major technique to service in competitive market.

Products offered by banks have been changing over years, particularly in recent years. These products are getting refined and revised in the light of customer needs, but not promptly enough or adequately and dissatisfaction arises. A large portion of customer's complaints arises because of the disparity between customer expectations and bank services. Very often, there are abnormal delays in receiving/making payments and customers have to wait indefinitely without anybody attending to them properly at the counter. This leads to mounting frustration among customers. Moreover, the procedures laid down at the banks are lengthy and cumbersome. Even the issue of cheque book takes twenty to thirty minutes because the officer is always busy with cheques/vouchers and registers. Even updating of pass book also takes a long time.

The Working Group on Customer Services in Banks set up by the Government of India under the Chairmanship of Mr.R.K.Talwar in 1975, has listed the following factors for customer dissatisfaction or customer grievances :

*(i)* delay and inaccuracy in putting through transactions ;

*(ii)* delay and inadequacies in correspondence ;

*(iii)* delayed, faulty and unhelpful decision-making ;

*(iv)* absence of elementary discipline;

*(v)* undue emphasis of staff on observance of rules and procedures;

*(vi)* inconvenience associated with credit apprehension ;

*(vii)* lack of uniformity in bank charges ;

*(viii)* general attitude of unconcern and apathy for clients.

Delivery system for customer services comprise five elements : speed, timeliness, accuracy, courtesy and concern. The present Customer Service System lacks motivation and initiative, thus adversely affecting the services offered. Neither the branch manager nor his staff take initiative in advising the customers on the choice of deposit plan, mode of operating an account, choice of credit facility or how to draw the best possible benefit from the banking schemes and the services. They are generally left to themselves, their friends and common sense, to take such decision.

## Recommendations of Working Group :

The Working Group, headed by Mr. R.K.Talwar, made a full scale review of the whole gamut of the issues involved and made wide ranging recommendations to improve customers services. It was stated in the report that banks must continuously assess and reassess how customers perceive their services, what are the new and emerging customer expectations and how these can be satisfied on an on-going basis. It has also been emphasized that customer service is an extremely dynamic concept. What is considered to be good customer service today may be an indifferent service tomorrow and bad one the day after.

The majority of the recommendations made by the Working Group on Customer Service in Banks were implemented in most banks. Bank management has also been alive to the situation and in the past a great deal of time and effort have been spent in the area of improving banking services. And yet the fact is that customers remain dissatisfied and complaints continue to pour in about delays in collection, remittance, transfer of accounts and most of all discourteous counter service.

## Redressal of Customer Grievances : Ombudsman Scheme

In exercise of powers conferred under Banking Regulation Act, 1949, the Reserve Bank of India announced the OMBUDSMAN Scheme, on 14th June 1995 covering all the scheduled commercial banks in India. This scheme was further extended to 134 scheduled primary co-operative banks on 17th June, 1995. Regional Rural banks have been kept out of the purview of the scheme for the time being. Ombudsmen have since been appointed for all states of India.

## The Banking Ombudsman :

Disputes will invariably arise between banks and their customers. When they do, it is normally in the interests of both sides to settle them amicably between themselves. For example, a missing credit transfer can usually be found and an apology is usually sufficient. If a dispute cannot be resolved in this way, then resort to legal action has always been possible. However, this takes time, costs, money and cause bad publicity and distress. Indeed, in relation to the amounts involved and the increasing competitiveness of the financial marketplace, it is often commercially far better for a bank to stand a small loss than fight- if the customer has the resources and determination to pursue the claim.

Nevertheless, the vast numbers of cheques and automated payments processed each day and the increasing use of ATMs and electronic funds transfer create more opportunity for fraud and greater risk of error. Mistakes will happen and disputes will ensue. Against this background the Banking Ombudsman was set to resolve disputes between banks and customers and investigate customer complaints.

Ombudsman is a mechanism for redressal of customer grievances in a quick and less expensive manner. The ombudsman attend to customers complaints related to certain key areas which remain unresolved at the bank level and facilitate satisfaction of such complaints.

Indian Banks' Association has favoured Ombudsman for banks for redressal of bank customer grievances so that customer complaints are heard, and speedily dispensed by Ombudsman who should be a retired high court judge. This saves the customer the delay involved in going for long drawn litigation. The appointment of Ombudsman is expected to result in improved customer service and provides quality and speedy redressal of grievances.

Both banks and customers stand to gain from the existence of the Banking Ombudsman. The office helps to maintain and improve public confidence in the banks' operations while to customers the office offers a way to effectively pursue complaints to redress their grievances.

### Benefits of Ombudsman :

The setting up of the Banking Ombudsman is a landmark in the Indian banking industry. The changed banking scenario calls for fair and effective redressal of complaints when things go wrong or some dissatisfaction arises.

The main advantages of the Ombudsman scheme are :

*(i)* It is inexpensive, i.e. the service is available absolutely free to the customer.

*(ii)* Ombudsman is a independent authority from banks themselves and his decisions are binding on banks.

*(iii)* Ombudsman is only a one man team because in most of the disputes neither the complainant nor the banks are represented, though they can be represented.

*(iv)* Ombudsman functions informally. It does not rely upon the cases put up to it by the relevant parties. In fact, it goes deep into the issue and conducts independent investigations before deciding the case. Therefore, fairness and natural justice constitute the essence of the scheme.

*(v)* The awards of the ombudsman are binding on the banks, but if the complainant does not accept the Ombudsman's decision, he has the right to proceed through the court in the usual way.

The existence of the Ombudsman scheme itself prevents some dispute between customers and banks.

### Classification of Customer Complaints :

Customer complaints may be broadly classified into two categories :

*(a)* Complaints concerning the deficiency in service and

*(b)* Complaints concerning non-observance of the RBI directives on interest rates, delay in sanction or delayed disposal of loan applications in particular and other directives in general.

### Complaints concerning the deficiency in service.

The banking ombudsman will look into complaints regarding deficiency in services such as :

- Non-payment/inordinate delay in the payment or collection of cheques, drafts/bills.
- Non-acceptance of small denomination notes and for charging of commission.

- Non-issue of drafts.
- Non-adherence to prescribed working hours by branches.
- Failure to honour guarantee/letter of credit commitments by banks.
- Claims in respect of unauthorized or fraudulent withdrawals from deposit accounts, etc.
- Complaints pertaining to operations in any account such as delays, non-credits of proceeds to parties accounts, non-payment of deposit of non-observance of RBI directives, applicable rate of interest on deposits.
- Delays in receipt of export proceeds, handling of export bills, collection of bills, etc. provided the said complaints pertain to the bank's operations in India.
- NRI complaints in relation to their remittances from abroad, deposits, and other bank related matters.

## Complaints regarding loans and advances :

Complaints concerning loans and advances relate to :

- Non-observance of RBI directives on interest rates.
- Delays in sanction/non-observance of prescribed time schedule for disposal of loan applications.
- Non-observance of any other directions or instructions of RBI, as may be specified for this purpose.

## Role of Ombudsman in Resolving Complaints :

Ombudsman can take up to one month just to decide whether the complaint falls within his jurisdiction. Having found the case suitable for consideration Ombudsman will first try to find an amicable settlement between the bank and the complainant. If that does not work out, he can make a recommendation. However, this recommendation is not final and the customer has an option to refuse the recommendations if he thinks it is unfair to him. Even if he accepts, banks can disagree. However to make the bank accept his recommendations, Ombudsman can take the help of Reserve Bank of India.

The Banking Ombudsman shall not make any recommendations or pass any award for an amount in excess to the complainant as a direct consequence of the commission or omission of the bank for an amount exceeding Rs. 10 lakhs, whichever is lower. In case, the bank defies the award, the matter would be referred to the RBI, which would take action under section 35 of the Banking Regulation Act.

The Banking Ombudsman may reject the complaint at any stage if it appears to him that the complaint is made without any sufficient cause or that it is not pursued by the complainant with reasonable diligence or that, prima facie, there is no loss or damage or inconvenience suffered by the complainant.

## MODEL QUESTIONS

**Section - A**

1. Define a Banker.
2. Who is a customer?
3. Can the customer demand the same identical currency notes deposited with the bank?
4. Why is a banker considered as Privileged debtor?
5. What is a Garnishee order?
6. What is banker's lien?
7. What are the circumstances in which a banker can exercise his right of lien?
8. What do you understand by "Right of Appropriation"?
9. Is a Banker justified in charging compound rate of interest upon his customers account?
10. Write a note on Law of Limitation.
11. What is relationship management?
12. Define CRM.
13. Who is an Ombudsman?
14. What are the benefits of customer relations to a customer?

**Section - B**

1. What do you understand by "Duration Theory"?
2. How does a bank debt differ from ordinary debt?
3. Write a note on "Right to combine accounts".
4. What is the role of a banker while acting as lessee in the case of safe deposit locker facility?
5. What are the agency services rendered by commercial banks to the their customers.
6. Comment on their banker's obligations to maintain the secrecy of the customers accounts.
7. Is there any difference between non-trader and a trader while paying compensation for the dishonour of his cheque?
8. What are the risks for a banker in disclosing customer's account?
9. Distinguish between particular lien and general lien.
10. What are the conditions for exercising lien?

11. What are the expectations to the right of lien?
12. What are the conditions for exercising the right of set off?
13. What do you understand by incidental charges? What are the circumstances in which a banker charges them?
14. Explain the importance of customer relations.
15. What are the benefits of customer relations to a banker?
16. What do you mean by Custómer Relationship Management?
17. Explain the importance of CRM in banks.
18. What are the factors responsible for customer grievances?
19. What are the benefits of Ombudsman.

**Section - C**

1. Explain the general relationship between a banker and a customer.
2. What are the rights and duties of the banker regarding Deposit Account?
3. What are the consequences of wrongful dishonour of cheques?
4. Is the banker legally obliged to maintain the secrecy of his customer's accounts. In what cases a disclosure is justified.
5. What are the special features of relationship between banker and customer?
6. How are customer grievances redressed in commercial banks?
7. What are the steps taken by Government for customer grievances in banks?
8. Explain the role of Ombudsman in resolving complaints.
9. What are the classifications of customer complaints?

# 11

# LOANS AND ADVANCES I

One of the important functions of the commercial banks is to raise the resources from the areas where it is available and to arrange for the transfer of such funds to such areas where it is needed most. A crucial decision to be taken by the bank administration is the use of such deposits and its own funds (capital and reserves) to enable the bank to earn profit. It should be noted that the borrowed funds of any commercial bank will be much more than its paid-up capital although the minimum paid-up capital has been raised to Rs. 100 crores quite recently.

Since the banks are dealing with public money, the bank should judiciously employ all its funds to achieve the objectives of the bank. The bank cannot lend the entire funds as the depositors are likely to withdraw their deposits at any time. If the banks have received deposits for a long period, they can think of long-term investment and higher profits without maintaining large reserves at the bank. However, if they have received money for short periods as in the case of current account deposits, the banks should be extra careful while lending these funds as the deposits are withdrawable at any time without giving any notice. A bank's capacity to attract deposits depends primarily on the confidence it enjoys with the public. If the bank is not able to collect the money lent to the borrowers in time, its ability to repay the depositors is diminished and the confidence on the bank will be shattered if the bank does not honour customer's demand instantaneously. Hence, the bank should take a decision to lend primarily on the basis of the availability and the nature of funds, RBI guidelines and investment policy of the bank.

Banks act not merely as creditors for borrowers but more as the custodian for deposit customers. Therefore, a bank is not only answerable to its shareholders but also to its depositors at large. Its activities, viz., method of lending, lending rate, group to which it lends etc., are closely watched by the public, RBI and the Government. In this context, bank lending has a special significance.

In the recent years, banks are more careful and follow the norms of lending, as there has been large number of bank scams followed by investigation and litigation. The banks are now careful and take adequate precautions while lending against securities. In case the borrower fails to pay the loan as per the terms, the bank will take legal action against the defaulter. Holding right type of securities would ease the banker's position to recover the dues from the borrower. Different types of securities such as gold and gold ornaments, fixed deposit receipts, goods, document of title to goods etc., are offered by the customers. Each type of security has its own feature to guard against the banker's risk. The banker would prefer to gilt-edged liquid securities, as they are easily convertible into cash at times of emergency. But such types of securities can be offered only by a few borrowers. Most of the others may offer the assets which may be available with them. Hence, banker must have a special knowledge of the various types of securities so that he can lend safety. Although there are certain standard norms for lending against various kinds of securities, the banker should deal with each case separately.

A prudent banker is cautious in investing his funds so as to bring maximum benefits to the shareholders without affecting the depositors. The guiding principles of investment policy are safety, liquidity and profitability. As time changes, the principles of lending also change. The traditional banker insisted upon security and profit. The social control and nationalisation of banks have transformed the concept of bank lending. Now no one can claim from the bank any loan merely on the basis of adequate security. The banks have been directed to meet the needs of priority sector. There has been a shift from security-orientation to purpose-oriented loan. However, the fundamental principles of lending cannot be dispensed with.

## PRINCIPLES OF LENDING

### 1. Safety

The term "safety" is inter-related with security. Since a banker deals with other people's money, the banker should ensure the safety of such funds and security of such depositors. If the banker is reckless in his investment policy, the safety of such investment is sacrificed at the cost of the depositors who lose their security. In case a banker is not able to get back his investment, he cannot imagine to meet his commitment and consequently loses the confidence of the depositors. Once confidence is lost, that is the end of the business.

The traditional banker emphasises the safety of funds and insisted upon security on the following grounds:

*(i)* The banker can exercise some degree of control over his customers' behaviour.

*(ii)* The customer understands the consequences of charging the security to the bank; he may have genuine interest in repaying the loan. Otherwise, some may feel that unsecured loan is a gift.

*(iii)* The banks can sell the security in order to meet the depositors' claims if the borrower fails to pay his debts in spite of his efforts to recover it.

*(iv)* Failure to collect loan may lead to insufficient funds at the hands of the bank, leading to serious consequences like bank failure.

Regarding securities, the value, in some cases, deteriorate in course of time. The banker will try his best to realise his money even under adverse conditions. If the security becomes inadequate, he may ask his customer to provide more security or ask the customer to arrange for repayment of a portion of the loan. However, if the banker seriously insists on security, those who cannot afford to give any security may not avail of any bank loan at all.

### 2. Liquidity

Liquidity, in banking terminology, means the ability to convert the assets into cash without any loss of time and value. The traditional banker usually supported his loan with tangible security which offers a cushion for safety. Whenever there is a withdrawal, the banker should unhesitatingly and without any delay honour his customers' demand. In case the banker delays repayment due to insufficiency of funds, the news might spread like wild fire, leading to spread of false rumours about the solvency of the bank. If all the customers demand withdrawal of their deposits at the same time, no bank can survive, as they will not have adequate cash to pay back the depositors although the bank may be solvent at that point of time. Therefore, a bank should be careful in the use of its funds without giving any opportunity at any time to lose faith in the banking system. Fixed assets like land and buildings, as securities, may pose problems of sale at times of emergencies.

### 3. Profitability

The third principle is the profitability. A bank is not a philanthropic institution. It is a business unit and it should make adequate profit to meet the banking and administrative expenses and to pay a reasonable return to its shareholders. The profitability of the bank depends on the quantum and nature of deposits and its investment policy. The bank pays interest on deposits and receives interest on loans/investments. The difference between the lending rate and the borrowing rate is the profit. If the bank invests all its resources, it may not be able to meet the demands of the depositors. Therefore, it should maintain a portion of the deposits as cash reserve to meet such emergencies. How much cash reserve should be maintained with the bank is a question to be answered by a banker based on his experience and expertise as withdrawals may vary from time to time depending upon the nature of deposits.

A shrewd banker should draw an imaginary line between safety, liquidity and profitability. He never takes too much risk at the cost of the depositors. "The secret of successful banking is to distribute resources between the various forms of assets in such a way as to get a sound balance between liquidity and profitability so that there is cash to meet every claim and at the same time enough income for the bank to pay its way and earn profits for its shareholders".

Investment is a difficult technique at the present juncture as there are various hurdles for a bank. First of all, a bank may have to maintain 10 - *15%* of its deposits depending on the situation, to meet the depositors' needs. Secondly, a scheduled commercial bank should deposit 14% of its deposits with RBI as cash reserve to inspire confidence among the public. The banks are also to maintain statutory liquidity ratio of 38.5% leaving only a small percentage at the disposal of the managers to decide on their lending.

Keeping in mind the expected lending rate, a banker may grant loan but he should not be carried away by the attractive interest offered by some of the borrower-customers. The general principle of lending is 'greater the risk, higher the rate.' Usually, *the interest is linked with the bank rate.* The interest rate varies according to the market rate. He may have to give due consideration to the safety of the loan. Experienced and successful bankers strike an intelligent balance between safety, liquidity and profitability.

In order to receive certain social obligations, the commercial banks have been asked to lend at a concessional rate of 4% p.a. to certain categories of borrowers from the weaker section of the community. The loss in this category of loans will be compensated by the higher rate of profits charged on some other customers.

## 4. 3-C's of the Customer

The 3-C's: *Character, Capacity and Capital* of the borrower may have to be ascertained carefully. The banker may have to use his judgment and take a firm decision as to whether the borrower will repay as agreed upon. Character does not simply refer to the moral character of the individual. It refers to his honest financial dealings with others. It is virtually impossible to assess one's character after the first meeting. Some customers may have money but they may not have the willingness to repay the loan whereas some others may take every effort to repay their dues whatever difficulty they face. Such characters may have to be identified by the banker through proper inquiries. A more reliable method of ascertaining the creditworthiness of the borrower is to examine whether he has honoured his other financial commitments in time.

*Capacity of the* borrower may refer to his *technical qualifications and the know how in the line of business* for which the loan is sought. It refers to the resourcefulness of an individual. Capacity also refers to the *ability to repay the loans* in time. The banker has to ascertain whether his borrower has a regular flow of income.

Apart from this, the bank may also see whether the customer has *enough capital in the form of assets - movable and immovable* assets in his name. Capital refers to his stake in the business. A customer may have vast landed property which do not give him any returns due to some reason or other. Such securities are of little value.

## 5. Purpose of the Loan

A lender "lends" money and does not give it away. Even though, there is cent per cent security, if the project is a failure, the bank will have the problem of recovering funds. Money cannot be lent for speculative and unproductive purposes. The *purpose of the loan* must be *legal, productive and commercially viable.* The proposal should *project future flow of funds.* The banker should be satisfied with the proposal. The banker should have confidence in the ability of the borrower to make use of the funds in an advantageous manner. If necessary, he may consult the technicians about the feasibilities of the project. He must ensure that there is an adequate surplus to cover the repayment of loan, after meeting his other commitments.

## 6. Recycling of Loan

A good proposal would facilitate continuous recycling of funds in preference to locking up of funds.

## 7. Spreading the Risk

According to H.P. Sheldon, in his book on "Practice and Law of Banking", the banker should spread over the risk. He suggests that *a bank should invest in various industries in different areas and grant loans in varying proportions* so that the loss in one area, if any, *may be compensated* by the *profit* in other area.It is also wise to give small amounts of loan to large number of customers, apart from the above principle.

### 8. Refinance

The bank may look for refinancing facilities from RBI, IDBI, or NABARD. Between two eligible proposals, he should give weightage for the proposal which carries refinance facilities.

### 9. Amount

Another pertinent question asked frequently by the banker is the *quantum of loan.* Most of the borrowers ask for an amount more than what they normally need. If the bank, on the basis of the security offered by him, grants such amounts, he may face problems in the future. Similarly, if the advance is inadequate, the bank may have to lend more to protect the previous lending. If he refuses to grant additional sum, the project may fail. The customer may not be able to pay back the loan; consequently, the bank will suffer.

The bank may insist upon the *borrower's matching contribution. The* customer cannot expect the bank to lend him the entire amount. If the borrower has invested reasonably in the project, he will have commitment to his profession and will also bear risk.

### 10. Priority to Weaker Sections

With the nationalisation of 20 commercial banks, the bank lending has a different dimension in order to achieve the social obligations. The Government is encouraging the banks to direct their lending towards priority sector. Under the compulsive pressure of social banking, banks were required to lend 40% of their advances to priority sector. National targets for advances to priority sectors as a whole with sub-targets for weaker sections of the society have been laid down, which must be attained by the public sector banks within the prescribed period. A banker should follow the RBI guidelines relating to the lending of funds.

### 11. Public Interest

Although a commercial bank is primarily concerned with its own funds, it should also consider the national interest and the borrowers' interest too. Like a money-lender, the banker should not exploit the borrower by charging exhorbitant rates of interest.

## PROCEDURE FOR APPRAISAL OF CREDIT PROPOSAL AND FIXING CREDIT LIMITS

For an outsider, bank lending may appear to be a simple affair. But lending of funds is not that easy as one imagines. A banker is guided by various considerations. Primarily, a banker may find the amount received from various deposit accounts would be inadequate to meet the innumerable proposals from the borrowers seeking financial help for various purposes. With the rapid industrialisation and development of various sectors of the economy, the banker's task is to choose the right type of borrower. Since a banker deals with other people's money, he exercises utmost caution and employs a number of modem tools of appraisal before sanctioning the loan to selected borrowers. The selection of a good borrower is an art. The banker selects such borrowers and arranges for making such advances, keeping in mind the principles of lending, particularly if it is a long-term credit. Usually advances are made by way of - *(a)* overdrafts, *(b)* cash credit, *(c)* discounting bills of exchange, and *(d)* loans and advances.

Overdraft is a temporary financial accommodation usually available to businessmen to meet their urgent needs. Cash credit is mostly a secured credit. Only a small limit is often sanctioned by the bank manager. While overdraft is granted on personal or just current accounts, cash credits are sanctioned for the benefit of industrialists, businessmen and others. The borrowers may prefer cash credit as they have the liberty to draw in instalments as and when required by them, but may have to pay interest only on the amount actually outstanding. The banks also purchase and discount commercial bills to finance genuine trade transactions and movement of goods. Bills are to be supported by documents of title to goods such as invoice, railway receipts, lorry receipts, bills of lading etc. Loans may also be granted by the bankers on the basis of certain movable or immovable securities. Whatever the type of advances they make, the banks adopt certain procedure.

The first step for a borrower to avail of a bank loan is to get the prescribed application form from the respective branch from where he intends to obtain a loan. Different forms of applications are available for different categories of loans. The RBI has also given direction to the commercial banks that they should lend 40% of their advances to the priority sectors, such as agriculture, small-scale industries, small borrowers etc. The borrower obtains the necessary application for a bank loan. The application form is available at free of cost.

The next step is to fill in the application. Many banks make the necessary applications available to their customers in the local language also. The application calls for the entire range of details and information necessary for ensuring sanction and safe return of money lent. The application should be complete in all respects. All the necessary documents in support of the claims made in the application form are also attached with the application and submitted at the bank.

Once the banker receives the application, he allots a serial number and enters in the Loan Application Received Register. The register has different columns for recording the following particulars :

(i) Serial number.

(ii) Date of receipt of the application form.

(iii) Name of the Applicant.

(iv) Amount of loan.

(v) Nature of the loan applied for (agriculture, SSI, small business etc.).

(vi) The manner of disposing of the application.

The loan application form is the base for the banker to decide whether to sanction a loan or not. The bank manager or his field staff will thoroughly scrutinise the application form and the relevant documents. This process is known as "Appraisal of the Loan." Normally the manager will also have an interview with the borrower. The following information will be ascertained by the bank manager :

### 1. Particulars of the Borrower

The manager learns, from the application the details of the borrower, like the name, address, his ability, integrity and experience, his establishment, the nature of his business, his reputation in the market etc.

### 2. Purpose of the Loan

The purpose of the loan is very important. The banker rarely lends money for unproductive purposes. In case of a new business, he may ascertain whether the money will be used for long-term capital outlay, i.e., for the purchase of plant and machinery. If so, he takes adequate care as the bank primarily lends for short-term purposes. The banker takes extra care if the loan applied for is for the redemption of previous loan/loans. Normally commercial banks do not grant credit for such purposes.

### 3. Security

The banker looks at the security offered by the borrower and finds out whether it can be easily sold in the market without any loss of time and value. He verifies the validity of the title to such security or securities. He may examine carefully whether he can have adequate 'Margin' in such securities. The difference between the market value of the securities and the amount lent against them is known as 'Margin'. In case there are sureties for the borrower, the details of such sureties and references will be verified.

Although the banks insist upon securities, they do not completely rely upon securities. If the banker feels that the project/proposal is unsatisfactory, he will decline the proposal without any hesitation even if the securities are too good. Security is taken as the last resort for the bank to get back the money by realising the security because :

*(i)* The customer may suffer in venturing into such unrealistic project. Further damage is done to him by selling his securities at odd times at low prices.

*(ii)* The banker, as expected, may not be able to realise the securities in certain cases; legal hurdles may arise.

*(iii)* Realising such securities is time-consuming and expensive, in certain cases; the value of such securities may fall.

*(iv)* If the bank resorts to sale of such securities, there may be adverse publicity against the bank, affecting its reputation.

*(v)* Last but not least, there is disharmony between the banker and the borrower.

## 4. Amount of Loan

The banker examines the relationship between the amount required by the borrower for his project and the amount asked for in the application. He verifies, using certain techniques, whether the amount is adequate to take up the proposed project. There is a misconception among the borrowers that the bank will normally grant lesser amount than requested. Therefore, there is a tendency to inflate the figures in the project proposal. The main concern for the bank manager is to determine the right quantum of loan required for the project. If the bank grants more, the customer may spend lavishly and waste it. But at the same time, if it is inadequate, the manager may have to lend more subsequently to protect the previous lending. If he refuses to grant additional sum, the project may fail and the customer may not be able to pay back the loan. Consequently, the bank will suffer.

The banker carefully ascertains the amount of loan, allowing provision for emergencies. In case, the bank feels that he cannot agree for the requested amount, he may ask the necessary amendments. The entire investment need not be contributed by the banker himself. He may insist on the borrower's contribution.

A borrower may approach a bank for three types of loan:

*(a)* Short-term loan;

*(b)* Medium-term loan; and

*(c)* Long-term loan.

*Short-term Credit* : Traditionally banks provide short-term credit only. The period of loan normally ranges between 3-6 months. Short-term loans are required by traders and manufacturing units to build up their inventory. The short-term finance depends upon the working capital cycle of the business. Short-term credit is also needed to meet operational expenses and long-term credit is needed to meet operational expenses and long-term credit needs of the customers. It is a temporary financial accommodation during the period between the time of purchase of raw materials and the time of sale of finished goods. For example, a cracker-manufacturing unit may have to build up its inventory from the month of April. But only in November, just before Deepavali, he may sell his stock and pay back the loan.

Short-term finance may be affected through cash credit against pledge, hypothecation of stock, book debts or supply bills. In the case of certain credit sales, banks may also resort to discounting such commercial bills.

*Medium-term Credit:* Banks, in certain special cases, grant medium term loans to the borrowers. The period of loan normally ranges between 2 – 5 years. Such medium-term loans are required to expand their business, renovation etc. In business where the working capital cycle is longer, the medium-term loans are granted to meet their working capital needs also.

*Long-term Credit:* The commercial banks hesitate to grant long-term credit, as they cannot afford to lock up their funds in long-term ventures. The banks, may, in certain exceptional cases, resort to long-term credit, ranging between 3-7 years. Long-term finance is required to acquire fixed assets like plant and machinery, land and buildings etc. They also lend for renovation or modification, etc. Banks may lend individually or in consortium with other banks or financial institutions. At present some commercial banks venture into housing loans ranging from 5-12 years.

## Areas of Probing

Whether the type of loan is short-term, medium-term or long-term loan, the banker adopts an overall credit appraisal procedure which covers certain common areas to probe in addition to the special attention, towards the specific category of credit.

## Credit Appraisal

Credit appraisal is a technique by which a banker estimates the soundness of a credit proposal by careful analysis. Credit appraisal leads to finding out the quantum of credit required for a borrower and the safety of such credit. In the recent years the banks and financial institutions have developed certain sophisticated techniques for ascertaining credit limits and to decide whether it would be worthwhile to accept such proposals.

Traditionally commercial banks are lending short-term credit needs, meeting the working capital gap. There is a close relationship between the success of the proposal and safety of the bank. Therefore, the banker takes adequate care in selecting the right proposal and looks for various particulars like sales, cost of sales, expected profit, general and administrative expenses, tax factor, indirect income etc. The banker may also ask for current assets and current liabilities.

The banker may ascertain the maximum permissible bank finance for the working capital as per the Tandon Committee Report, towards fluctuating demand credit, fixed loan, discounting bills etc. Appraisal of loan application is the starting point for fixing credit limit for the borrower. The banker evaluates the proposal taking into account the following:

*A. Approval :* The banker examines whether the proposed project submitted has been approved by the respective bodies. In the case of a company, there should be provision for such a project as per the Memorandum of Association and Articles of Association. In addition to this, the Directors' approval is necessary. The banker may satisfy himself as to whether the project has the legal sanction in terms of the required licenses, approvals, and clearances from the appropriate authorities or Government.

*B. Technical Feasibility :* A new project submitted with the banker for consideration of financial assistance requires a thorough scrutiny. One of the important considerations affecting the feasibility of the project is the type of technology proposed to be employed by the borrower. The banker ascertains, if necessary, with the help of the experts in the field, as to whether the technology is the latest or outdated, capital-intensive or labour-intensive etc. He also examines the borrower's capability in case of changes in the product or shift in consumer preference. The experts may also give their approval after considering the availability of raw materials, labour, fuel, power, water, transport, market technology etc. Location of the project is another important factor for the success of the project. In case of a manufacturing unit, proper location may be related to adequate supply of raw materials, availability of power, water, labour and other infrastructure facilities.

*C. Financial Feasibility :* The nationalisation of commercial banks in 1969 has a tremendous impact on the lending policies of the commercial banks. The security-oriented approach has been relegated to the background. Instead the thrust is more on purpose and performance. Due to these changes in the policies, the bankers assess the project on the above lines, by examining the financial statements and analysing the balance sheets. The bankers evaluate the project by using certain important techniques of financial evaluation for lending decisions, *viz.*, ratio analysis, break-even analysis, cash flow and fund flow analysis.

## 1. Ratio Analysis

Ratios refer to the numerical or quantitative relationship between two items/ variables. It is an invaluable aid to management in the analysis of the data. Although there are many ratios for evaluation of a firm, a banker may use only a few ratios related to his needs. The banker is to judge not only the profitability of the firm but also the cash flow in the firm, as the repaying capacity of a borrowing concern is not influenced by profit alone. Some of the ratios widely used by the bank at the time of project appraisal are as follows :

*(a)* Current Ratio $= \dfrac{\text{Current Assets}}{\text{Current Liabilities}}$

Current ratio states the relationship between *current assets* and current *liabilities.* It is an *index of the firm's financial stability.* Current assets are cash and other assets which could be converted into cash in the near future. Current assets comprises of cash, bank, short-term investments, bills receivables, book-debts, inventories etc. Similarly, current liabilities are those which are to be settled in the near future, viz., creditors, bills payable, income tax, overdrafts etc.

An ideal current ratio is said to be 2:1. A high current ratio is an assurance that the firm will have adequate funds to meet current obligations. However, one of the limitations is that current ratio fails to indicate the rate of liquidity of individual components. For example, a large inventory does not mean cash. In credit analysis, a banker will not be satisfied with the mathematically good current ratio. What is required more is the qualitative aspect of the composition of the current assets. Hence he should also look for liquid ratio.

*(b)* Liquid Ratio $= \dfrac{\text{Liquid Assets}}{\text{Liquid Liabilities}}$

Liquid ratio is a rigorous test for ascertaining the liquid character in the firm. It examines the relationship between the liquid assets and liquid liabilities. This can be worked out only if the current assets are classified into liquid asset and deferred assets. Similarly, the current liabilities may be classified as liquid liabilities and deferred payments. This classification can be effected by establishing a simple rule that all assets and liabilities are liquid if they are expected to be realised or paid within a month. The components of liquid assets are cash, bank, debtors, bills receivables, immediate marketable securities etc.

*(c)* Net Profit Ratio $= \dfrac{\text{Net Profit}}{\text{Sales}} \times 100$

Net Profit ratio is the relationship between net profit and sales. It indicates the profitability of the business.

*(d)* Debt-Equity Ratio $= \dfrac{\text{Long - term Debt}}{\text{Shareholders' Equity}}$

This ratio shows the relationship between borrowed funds and owner's capital. This ratio is used for measuring the long-term financial solvency of a firm. The debt refers to the long-term debt alone and equity may include both ordinary and preference capital but excludes past accumulated losses. It is the ratio of the amount invested by outsiders with that of the amount contributed by owners (including preference shareholders).

Since the preference shareholders do not have the voting rights, a doubt has often been expressed as to whether preference capital should be taken into account while computing shareholders' equity. The exact treatment may depend on the purpose for which the ratio is used. If the banker intends to calculate the financial solvency of the firm, preference capital should be included. On the other hand, if the debt-equity ratio is calculated for contribution of eamings per share, it need not be taken into account.

*(e)* Capital/Asset Ratio = $\frac{\text{Fixed Assets}}{\text{Capital Funds}}$

This ratio states the relationship between the fixed assets and paid-up capital + reserves. Fixed assets are taken at its depreciated book value. This ratio may indicate as to whether the long-term funds have been effectively utilised. It may also indicate whether short-term funds have been invested in long-term assets. If any firm has done so, it may land itself sooner or later into financial constraints to meet its immediate obligations. The current ratio, in such concerns, may not be satisfactory.

*(f)* Cash-flow Ratio = $\frac{\text{Operating Profit + Depreciation}}{\text{Net Sales}}$

This ratio enables a banker to assess the cash generating capacity of the firm as well as the extent to which the funds are derived. Some firms may have a good net profit ratio. But their cash flow ratio may be poor.

## 2. Break-even Analysis

Break-even analysis is an analytical technique for studying the relationship between cost, volume and profit. It is a device used to determine the usefulness of the profit planning. As the banker is interested in getting back his money, he wants to make sure when the surplus is likely to be received by his unit. He may like to find the break-even point of sales volume at which the, total revenue is equal to the total costs. The break-even point is computed as follows:

$$\text{Break-even Point} = \frac{\text{Fixed Cost}}{\text{Contribution per unit}}$$

Contribution = Selling Price per unit - Variable Cost (per unit)

The break-even point gives the answer wherein the firm does not make either profit or loss when it manufactures/sells a particular number of units. This analysis is very important for the banker as the repayment of the term loans is generally scheduled to begin after the break-even.

Apart from the analysis of the data, the facts given in the project proposal are carefully examined and verified. The banker also checks the calculations shown in the Project Report. The banker also examines the feasibility report given by the technical experts. The experts may give their comments after considering the availability of raw materials, labour, fuel, water, transport, market, technology etc.

### 3. Cash Flow and Fund Flow Analysis

Cash Flow and Fund Flow Analysis are important analytical tools for banker for evaluating the employment of funds. Cash flow may be of two types - Actual cash flows and Notional cash flows. Actual cash flow refers to the actual movement of cash in or out of the business whereas the notional cash flow may refer to the increase or decrease in the current assets. The cash flow estimates are prepared to indicate the inflow and outflow of funds year by year of the concern covering the entire period of term advance. These estimates would help the banker to schedule the repayment of loan over a period of time, making provisions for certain allowances favouring the borrower. Cash Flow and Fund Flow Techniques help the banker to find out wherefrom the funds would come and how such funds would be applied. Once the fund flow and cash flow statements are favourable, it enables the banker to decide the case easily to the advantage of the borrower.

### 4. Return on Investment

The very first information that a banker seeks in a Project Report is the return on investment. He may compare this with the cost of capital. He may think of further appraisal of the project only if the return on investment is more than the cost of capital. There are four methods to evaluate the return on cost of capital:

*(a)* Pay-back Period Method.

*(b)* Average Rate of Return.

*(c)* Net Present Value Method

*(d)* Internal Rate of Return.

*(a) Pay-back Period Method* : Pay-back period method is a technique by which the banker finds out the number of years required to recover the original cash outlay invested in a project. The following formula can be adopted :

$$\text{Pay} - \text{Back Period} = \frac{\text{Cash Outlay}}{\text{Annual Cash Inflow}}$$

One of the limitations of this method is that it does not consider the flow of funds after the pay-back period. However, it is a useful technique for a banker who lends funds to the borrower.

*(b) Average Rate of Return (ARR):* Average rate of return is a method to determine the average annual profit during the lifetime of the project. It is

normally expressed in percentage. The following formula is adopted.

$$\text{ARR} = \frac{\text{Annual Average Profit}}{\text{Initial Investment}} \times 100$$

*(c) Net Present Value Method(NPV):* Net Present Value Method is the most classic method of evaluating the investment proposals. It is one of the discounted cash flow techniques, recognising the time value of money. Under this method, the future costs and revenues are discounted by a required rate of return in order to compare the present value of future benefits with the present value of investments. If the present value of future benefits exceeds the present value of investments, the banker will accept the project. Otherwise he may outrightly reject it.

*(d) Internal Rate of Return (IRR):* Internal rate of return is a technique by which the banker matches the present value of future benefits with the present value of the project and finds out the ' IRR. He may compare the internal rate of return with the expected rate. If the IRR is satisfactory, he may proceed further in evaluating the project.

## 5. Commercial Feasibility

Commercial feasibility involves the study of the product in relation to its current and future demands, market share, fluctuations in demand for the product due to changes in consumer preferences or technology etc. Normally increase in production may lead to reduction in the cost per unit. But exceeding a particular limit, it need not be true. The products manufactured by the firm should be sold in the market to enable the producer to move along the operating cycle, as the inventory is not cash. The capacity to repay the loans is dependent on the sales revenue of the project.

## 6. Managerial Competence

The banker also examines the organisational and managerial capabilities of the applicant. Managerial ability is the most essential factor considered by both commercial bankers and development banks in sanctioning the application. Sometimes the project may be technically sound, economically and commercially viable and financially profitable. But if it cannot be managed properly, it cannot be considered as a worthwhile project. Hence, the banker gives more weightage for the managerial competence of the applicant.

Moreover, the applicant may be over enthusiastic in his ideas. But he might have undermined certain realities. The banker takes into account the controllable factors and non-controllable factors. The controllable factors are the inputs, *viz.*, money, materials, machines, methods, etc. They are to be scientifically designed and combined. It is very difficult to predict the non-controllable factors like change of Government policy, competitors' behaviour, legal restrictions, political changes etc. All these factors are carefully visualized in advance before granting loans.

### 7. Socio-economic Viability

The banker and the financial institutions evaluate the project on the basis of the socio-economic viability. It is an assessment to know whether such project, as a whole, brings any social benefit to the nation to fulfil the national objectives. Some of the socio-economic benefits to the nation are employment generation, removal of regional imbalances, minimisation of inequalities in the distribution of income and wealth, development of import substitution, export-orientation, development of agriculture and other priority sectors, upliftment of weaker sections of the society etc. The banker may consider a lower rate of interest, low margin, longer repayment schedule etc., for certain types of projects. For instance, 4% per annum is charged towards the Deferential Interest Rates (DIR) Loans.

The banker, having thoroughly examined the application, may accept or reject the proposal or may also suggest to the borrower the necessary modifications in the project. Once he is convinced about the project, he holds an interview with the prospective borrower-customer to discuss in detail about the project, interest rates, repayment schedule etc. In certain cases, the banker may visit the location of the plant to study other details before making the commitment.

During the interview, the banker will discuss with the customer in detail about various aspects of this project proposal, particularly the amount of loan required, the borrower's contribution, security, repayment schedule, type of credit, interest rate etc.

In the case of working capital requirement, it is to be noted that the peak level of borrowing coincides with the peak level of production and credit sales. Taking into account all the above factors working capital limits may be fixed as follows :

Working Capital required = Working capital requirements – (Credit available from suppliers + Cash + Borrower's fresh contribution)

In the case of long-term loans, the banker should not undertake any risk and block his capital alone. Credit limit, in such cases, should be fixed taking into account the total cost of project, promoter's contribution, other sources of funds, working capital requirements, cash flow, debt-equity ratio etc. The bank normally expects the borrower to prove adequate stake in the cost of the project to ensure his continued interest and care in the project. The owner's contribution should be in the form of risk capital and the balance is provided by the bank.

## MODEL QUESTIONS

**Section - A**

1. State the principles of lending.
2. What do you mean by liquidity in banking terminology?
3. A bank is not a philanthropic institution. Why?
4. What is Current Ratio?
5. What is a Break-even Point?
6. State the two types of cash flow.
7. State any four methods to evaluate the return on the cost of capital.

**Section - B**

1. What is Credit Appraisal? How does a banker evaluate the proposal given by a client?
2. Write short notes on : *(a)* Technical feasibility; *(b)* Financial feasibility.

**Section - C**

1. What are the general principles which should guide a banker in making loans and advances to a customer?
2. What do you mean by "Credit Appraisal"? What are the procedures for appraisals of credit proposals adopted by a commercial bank?

# 12

# LOANS AND ADVANCES II

## TYPES OF BORROWINGS

## MODES OF CREATING CHARGE

Whatever security is offered by the borrower, the banker has to get it properly charged in his favour. Unless the security is charged in favour of the bank as per the requirements of law, he may not be in a position to realise the debt against such security. For example, a loan is sanctioned to a borrower with the stipulation for creating equitable mortgage of his property. Now, it is not merely enough that the bank possesses the title deeds of the property concerned. What is important to see is that the proper procedure, in accordance with the provisions contained in the Transfer of Property Act, 1882, is followed so as to constitute a valid equitable mortgage. The following modes of creating charge are common :

1. Pledge.
2. Hypothecation.
3. Lien.
4. Assignment.
5. Mortgage.

## Pledge

A pledge arises when goods or documents of title to goods are delivered by one person (called the pledger) to another person (called the pledgee) to be held as a security for the payment of a debt or for the discharge of some other obligation, upon the condition that the subjectmatter of the pledge is to be restored to the pledger as soon as the debt or other obligation is discharged.

Section 172 of the Indian Contract Act, 1872 defines pledge as "the bailment of goods as security for payment of a debt or performance of a promise."

Thus, a pledge is only a special kind of bailment, and the chief basis of distinction is the object of the contract. Where the object of the delivery of goods is to provide a security for a loan or for the fulfilment of an obligation, that kind of bailment is called pledge.

Advances granted by banks under pledge are commonly known as 'Key Loan.'

## Essentials of a Pledge

1. *Delivery of Possession :* For the validity of the pledge there must be delivery of goods to the pledgee. A transfer of possession is necessary to complete a pledge and it must be lawful possession properly given. Delivery of possession may be actual or constructive. Delivery of the key of the godown where the goods are stored is an illustration of constructive delivery. Likewise, delivery of documents of title to goods (*e.g.*, railway receipt, bill of lading, warehouse receipts, etc.) will amount to constructive delivery and would be equally effective to create a pledge.

   No doubt, the possession passes to the pledgee, the legal ownership remains with the pledger.

2. *As Security for Payment of a Debt :* It is essential that the goods should be delivered to the pledgee as security for a debt.

Another requirement of a valid pledge is that there should he a Contract to return the same goods after the debt is repaid.

## Who can Pledge?

Ordinarily, goods may be pledged by the owner or any person with owner's authority. A pledge made by any other person may not be valid. Thus, for example, where goods are left in possession of a servant, while the owner is temporarily absent, a pledge made by the servant was held to be invalid. Similarly, where certain goods are left in the care of a person for some special purpose, cannot pledge them.

Apart from the owner of the goods the following persons may also create pledge:

1. *Pledge by Mercantile Agent :* According to Section 178 of the Indian Contract Act, where a mercantile agent is, with the consent of the owner, in possession of goods or documents of title to goods, a pledge made by him while acting in the ordinary course of business shall be valid. The pledgee in such a case, however, should act in good faith and should have no notice of the fact that the agent has no authority to pledge.
2. *Person in Possession under Voidable Contract :* According to Section 178 A of the Indian Contract Act, 1872, where goods are pledged by a person who has obtained possession under a voidable contract, the pledge is valid, provided that the contract has not been rescinded at the time of the pledge and the pledgee has acted in good faith and without notice of the pledger's defect of title. However, this rule will not apply where the goods have been obtained by means of theft as a thief has no title and can give none.
3. *Seller of Goods :* The seller, after having sold the goods, if continues to be in possession of the goods or documents of title to goods, may create a valid pledge provided the pledgee has received the goods in good faith and without notice of previous sale.

## Right and Duties of the Pawner/Pledger

1. ***Duty to repay the loan :*** The pawner /pledger should repay the loan and interest as per the agreement and take back the pledged goods from the pawanee in time.

2. ***Right to receive the goods :*** The pawner/pledger has the right to receive the goods in the same condition when he parted with the goods, after discharging his contract. But if by any chance he makes default in the promise or fails to pay back, the pawnee may arrange to sell the goods after giving due notice to the pawner. The pawner has the right to redeem his goods before any sale is made. However, in the meantime, if any expenses had been met by the pawnee, these expenses can be reimbursed from the pawner.

3. ***Right to receive any increase in the goods :*** In case of any increase in the asset, the pledger will be entitled to revive the same from the pledgee.

## Rights and Duties of the Pawnee / Pledgee

1. ***Right to retain :*** The pawnee/ pledgee has the right to retain the goods till the performance of the promise or the repayment is made including the interest thereon. He can also recover all reasonable expenses incurred by him on such goods pledged.

2. ***Right to retain goods for subsequent loan :*** In case the pawnee / pledgee lends subsequent advances on the strength of the goods already pledged, the pawnee (as a banker) has the right to retain such goods for the subsequent loan also unless there is an agreement contrary to his effect.

3. ***Right to receive payment of the debt :*** The pawnee/pledgee has the right to receive payment of the debt including interest.

4. ***Right to extraordinary expenses :*** Sec. 175 of the Indian Contract Act provides for the right to the pawnee to receive from the pawner any extraordinary expenses incurred by him for the maintenance of the goods pledged with the pawner.

5. ***Right against the True Owner :*** A pawner/pledger might have obtained the goods under voidable contract i.e. by fraud/undue influence etc. When he pledges such goods with the pawnee, if the voidable contract had not been recinded, the pawnee acquires good title to the goods provided he acts in good faith and without the knowledge of the Pawner's defect of title.

## Pawnee/pledgee/options in case of default

In case of failure to pay the debt, the Pawnee has the following options before him :

*(i)* He can retain the pledged goods until such time the debt is paid back

*(ii)* He can file a suit against the pawner for the recovery of the debt;

*(iii)* He may sue for the sale of goods and the realisation of the money due to him :

*(iv)* He may sell the goods after giving due notice

*(v)* He can recover any balance from the pawner if the proceeds of the sale is inadequate to meet his claim. Similarly, if there is surplus, the Pawnee should pay back to the pawner.

## Precautions to be taken for accepting goods under pledge

First of all, the pledge must be regular and complete from legal point of view. As an evidence of the borrower's intention to create pledge, bankers obtain from him a document known as 'Letter of Pledge.' All the blank spaces in the letter of pledge should be properly filled in as per the terms of the sanction. The letter of pledge attracts stamp duty as applicable to agreements. It should also be ensured that the borrower has a right to pledge the goods in question, say, by inspection of the original invoices or cash memos which should be retained on the bank's records.

The goods should be stored in pucca built godown. They should be situated at convenient places so that periodical inspections may be carried out without any difficulty. The godown should have independent access as far as possible. A board should be put at the entrance of the godown stating that the goods are pledged to the bank. The goods must be adequately insured.

## Hypothecation

The term hypothecation has not been defined by any statute so far. Hart has defined it as under:

"Hypothecation is a legal transaction whereby goods may be made available as security for a debt without transferring *either the* property or its possession to the lender."

In other words, hypothecation is a right which a creditor has over a thing belonging to another and the right consists in the power to cause it to be sold in order to realise money due to him. The charge by way of hypothecation is created by an instrument in writing known as "Letter of Hypothecation.' Except immovable property, all forms of assets may be covered under a hypothecation arrangement. The common examples of securities which are covered under hypothecation are goods, machinery, fixtures and book-debts.

The asset hypothecated remains under the possession of the borrower and he is free to deal with it. Since the banks do not obtain actual or constructive possession of the goods, the borrower has ample opportunity of dealing with them fraudulently.

The usual hypothecation agreements obtained by banks contain a clause giving power to banks to enter the premises of the defaulting borrowers and take possession of the goods hypothecated without recourse to judicial proceedings. However, the validity and scope of the right, when challenged in a court of law, are doubtful. This apart, it is always a matter of practical knowledge that without the borrower's consent the bank will not be in a position to take possession of the security. After default, it is only rarely that we can expect a borrower to voluntarily hand over possession of the goods covered by the hypothecation agreement in favour of the bank.

In view of the above drawbacks of the hypothecation system, bankers generally prefer to grant pledge limits. Hypothecation limits (also known as 'Open Loan Limits') are granted only to trusted and reliable parties.

## Precautions taken by a banker while granting loans on hypothecation

It is interesting to note that the hypothecation agreement gives power to banks to enter into the premises of the defaulting borrowers and take possession of the goods hypothecated with the bank. But it is a known fact that the bank will not be in a position to possess the goods with out the consent of the borrower. Apart from this, since the goods are with the customer, he can sell the goods or hypothecate the same goods with another bank. Hence the following precautions should be taken by the banker in order to safeguard his interest although granting loans under hypothecation is quite risky.

Apart from taking the usual precautions - safety, liquidity, profitability, 3 C's of the customer, spreading the risk etc., the banker should take certain additional precautions:

1. The banker should make the customer to sign the Hypothecation Agreement bringing in all the clauses advantageous to the banker.
2. An undertaking should be obtained from the customer that he will not simultaneously hypothecate the same goods or borrow from any other agency on the strength of the same hypothecated goods.
3. The banker should arrange to fix up a name plate in a conspicuous place of the godown with the words "Hypothecated to Bank". In case a vehicle loan, these words should be clearly written on the vehicle.
4. The banker should arrange to get periodical return relating to the stock position in the godown and the drawing limit should be calculated accordingly. The banker should also arrange for periodical checking and surprise checking of the stock.
5. In case customer has hypothecated the goods with another bank, he should be asked to earmark his stock for indemnification. It is advisable that the borrower maintains separate record books to identify stocks hypothecated to different banks.
6. It is essential that the goods be insured against theft, fire and other risks etc.

## Assignment

When a party to a contract transfers his right, title and interest in the contract to another person or other persons, he is said to assign the contract. Thus, assignment is transfer of a right in favour of another person. The transferor is called the 'assignor' and the transferee and the 'assignee.' In banking, the subject- matter of assignment are 'actionable claims" which include book-debts, supply bills and life insurance policies. Debts which are sought to be assigned may be present or future, conditional or contingent.'

There are two types of assignments: *(i)* legal; and *(ii)* equitable. A legal assignment is an absolute transfer of actionable claim and not by way of charge only. It must be in writing and signed by the assignor. A written notice of assignment, containing the name and address of the assignee, should be given by the assignor to his debtor. In case, the assignor fails to do so, the assignee should himself serve a notice on the debtor of the assignor. An equitable assignment is one which does not fulfil the above requirements of a legal assignment. For obvious reasons, a lending banker always insists for legal assignments.

## Merits of Assignment as a Charge

Assignment of debt is not considered a good security for bank advances as it suffers from many drawbacks. First, realisation of the assigned debt depends upon the integrity and creditworthiness of the debtor of the assignor (i.e., the borrower). Secondly, the assignment is always subject to right of set-off by the assignor's debtor. If the debtor has any counter claim against the assignor, the bank as an assignee would get only the balance amount that is left after the satisfaction of the debtor's claim. Thirdly, if there happens to be a breach of contract between the assignor and his debtor, it will prejudice the bank's interests.

In view of the above drawbacks banks grant advance against assignment of book debts only to parties of good standing and repute. Advances against assignment of life insurance policies is, however, more common.

## Mortgage

A mortgage is the transfer of an interest in specific immovable property for the purpose of securing the payment of money advanced or to be advanced by way of loan, an existing or future debt, or the performance of an engagement which may give rise to pecuniary liability. The transferor is called a mortgagor, the transferee a mortgagee.

Immovable property normally consists of land, buildings, and anything attached to or embedded in the earth. For example, trees which are not cut are immovable property, as they are attached to earth. But when trees are sold to be cut and taken away, they become movable property.

There are in all six kinds of mortgages.

### 1. Simple Mortgage

In a simple mortgage, the mortgagor binds himself to pay the debt personally, and agrees that in the event of his failure to pay the mortgage money, the mortgagee shall have the right to cause the property to be applied so far as may be necessary by means of a decree for the sale of property. If the mortgaged property is not sufficient to discharge the debt, the mortgagee can bring a personal action against the mortgagor and obtain a decree which like any other money decree, can be executed against other properties of the mortgagor. Thus, the mortgagee cannot sell the property himself. In case of default in payment, he will have to file a suit in a court of law for sale of the mortgaged property. In simple mortgage, no right of possession or foreclosure is available to the mortgagee.

### 2. Mortgage by Conditional Sale

In this type of mortgage the property is mortgaged with the condition that, in the event of a failure by the debtor to repay the debt at the stipulated time the transaction should be regarded a sale, and, in case the loan is repaid within the stipulated time, the sale shall be invalid, or, on condition that on such payment being made the buyer shall transfer the property to the seller.

Thus, for the all practical purposes, this type of mortgage is a sale of the mortgaged property with a condition for repurchase by the mortgagor by repaying the loan. It will be noted that the mortgagor transfers the property with the following three conditions:

(*a*) If the loan is repaid, the sale becomes void;

(*b*) If the loan is not repaid at the stipulated time, the sale will become absolute and binding and

(*c*) When the debt has been repaid at the stipulated time, the mortgagee shall re-transfer the property to the mortgagor.

## 3. Usufructuary Mortgage

Section 58 (d) of the Transfer of Property Act defines a usufructuary mortgage as under :

> "Where the mortgagor delivers possession or expressly or by implication binds himself to deliver possession of the mortgaged property to the mortgagee, and authorises him to retain such possession until payment of the mortgage money, and to receive the rents and profits and to appropriate the same in lieu of interest, or in payment of the mortgage money, or partly in lieu of interest and partly in payment of mortgage money, the transaction is called a usufructuary mortgage."

Thus, in this type of mortgage the mortgagor has to deliver possession of the property to the mortgagee. If possession is not given, the mortgagee can sue for possession. The usufructuary mortgage has the following characteristics :

(*a*) Possession of the property must be delivered to the mortgagee;

(*b*) There is no personal liability on the part of the mortgagor to pay;

(*c*) The mortgagee is entitled to rents and profits in lieu of interest or principal or both; and

(*d*) The mortgagee however is not entitled to foreclose the mortgage or to sue for sale.

## 4. English Mortgage

Section 58 (e) of the Transfer of Property Act, 1882 provides :

> "Where the mortgagor, binds himself to repay the mortgage money on a certain date, and transfers the mortgaged property absolutely to the

mortgagee but subject to a proviso that he will re-transfer it to the mortgagor upon payment of the money as agreed, the transaction is called an English Mortgage."

Thus, the essential features of an English Mortgage are as under:

*(a)* The mortgagor binds himself to repay the mortgage money on a certain day. In other words, there should be a personal undertaking to pay;

*(b)* The mortgaged property is absolutely transferred to the mortgagee and

*(c)* Such absolute transfer is subject to a provision that the mortgagee will retransfer the property to the mortgagor upon payment of the mortgage money on the fixed day.

## Distinction between English Mortgage and Mortgage by Conditional Sale

An English mortgage looks like a mortgage by conditional sale but there are obvious differences between the two.

*(i)* In English mortgage there is a personal liability undertaken by the mortgagor to pay the debt. In a mortgage by conditional sale there is no personal covenant (agreement) for repayment of the mortgage money and the mortgagee has his remedy against the mortgaged property only.

*(ii)* In an English mortgage the ownership in the mortgaged property is absolutely transferred to the creditor (i.e., the mortgagee) which, however, may be divested on repayment of the loan on the fixed day. In a mortgage by conditional sale, the mortgagee gets only a qualified ownership which may, however, ripen into an absolute ownership in default of payment of the mortgage money.

## 5. Mortgage by Deposit of Title Deeds

This type of mortgage is called equitable mortgage in English law. In this transaction, a person delivers to the creditor or his agent documents of title to his immovable property with an intention to create a security, and obtains a loan. The requisites of the mortgage are: (i) a debt, (ii) deposit of documents of title to the property (i.e., title deeds) in a notified town, and (iii) an intention that the deeds shall be security for the debt.

A mortgage on immovable property, to be valid, must be in writing and attested by two witnesses and the document must be registered. But in the case of a mortgage by deposit of title deeds it need not be registered and an oral agreement between the borrower and the creditor followed by the delivery of the title deeds is enough. No stamp duty is payable on this type of mortgage. For creating an equitable mortgage, the owner of the property calls at the bank's branch in a notified town and delivers to the Branch Manager/official of the branch the title deeds of the property. The Branch Manager/official makes a noting in the security register which is also called Memorandum of Oral Assent. The noting *inter alia* contains the name of the person i.e., the owner of the property who delivered the title deeds, details of the property mortgaged, the amount of loan borrowed etc., and it is dated and signed only by the Branch Manager/official. The mortgagor should not sign thereon. The title deeds so deposited by the borrower will remain in the custody of the bank until the debt is liquidated.

An equitable mortgage can be created only in the specified towns in India and not at all the places. The places where the equitable mortgage can be created are, Delhi, Mumbai, Calcutta, Chennai, Agra, Adoni, Ajmer, Allahabad, Alwar, Bangalore, Bellary, Cochin Coimbatore, Jaipur, Jodhpur, Kanpur, Rajahmundry, Udaipur, Vellore, Eluru, Pali, Bhilwara, Bikaner, Narayanganj, Mysore, Tuticorin, Madura, and in certain otherplaces notified from time to time by any State Government in its Official Gazette. No doubt, the equitable mortgage can be created only in certain specified towns, but the property may be situated anywhere in India.

An equitable mortgage has two fold advantages. First, the borrower saves the stamp duty on the mortgage deed and registration charges. Secondly, it is easy to create and thus save time. Therefore, it is very popular amongst bankers as well as the borrowers.

### 6. Anomalous Mortgage

A mortgage which is not a simple mortgage, a mortgage by conditional sale, an usufructuary mortgage, an English mortgage or a mortgage by deposit of title deeds is called an anomalous mortgage.

Thus, an anomalous mortgage is a combination of various other mortgages. For example, an usufructuary mortgage may be created with the right of sale to the mortgagee.

## LIEN

Lien means the right to retain the goods of some one else. Lien does not give any right for the holder to sell except retaining the property until his demand is satisfied unless such right is expressly conferred by the statute.

There are two kinds of lien :

*(a)* General Lien.

*(b)* Particular Lien.

General lien is the right to retain goods in respect of the general balance due to him. For instance, a customer has taken two loans form the bank -

one with the security and the other without any security. In case the borrower fails to pay a loan taken from the bank without any security, the banker can still retain the security and refuse to release it unless the amount due to him from the loan account, although taken without any security, is settled.

Particular lien is applicable to craftsmen like repairers, tailors and goldsmiths. An illustration would clearly distinguish between general lien and particular lien. For instance, a person gives a piece of cloth to a tailor for stitching a shirt and has not taken it back. Some time later, he gives another piece of cloth to the same tailor for stitching pants. These are two different contracts at different times. If the customer wants to take delivery of only pants, the tailor cannot force him to pay for stitching the shirt too to take delivery of pants.

While the craftsman possessing particular lien cannot combine both and consider it as one, the banker can exercise general lien and exercise his right. The general lien enjoyed by a banker is more than ordinary lien. It is an implied pledge.

A general lien may arise by usage, express agreement or during the ordinary course of business. In a leading case, *Brandao Vs. Barnett (1846),* Lord Campbell remarked, "Bankers, most undoubtedly have a general lien on all securities deposited with them as bankers, by a customer unless there can be express contract or circumstances that show an implied contract inconsistent with the lien." The Indian Contract Act, 1872 is also very clear. According to Section 171 of the Act, "Bankers, in the absence of an agreement to the contrary, retain as a security for a general balance of account any goods and securities banked to them."

## Loans, Overdraft and Cash Credit

Credit facilities extended by commercial banks may be classified into four categories : *(a)* Loans, *(b)* Overdraft, *(c)* Cash credit, and *(d)* Bills Purchased/ Discounted. These advances may either be : *(i) Secured which* are granted against the security of some tangible assets; or *(ii) Unsecured for* which the bank holds no tangible asset and which are allowed against personal credit of the borrower.

### Loans

A loan account is not a running account and the amount is disbursed to the borrower only once. In some cases, however, the disbursement may be even in stages as per the requirements of the party *e.g.*, crop loans or loans for constructions. Once the borrower pays in money in a loan account, he cannot withdraw the same. No chequebook is issued. Loans may be of two types :

(i) *Demand Loans,* which are repayable on demand by the bank *e.g.*, loans against banks own time deposits.

(ii) *Term Loans,* which arc granted for a specified period. In a term loan, the repayment is phased in instalments at the time of sanction of loan. In the case of term loans, bank now obtain from the borrowers what is known as 'Articles of Agreement.' It contains terms and conditions of the loan and the number and amount of periodical instalment.

## Overdraft

Overdraft means allowing the party to overdraw his account. It is allowed only to current account holders.

Under an overdraft arrangement, a customer is allowed to draw cheques up to an agreed limit over and above the credit balance in the account. For instance, a customer has been sanctioned overdraft limit for Rs. 50,000/-. A cheque for Rs. 80,000/- is presented for payment when the credit balance in the account is only Rs. 30,000/-. The cheque will be passed for payment in view of the overdraft limit enjoyed by the party. No sooner the party adjusts the overdraft of Rs. 50,000, which was created on account of the cheque having been paid, he can again draw cheques up to the stipulated limit of Rs. 50,000. Thus, unlike loan accounts, an overdraft is a running account. The overdraft may be classified into two categories:

(i) *Clean Overdraft :* It is usually in the form of temporary accommodation to meet the party's sudden requirement. It is allowed purely on the personal credit of the party for which bank holds no tangible asset. Overdraft against cheques in clearing also falls under this category.

(ii) *Secured Overdraft :* Here, the party is granted regular limits. It is usually allowed against bank's own time deposits, shares, government securities, government supply bills, book-debts, and hire purchase hundies and outward bills for collection.

## Cash Credit

Cash credit account is an operative account against a credit limit granted by the bank. The customer withdraws the money from time to time as per his requirements subject to the agreed limit. Cash credit accounts are considered as secured advances as they are generally allowed against pledge or hypothecation of goods. In some instances, however, cash credit may be granted against personal securities.

Cash credit limits for the parties are fixed by the banks after properly assessing their actual requirements on the basis of the working of the unit. While processing a proposal for cash credit limits, a banker usually takes into account production, sales, inventory levels etc.

Although the cash credit advances are repayable on demand, in practice however, they roll over a period of time and thus they are permanent source of finance to business enterprises. Banks make periodical review of the limits with a view to revise them depending upon the past performance and future plans of the borrower.

## MODEL QUESTIONS

**Section - A**

1. State the modes of creating charge on securities.
2. Who is a pledger and pledgee?
3. Who can pledge?
4. What do you mean by Key Loan?
5. State the two types of assignments.
6. State the six kinds of Mortgages.
7. State the difference between General Lien and Particular Lien.

**Section - B**

1. Write short notes on 'Lien.'
2. Distinguish between pledge and Lien.
3. What are the essentials of a pledge and who can pledge?
4. Write a brief note on 'Hypothecation.'
5. Briefly discuss about 'assignment.'
6. What are the modes of securing advance? Elaborate.
7. Define pledge and explain the rights and liabilities of the bank in respect of pledged goods.
8. Distinguish between Pledge and Hypothecation.
9. What are legal and equitable mortgage? Explain their relative merits and demerits.
10. Write notes on

    *(a)* Overdraft

    *(b)* Cash credit

    *(c)* Loans

**Section – C**

1. Discuss the different modes of creating charge.
2. What do you understand by 'mortgage'? Explain the different kinds of mortgage.

# 13

# LOANS AND ADVANCES III

## ADVANCES AGAINST GOODS

India is an agricultural country where a large portion of the bank advances are secured by goods, such as cotton, wool, wheat, manufactured goods etc. Over 60% of the total bank advances are secured against manufactured goods and agricultural produce. Although the traditional bank shy away from these kinds of collateral securities due to its inherent risks like deterioration in the quality, loss of weight, difficulty in the supervision etc., the modern bankers consider them otherwise and lend short-term loans against them. In the case of such collateral securities, the primary security is the credit worthiness of the borrower and the goods is only a supportive security. However, the bank can sell the goods and realise their dues either fully or partly from the sale proceeds.

The term goods is a comprehensive term. It includes produce, commodity and merchandise including raw material, work-in-progress, finished goods and goods in transit. The Indian Sale of Goods Act 1930 defines the term Goods as "Goods" means every kind of movable property other than actionable claims and money and includes stock and shares, growing crops, grass and things attached to or forming part of the land which are agreed to be severed before sale or under the contract of sale".

The commercial banks help the farmers in marketing their produce by granting advances even on standing crops. They also finance the merchandise in the distribution of the commodities. Industrial advances are granted against goods to meet the working capital needs of the company. Goods are broadly classified into food articles, industrial raw materials and finished goods.

## Merits

1. *Tangible Security :* Goods are tangible securities and are better than guarantees or bill of exchange because the banker can sell the goods straightaway and recover his dues. The principle of 'something is better than nothing' suits to this security.
2. *Ready Market :* While securities like land and buildings are not easily saleable, goods have a ready market. Some of the goods like wheat, sugar, cotton etc., can be easily sold whereas industrial goods of seasonal variation may not have ready marketability.
3. *Price Stability :* While there is a wide variation in the prices of certain luxury goods due to changes in demand, technology, fashions and tastes of the people, goods which are necessaries of life such as rice, wheat, sugar, cotton etc., do not change widely. Bankers accept such securities whose prices do not vary widely.
4. *Short-term Loans :* In principle, bankers lend for a short period against goods, as they are likely to deteriorate over a period of time. For instance, perishable goods like rice and wheat can attract loan only for 3-6 months. Moreover, short-term loans are associated with lesser risk than long-term loans.
5. *Easy Valuation :* There is no need for any technical expertise to evaluate the prices of essential goods, as the prices of such goods are readily available in the market reports. The banker himself can know the prices and price trend easily.

## Limitations

1. *Deterioration in Quality :* Although the bankers are careful in lending against certain types of goods, it may be inevitable that they have to lend against certain goods which may deteriorate in quality over a period of time. For instance, moisture affects sugar, jaggery, salt etc. Paddy and rice and wheat may lose weight in the summer and are affected by pests and rodents.
2. *Reduction in Price :* The prices of certain luxury goods are likely to vary very widely. In case there is a fall in price due to changes in technology, demand, fashions, new innovations etc.,. The bank may not be able to realise the entire loan in such cases. If the borrower dies, becomes insane or insolvent, it would be difficult to recover the full amount as the value of the goods has gone down sharply.
3. *Frauds :* There is enough possibility of dishonest traders indulging

in adulteration by which the quality of the goods would be affected. Although it would be easy to standardise the industrial products with "ISI" marks, it would be difficult to identify the variation in the quality of the agricultural produces. Moreover, when goods are kept in containers in large quantities, checking each and every container is difficult. There have been instances where the containers contained only water instead of oil. Hence, there is ample scope for frauds and the banker will be facing such risks.

4. *Maintenance of Goods :* The banker should find a right place to store the goods properly. In India, storage facilities are rare and warehouses should be reliable. Apart from this, the banker should periodically check the goods stored in such warehouses, however reliable such warehouses may be. The cost of storage will increase the debt.

5. *High Transport Cost :* In case of default of repayment, the banker arranges for taking delivery of the goods from the godown and transport them to the market for sale. This is an added responsibility on the part of the bank. In case the price is not favourable, there could be some delay in making the necessary adjustments.

## Precautions

The following precautions should be taken by a bank before lending against goods as securities :

1. *Knowledge of the Borrower :* A banker should have a thorough knowledge about the customer. He must see whether the borrower is a dealer in the goods/commodity and possesses the necessary license. The 3-C's of the customer - Character, Capacity and Capital may be ensured. The banker should examine the banker's previous experience with the customer. In case the borrower had financial dealing with other bank/banks, the banker should be extra-cautious. He should enquire with the other bank about the financial dealings.
2. *Knowledge of Goods :* It is essential that the banker must have the working knowledge of the feature of the commodities on which the loan is granted. The banker can go through the market surveys and reports appearing in the daily newspapers and update his knowledge on price trends.
3. *Short-term Loans :* The banker should see that he lends only short-term loans for a period of 3 - 6 months to provide working capital for the business. In case funds are locked up for long periods, the bank may face liquidity crisis. The bank faces only lesser risk in case of short-term loans.

4. *Nature of Goods :* The banker should not encourage lending against

perishable commodities. He may lend against essential goods due to certain advantages like stability in price, easy salability and wide acceptability.

5. *Frauds :* There is adequate scope for frauds being committed by dishonest traders. The banker should check whether there is "ISI" mark in the case of industrial goods. Although it would be difficult to ensure the quality of agricultural goods, experienced bankers would avoid unfamiliar goods.

   The banker should take special care in verifying such goods kept in the containers. He should ensure that there is no false platform raised in the case of loose storage. Bags, bales, cases or tins should be arranged in the warehouse in an easy countable manner. Though it would be difficult to check every container or bag, at least random sample check should be made to satisfy himself about the accuracy and quality of the goods.

6. *Warehouse and Insurance :* The banker should see whether the goods have been stored in a licensed warehouse. It is always necessary that the goods are stored in first class godowns with independent access. The banker should advise the customer to choose a pucca godown (not a shed) easily accessible by rail or road. He should also see the surrounding area whether there are any risky business ventures like petrol bunks, explosive factories etc. The floor of the godown should be damp-proof and leak-proof, without having too many windows and doors. In short, the warehouse should be strong enough to withstand the vagaries of the weather.

   The banker should physically check the goods kept in the warehouse and verify with registers kept in the godown. He should ask the borrower to arrange for preparation of a godown - chart indicating the quantity of goods and location of goods in the warehouse. Once the banker takes charge of the godown, he should put his own locks and also put up a nameplate outside the godown indicating hypothecation of goods with the bank. A good and reliable watchman should also be appointed by the bank and the charges may be debited to the customer's account.

7. *Insurance :* Even before granting the loan to the customer, the banker should see that the goods are insured fully against all sorts of risk as fire, theft, flood etc.

8. *Other Precautions :* Special attention should be paid to distinguish between hazardous and non-hazardous goods. Hazardous and non-hazardous goods should be kept in separate warehouses.

The banker should also arrange for periodical inspection of the goods by the bank staff.

Finally, while sanctioning loan, the banker should ensure that adequate margin is maintained, particularly in the case of goods where wide fluctuations in prices are common.

## DOCUMENTS OF TITLE TO GOODS

When goods are purchased for cash, the buyer gets the cash bill along with the goods. The bill is a document of title to the goods he has bought. Similarly, there are other documents of title to goods. When the seller transports his goods to the buyer through rail, the Railway receipt sent by the seller to the buyer is also a document of title to goods. According to Section 2 (4) of the Sale of Goods Act, 1930, "Document of title to goods includes a bill of lading, dock-warrant, warehouse keeper's certificate, wharfinger's certificate, railway receipt, warrent or order for the delivery of goods and any other document used in the ordinary course of business as proof of the possession or control of goods, or authorising or purporting to authorise, either by endorsement or by delivery, the possessor of the document to transfer or receive goods thereby represented".

A document of title to goods represents actual goods in the possession of the owner or someone else. It confers on the purchaser the right to receive the goods and the right to transfer it to some one else by mere delivery or by endorsement or by both. The transferee can take delivery of the goods in his own right. The familiar documents of title to goods with which the bank loans can be granted are:

Cash receipt/Invoice, Bill of lading; Dock warrent; Warehouse-keepers' certificate; Delivery orders; Railway receipts/lorry receipts.

*Cash Receipt/Invoice :* A cash receipt is a receipt issued by the seller to the buyer for having received the cash in exchange of the goods. Similarly, an invoice represents a document relating to the credit sale showing the nature and value of goods.

*Bill of lading :* A Bill of Lading is a document issued and signed by the captain of the ship acknowledging the receipt of the goods for transporting the goods from one port to that of the another. It is prepared in triplicate and duly stamped. One of the copies will be retained by the Captain and the other two are handed over to the consignor. The consignor, along with other documents, sends one copy of the bill of lading to the buyer who can take delivery of the goods in his place.

A bill of lading contains the description of the goods specified therein. It is merely an acknowledgment of the goods received for transport but does not certify its contents. The description of the goods in the invoice should tally with that of the bill of lading. Legally it is also an acknowledgment of the goods received by the captain of the ship.

### Railway/Lorry Receipt

A Railway Receipt is also a document of title to goods issued by the railway authorities for transporting goods from one destination to the other. Though it is not a negotiable instrument, it can be transferred by endorsement and delivery. Hence, the consignor insures the goods during transport against fire, loss or damage. The endorsement on a railway receipt does not confer on the endorsee the right to sue the railway for short of delivery or non-delivery of goods as the goods are transported at the owner's risk. Lorry Receipts/Motor receipts has not attained the status of document of title.

### Dock Warrant

Dock Warrant is a document issued by the dock authorities of a dock or warehouse stating the receipt of the goods described in it. It also contains the name of the person/party to whom the goods would be delivered or to his order. A dock warrent can be transferred by endorsement and delivery. It also contains the description of the goods consigned, numbers, gross weight etc.

### Delivery Orders

A delivery order is a document issued by the seller addressed to the warehouse-keepers to deliver the goods mentioned therein or part thereof to the person mentioned therein. Either the owner himself or his assistant may fill in the name of the person who is authorised to take delivery of the goods. Jute and Tea Delivery Orders are normally accepted as good security for bank advances. A delivery order is recognised as a document of title to goods.

### Merits

Apart from the honesty and reliability of the customers, the documents of title to goods serve as additional securities for bank advances. Documents of title to goods, if properly assigned in favour of the bank, can be accepted by banks as good securities. Although the goods are not with the bank, the right to sell the goods, in case of default, is with the bank.

A bill of lading contains the description of the goods specified therein. It is merely an acknowledgement of the goods received for transport but does not certify its contents. The description of the goods in the invoice should tally with that of the bill of lading. Legally, it is also an acknowledgement of the goods received by the captain of the ship.

## Precautions

The following precautions should be taken by a bank while lending against document of title to goods :

1. Since document of title to goods is only an additional security, the banker should fully rely on the integrity and honest of the borrower. He should examine whether the borrower is dealing in the type of goods for which he surrenders the documents of title.
2. The banker should examine the contents of the documents of title carefully and see whether it is genuine. He must check whether it contains any adverse conditions or remarks which are prejudicial to the banker.
3. The banker should also verify whether goods mentioned in the documents of title are insured.
4. The following documents should also be obtained in case of lending against documents of title:

   *(a)* Certificate of packing.

   *(b)* All copies of the bill of lading.

   *(c)* Insurance policy.

   *(d)* Copies of the invoice.
5. While advancing against warehouse-keeper's receipt, the banker should examine whether the warehouse is licensed as per the law governing the State. The banker should examine whether a part of the goods has already been delivered from the warehouse. Although a banker may be advancing against documents of title to goods, there is nothing wrong in physically examining goods to estimate the correct value of the goods. Steps may be taken for physical verification. In case of part-withdrawal of goods from the godown, the banker can permit only after ensuring the repayment of the proportionate loan and interest. This may be done only through issue of delivery order by the bank. The banker should also check whether rent, insurance and other charges have been paid up-to-date.
6. In the case of loans against delivery orders, the banker should see that the document is transferred in the name of the bank.

## Life Insurance Policies

Life Insurance Policy is a contract between the insured and the insurer wherein the latter promises to pay a specified amount after the expiry of a certain period or on the occurrence of the death of the assured. Usually, the contract provides for payment of premium on the port of the insured also. The LIC of India issues several kinds of LIC policies which are accepted as a good security by a banker and loans are granted against them. There are three kinds of life policies issued by the LIC : *(i)* Whole-life Policy; *(ii)* Endowment; and *(iii)* Annuity Policy.

A whole-life policy is one wherein the amount is payable at the death of the insurer. In an endowment policy, the amount will be payable to the nominee at the death of the insured or at the maturity to the insured whichever is earlier. This type of policy is very popular. Endowment policy is issued by LIC 'with profit' and 'without profit'. LIC declares Bonus on Endowment Policy 'with profit'. In the case of Annuity Policy (not very popular) a lump sum is paid by the insured to the LIC in the beginning and periodical payment as per the contract is paid to the insured till his death.

The main objects of taking Life insurance policies are to make a provision for dependents in cases of untimely death of the insured, to make a provision for old age and retirement and to obtain a Loan from LIC for construction of house by the policyholder.

At present, the LIC grants loans on its own unencumbered policies up to 90% of the surrender value. The banks also consider Life Policy as a good security and grant loans up to 80-90% of its surrender value.

Surrender value is the amount payable to the insurer if he abandons the policy and pays no further premiums. A LIC Policy can fetch the surrender value only if the premiums have been paid atleast for a period of two years.

## Merits of Life Policies

The banker prefers Life Insurance Policy as a good security for granting loans due to the following reasons:

*(i) Excellent Security and Guaranteed Repayment :* Since Life Insurance Policies are issued by Life Insurance Corporation of India and Post Offices, they are accepted as good securities. There is a guaranteed repayment by LIC or Post Office. In case of the borrower's default in paying the premium or untimely death, the banker can surrender the policy as per the procedure and receive the surrender value from the LIC. Even when the policy matures, the payment is received by the bank. In all these cases, the formalities are quite simple.

*(ii) Assignment of Policy :* Life Policy can be assigned in favour of the lender. Hence, the assignment can be registered in favour of the bank. Once the policy assigned and registered with the LIC , the bank gets the legal title and the amount is payable only to the bank. Moreover, the policy remains with the bank as a safe security. This security does not incur any expense or supervision.

*(iii) Increasing Value of the Policy :* The surrender value of the policy continues to increase on account of payment of subsequent premiums

and declaration of Bonus. The banker need not worry about the fall in the value of the Life Policy at any time.

## Risk Factors

(i) *A Contract of Uberrimae fidei* : A contract of insurance is a contract of *Uberrimae fidei i.e.*, a contract of utmost good faith. It requires the insured to reveal all the material facts concerning his life to the insurance company. Failure to do so or giving false information will nullify the contract. This is a clause in the LIC contract whereby the insurance company would avoid its liability in case of concealment of any material fact known to the insured. A banker has no means of knowing exactly whether the insured has perfectly adhered to this clause.

(ii) *Default in Payment of Premium* : The validity of the life policy depends on the regular payment of premiums. In case the insured stops paying premium at the appropriate dates, the policy gets lapsed. Consequently, the banker may not get even the surrender value. Hence the banker is entrusted with the task of monitoring the regular payment of premiums with the LIC.

(iii) *Draw back on Assignment of policy* : One of the serious limitations of this security is relating to the assignment of the policy. In case the life policy has been assigned on an earlier date to some one else, the banker will be at a loss.

(iv) *Risk in case of suicide* : Life Policies, in certain cases, may include a 'suicide clause' which may prevent the payment in case the insured commits suicide.

(v) *Other Hazards* : The policy may restrict an insured from taking up certain hazardous jobs like working in an explosive unit. Failure to adhere to this cancels the original agreement and LIC may evade the payment on this ground.

## Precautions

A banker should take the following precautions while lending against life policies :

1. To meet the increasing needs of the people, different kinds of policies are issued by the LIC and Post Offices. Firstly, the banker should ascertain the kind of policy with which the loan proposal is made. Due to the advantages associated with, the banker would prefer it an endowment policy as endowment policy is payable at the expiry period or on the death of the insured whichever is earlier. It should be remembered that some of the policies not eligible for obtaining a bank loan are :

(i) Policies issued under Married Woman's Property Act.

(ii) Policy issued for the purpose of payment of Estate duty.

(iii) Children's endowment policies.

2. The banker should ensure whether the assured has an insurable interest when a policy is presumed to exist when a person insures his or his wife's life. A father has insurable interest in the life of his son provided he is dependent on his son.
3. The bank should verify whether the premiums have been paid regularly. The banker could ask for the latest premium paid receipt before deciding to grant the customer a loan. He should also obtain an undertaking from the borrower that he would continue to pay the premiums regularly and submit the receipts to the bank as and when it falls due. Apart from this, the banker should obtain an authorisation letter from the customer that he would be allowed to pay the insurance premium on behalf of the customer and debit his account if the insured fails to pay the premiums in time.
4. The banker should examine the conditions of the policy. Conditions such as restrictions on assignment of the policy may prevent the banker from lending against such securities.
5. It is absolutely necessary that the age of the policyholder should have been admitted by the LIC. Till such time, the LIC does not ensure any liability. Hence, the banker should get the age admitted by the LIC either by a separate letter or by an endorsement on the policy if not done earlier.
6. It should be ascertained whether the policy is not already assigned/ encumbered. The policy should be got assigned in favour of the bank. For this, the policy should be sent to the branch of the LIC where it is being served. The charges in connection with the legal assignment should be debited to the customer's account.
7. The surrender value of the policy should be calculated as per LIC's booklet by verifying the latest premium paid receipt. Normally a policy will acquire surrender value only after three years from the date of issue. Generally a margin of 10% is maintained.
8. Advances against Postal Life Insurance Policies are generally granted only to employees. Hence, care should be taken to get the policy assigned in the format specified in the bank circular and the same should be registered with the Post Master General of the circle.
9. Once a banker grants loan on Life Policy, he should monitor the repayment of the loan and regular payment of premium. In case the borrower fails to submit the premium receipt, the bank should check

with the company for regularity of payment of premium to ensure that the policy is kept alive. If defaults are there or if the depositor dies, the policy should be surrendered as per the procedure and the advance be adjusted from the proceeds.

10. A Register should be maintained by the bank to record the particulars relating to the assignment. On repayment of the advance, the bank should check the accounts once again and see whether there is any outstanding payments. After collecting the dues to the bank, the policy may be reassigned.

## ADVANCES AGAINSTS STOCK EXCHANGE SECURITIES

Securities which are bought and sold through stock exchanges are called "Stock Exchange Securities". They are classified into three categories:

(a) *Government Securities* : Securities issued by Central/State Governments are known as Government securities. They are Stock, Bearer bonds and Promissory Notes.

(b) *Semi-Government Securities* : They include bonds and other securities issued by Port Trusts, Public bodies like Municipality/Corporation etc.

(c) Shares and Debentures issued by private and public limited companies.

As stock exchange securities are held in large blocks by rich and upper middle class people residing in major cities like Chennai, Mumbai, Delhi and Calcultta, advances against these securities are common. The banks also realise that the money lent on these securities are easily realisable. Government and Semi-government securities are termed as 'gilt.-edged' securities as they are issued by Government and Public bodies like Corporation and Municipalities. They are easily realisable. The principal forms of Government securities are:

(a) *Inscribed Securities* : These are certificates indicating the name of the shareholder in the books of public debt office. These securities can be transferred only by a transfer deed by registering transferees name with the public debt office. The transfer is not done by endorsement or by simple delivery.

(b) *Bearer Bonds* : Bearer bonds are certificates issued for a specified sum. They are considered as loan bonds payable to the bearer. They need only simple delivery for transfer of ownership.

(c) *Promissory Notes* : Promissory notes are issued by the President of India in the case of Central Government and by the Governor of the State in the case of State Government for raising special loans. It is a promise to pay the specified sum of money to the holder of the promissory note or endorsee on a stipulated date. A promissory note is a negotiable instrument and the ownership can be easily transferred by endorsement and mere delivery. The bankers view Government securities as gilt-edged securities and consider them as safe security. They prefer to Government securities, as they are sure of getting back their loan without any loss. However banker should carefully examine their validity, legal title, charges on them, valuation etc.

## Shares and Debentures

Shares and debentures are commonly accepted as securities by the bankers. They are issued by private and public companies under the Indian Companies Act, 1956. There are two kinds of shares - Equity and Preference shares. While equity shareholders are the real owners who can exercise their voting rights, the preference shareholders are merely creditors of the company enjoying a fixed rate of dividend irrespective of the company's performance.

## Debentures

A debenture is a loan bond issued by a company. It carries a predetermined interest, payable on maturity. Debentures are issued for varying periods up to 10 years. Companies may issue different types of debentures. Debenture holders are the creditors of the company and they are regularly paid the predetermined rate of interest whether the company makes profit or not. Debentures may be issued in one lump sum or in series of Rs. 1,000/- each.

Like issue of shares, debentures may be issued at a discount or at a premium or on par. In banking business, the bankers prefer to mortgage debentures as it is accompanied by a floating charge created by a borrowing company over its assets; but mortgage debentures may also include fixed charges over some specific assets such as land, buildings, machinery etc.

## Merits of Stock Exchange Securities

1. *Reliability :* Compared with other forms of security such as guarantees, stock exchange securities are more reliable as the banker has something tangible with him to recover the loans. It is easy for the banker to verify the ownership of the documents as the shares and debentures are issued in the name of the owners.

2. *Security :* Shares and debentures of reputed companies may also be considered, as gilt-edged securities as the market value of the shares are much more than their face value. They are well recognised and are easily saleable.

3. *Ready Market :* The prices of shares are quoted in the Stock Exchange. Shares and debentures of reputed companies are easily reliable than those of other kinds of securities such as lands, buildings and other

kinds of goods. In case of default, the sale may often be less time consuming and inexpensive.

4. *Price Stability :* Although there may be variations in prices of shares and stocks, reputed company's share prices do not fluctuate widely. Normally a banker keeps a margin for such fluctuations. In case of default, the bank can sell the shares/debentures even without any co-operation from the customer.
5. *Dividends :* Every year companies earn profits and dividends are declared to the shareholders. A banker can make the necessary arrangement with the company for receiving regular dividend. Dividends received may be adjusted with the borrower's debt.
6. *Transferability :* Shares can be freely transferred by one person to another. By registering the shares/debentures in the name of the bank, a prefect title can be obtained.

## Demerits

The following are the limitations of lending money against shares/stocks :

1. *Partly paid shares* possess a problem to the banker, as the banker remains liable to pay future calls if such shares are taken in the name of the bank.
2. *Liability for Omission Regarding Distribution of Notices : The* bank must ensure that all notices received from the company are passed on to the customer positively. In case of receipt of a notice relating to issue of right shares and failure to pass on to the customer, the banker will be held liable for any loss suffered by the customer.

   Generally, a company will have a right to forfeit its shares if the shareholder fails to pay any calls due on them. However, this right of lien will not be available against such debts which the company might have contracted after receipt of notice of pledge by the company from the bank. If, by any chance, the banker fails to pass on the notice to the customer (borrower), the banker will be held liable for the loss suffered by the customer.
3. *Legal Formalities and Expenses :* The bank normally prefers to legal mortgage in which case the shares must be transferred in the name of the bank. Legal mortgage has certain formalities which are to be completed and it requires expenses in the form of stamp duty, registration etc.
4. *Forgery :* It should be noted that duplicate share certificates are also issued by the companies. It is possible that the same certificate could have been pledged with other banker/lenders. If the shares are

registered in the name of the bank with forged signatures of the shareholder, although a bank has acted in good faith, it is bound to compensate the loss suffered by the company.

5. *Fluctuation in Prices :* When the economy is lull, the share prices are likely to be affected. The prices of some companies are affected if there is mismanagement, strike, lock out, difference of opinion among the directors etc. The violent fluctuation in prices will affect the bank. One cannot predict as to when these problems would emerge.

6. *Shares of Private Companies :* Normally banks do not favour shares of private companies. It would be impossible for the banker to judge the financial position of the company, as private companies are not bound to publish their balance sheets. a

   Moreover, the shares of private companies cannot be easily bought and sold since estriction on the transferability of shares is incorporated in the definition of a private company.

7. *Restriction for Advances against Shares :* Under Section 19 (2) of the Banking Regulation Act, 1949, a bank cannot hold shares of any company as pledgee, mortgagee or absolute owner of an amount exceeding 30% paid-up capital of the company or 30% of its own paid-up capital and reserves whichever is lower. In the case of block loans, the banker should verify his records and see that he does not exceed the limit.

## Precautions taken by a Bank while Lending against Shares/ Debentures

1. *Selection of Share/Debentures :* The Head Office is entrusted with the responsibility of identifying corporate securities. It sends the list of approved corporate securities to all the branches of the bank. While appraising the loan application, the first thing to be done by a banker would be to check whether the proposed share/ debenture offered as security by the borrower is approved by the Head Office. In case of non-inclusion in the bank's approved list, he should arrange for getting clearance from the Head Office if the manager feels that he is a reliable customer. For inclusion of such securities in the list, the Head Office considers the nature of company's business, management of the company, past working results and market trends in prices of shares of the company and so on.

2. *Share Prices :* While lending on the strength of the shares/ debentures, the banker should verify share prices. He should also check closely whether the prices quoted are with or without dividend/

interest. In case the quoted share price includes dividends/interest, the dividend or interest part of it should be deducted from the price.

3. *Type of Security :* The banker should accept the right type of security which he considers safe at that point of time. Debentures and preference shares are to be preferred than ordinary shares as they are reliable prior to equity shareholders in case company goes into liquidation. Moreover, the dividends and interest of these securities are also paid to the holders prior to equity shareholders. Finally, the banker does not gain anything even if the market value of the equity shares go up.

4. *Fully Paid-up/Partly Paid-up Shares :* The banker should never lend money on partly paid-up shares due to the following reasons :

   *(a)* In case the borrower fails to pay the calls-in-arrears on shares, the bank may be forced to pay them because failure to pay the calls would result in forfeiture of shares.

   *(b)* Since the banker has obtained the legal mortgage, he would become liable for payment of calls in arrears.

   *(c)* The market price of such partly-paid shares are much lower.

   *(d)* Even in the case of retransfer of such shares in the name of the borrower, the banker continues to be liable as a contributory shareholder at least for a period of one year from the date of transfer. In case of liquidation of the company during this period, the banker will be liable as a contributory shareholder. Hence, it is advisable not to lend any money against partly paid-up shares.

5. *Restrictions on Advances against its Own Shares :* The Indian Companies Act, 1956 prohibits the acceptance of its own shares as security for any loan granted by the bank. Hence, the bank's own shares should not be accepted.

6. *Shares of Private/Public Limited Company :* The banker should check whether the shares are related to any private limited company. If so, shares cannot be easily transferred. The Articles of the company restricts the transfer of shares.

7. *Listed Securities :* The banker should verify whether the shares/ debentures of public limited companies are listed with the recognised stock exchanges. If so, the prices are published regularly. In case of securities which are not listed, he has to verify closely the share prices.

8. *Margin :* The bank should keep a margin of safety as the prices of these shares/debentures may fall at certain times. Usually the banks prefer to have 25% margin on preference shares and 40% - 50% on equity shares.

9. *Short-term Loans:* While granting loans on stock exchange securities, the bank should arrange for short-term loans. Investment for longer periods would be against the principles of lending in commercial banks. The advances sought should be commensurate with the line of activity and net worth of the borrower and the finance extended should be need-based.
10. *Genuineness :* The companies issue duplicate certificates in case of loss of such original certificates. The genuineness of the certificate should be checked carefully. Even fake certificates can be presented by some borrowers. In order to safeguard himself, the banker should check the official seal of the company. They should also see that the certificates are signed by atleast two directors of the company and one officer of the company. The banker should also check whether the shares/debentures submitted as security bear the name/names of the borrower.
11. *Creation of Charge :* As per the RBI guidelines, if the advance amount exceeds Rs. 5 lakhs, the shares should be got transferred in the name of the bank. It is absolutely necessary that a bank should create its charge in its favour. Such charges can be created either by giving a legal title or by creating an equitable title.

    A legal title is one by which the borrower executes a transfer deed and arranges for entering the name of the banker or his nominee as shareholder in the books of the company subject to the agreement that the securities will be retransferred to the customer when advance is repaid.

    In the case of equitable title, the borrower deposits the share certificate with the bank without any registration but with the intention of creating a charge over them. However, no transfer is made in the books of the company. It is mere possession of the share certificates.

    The banker should check thoroughly whether any equitable charge has already been made. The banker should not accept the shares or debentures standing in the name of the borrower. The banker should not prefer to third party securities.
12. *Notice to the Company :* The banker should give a notice to the company informing that he has charge over the securities, particularly in the case of equitable title. Such notice will prevent the company from issuing a duplicate certificate.
13. *Possession of the Securities :* Unless the loan is fully cleared, the bank should not part with the securities.
14. *Purpose of the Loan :* Loans/advances shall not be considered for

speculative purposes. Loans can be granted for meeting contingencies and need of personal nature and for subscribing to rights/new issue of shares/debentures.

15. *Repayment Schedule* : If the advance exceeds Rs. 5 lakhs, the repayment schedule should be approved by the RBI. Normally the repayment schedule should not exceed 2 years.

## ADVANCES AGAINST FIXED DEPOSIT RECEIPTS

Fixed Deposit Receipts are issued by the banks for the deposit made by the customers for a specific period ranging from 15 days to 5 years or more. They are popularly known as 'FDR's among the business circle. The rate of interest varies depending upon the term of deposit. The interest allowed by the bank is higher than interest allowable in other types of accounts. The longer the period of deposit, higher is the rate of interest. The rules governing the fixed deposits are printed on the reverse side of the FDR.

The bankers favour the FDR as a security as they are issued either by themselves or by their counter-parts (other banks). In case the customer needs money prior to the due date, although he may not be able to withdraw strictly from fixed deposit account, he can obtain a loan from the bank on the strength of the FDR. The banker sanctions the loan depending upon the requirement of the borrower subject to a minimum margin of 10% to meet unforeseen contingencies.

### Merits

1. The bank can safely make an advance against fixed deposit receipt, as it constitutes a good security for lending due to the following reasons :
   - *(a)* The banker knows the customer; he will be satisfied with the title of his own FDR as a security;
   - *(b)* The loan is granted only against his own liability or any other bank. Hence realisation or adjustment of accounts will be only a formality at the end.
   - *(c)* There is no variation in the value of the security as in the case of other securities;
   - *(d)* FDR is transferable.
2. The banker is aware of the due date of the fixed deposits. Hence, it would be easy to lend a loan against the fixed deposit for the remaining period. At the end of the period, the amount due to him along with interest receivable can be deducted/adjusted with the matured amount and the balance may be handed over to the depositor.
3. The lending procedure is not complicated and inexpensive. It is a

simple method of getting financial assistance from the bank. Similarly, the banker would feel that the lending procedure is very easy and inexpensive.

4. The banker is aware of the maturity date of the FDR. Hence, he can be sure of the term of the loan and the exact date of repayment of the loan.

## Precautions taken by a bank while lending against FIXED Deposit Receipt :

Although the Fixed Deposit Receipt is a desirable security, the banker should take certain precautions before lending money against FDRS:

1. The banker should ensure whether the fixed deposit receipts submitted by the borrower are owned by him and in his own name/ names. He should not encourage lending if the FDR is in the name of some one other than the borrower.

   In case of Fixed Deposit Receipts carrying two or more names as joint depositor and one of them is wanting to raise a loan on the strength of the FDR, the banker should ask for a letter of authority signed by all depositors authorising him (the borrower) to get an Overdraft or loan against the FDR. Even in the case of Fixed Deposit with the clause 'payable to either or survivor', the banker should ask for authority from the other person too.

   Loans against minor deposits can be granted after satisfying that the loan will be used for the benefit of the minor. A declaration should be signed by the father/ guardian and should be certified by the branch. Even in the case where mother is taken as a guardian for the minor, father alone can exercise the loan papers, *if he is alive.* In exceptional cases, loans and advances can also be granted on security of fixed deposits standing in the name of third parties. The 'Third Party Letter of Pledge' should be executed by the depositors.

2. The banker may grant a loan up to a maximum limit of 90% of the FDR including accrued interest for period completed. For deposit accounts with instalments like recurring deposits, interest accrued can be taken into account only if the account is regular.

3. The banker should make the borrower to pledge the FDR with the bank and request the customer to apply for overdraft/loan against such deposit.

4. After having received the FDR from the customer, the lien should be properly marked in the FDR, deposit ledger, pass book in the case of recurring deposit and maturity date should be incorporated for future follow-up.

5. Whenever loan is granted against FDR, the interest payable on deposit should be credited to the Loan account.
6. The banker should see that loans might be granted on the strength of the Fixed Deposit Receipt issued by themselves or of any scheduled bank or Central or State Finance Corporation. He must also see that the bank which has issued the FDR should not have a branch in that place. If there is any branch in that area, the customer may be advised to go to the branch to get the loan. Apart from that he should send a notice to the bank which issued the receipt intimating about advancing of money to the depositor.
7. If the deposit is issued by another branch of the same bank, the lending branch should ascertain from the branch whether any lien has been noted against the said FDR. After sanctioning the advance, the lending branch should inform the issuing branch to note its lien on their records. It should also be noted that the lending bank should not affix its stamp on the Fixed Deposit Receipt issued by another bank.
8. The bankers should grant only short-term loan against the FDRS. He should prefer to lend on FDRs which would be maturing for payment within the next six months. The borrower can also be advised to deposit the matured amount with the bank after maturity.

## ADVANCES AGAINST BOOKDEBTS

Book Debts are debts receivable from different debtors. They may represent money due to the firm on account of credit sales or service rendered to some persons or money paid on account. Book Debts are generally considered to parties of high repute. The bankers accept book debts only as a last resort and not as principal security as the banker might be loaded with the trouble of collecting such debts from unknown persons. The procedure is lengthy and cumbersome. Book Debts are normally permitted only to Joint Stock Companies, Small Scale Industry and Trading and Commission Agents.

Book debts are considered to be actionable claims. According to Section 130 of the Transfer of Property Act, book debts may be assigned to any one except to a judge, a legal practitioner or an officer of a court of justice. When a bank chooses to advance against book debt of a customer, equitable assignment is made by the customer instructing the debtor to pay the debt directly to the bank. The advances made against book debts are treated as clean advances. For the purpose of classification in statements and Balance Sheet and for sanctioning purpose, this is treated as secured advance.

### Merits

1. Although book debts are considered only as an additional security, it

is a common security for any businessman. There is ample chance of recovering the money directly from customers as most book debts are arising out of sale. In the normal course, the customer will pay back the debts, as continuity of purchase would exist.

2. Book-debts can be assigned as per the Law. Sec. 130 of the Transfer of Property Act permits the assignment of debt to anyone expect to a judge, a legal practitioner or an officer of a court of justice. Hence, there is a provision for legal transfer in favour of the bank.
3. The assignment of debt gives the banker all powers to recover the amount directly from the debtor. The banker can file a suit against the debtor for recovery of the dues.
4. The chance of failure to pay back is the debt by all debtors is very remote. In fact, by lending against book debts, the banker has reduced his risk among many.
5. In the event of failure to collect money from the customer, the banker can straightaway proceed against debtor. He can file a suit against the debtors without taking the consent of the assignor in case both borrower and the debtors default.

## Limitations

1. The banker's duty does not stop with getting assignment of debt in his favour but also to give a notice of assignment to the debtor. The banker would be safe only when a separate contract is entered by which the debtor agrees to pay the money to the banker directly.
2. From the banker's point view, the debtors are only third parties. The banker may not know about their financial position or financial dealings of the debtors. The banker should not become a collector of dues.
3. The debtors may have a counter-claim with the customer. The banker may not know anything about this when a list of debtors is given to the banker. Without thorough checking, enquiries and confirmation, if money is lent to the customer only on the strength of book-debts, there may not be a legitimate claim from the debtors. This would pose as a serious problem for the bank while collecting debts from the debtors.
4. The bank should check when the book debts had arisen. Sometimes, goods would have been sold by the customer to the debtors long time back. In case of long over dues, it would be difficult for the bank to collect the money. Moreover, some debts would have become time-barred as per the Limitation Act. The banker should also keep in mind that the Law of Limitation can be exercised by the debtor in his favour if the book debt is due for more than three years.

## Precautions

The following precautions should be taken by the banker while lending on the strength of book debts :

1. Primarily, the banker should be satisfied with the validity of the claim and must enquire about the reputation of the debtors about whom the banker does not know. Hence, the banker should ask his customer to list the transactions between him and his debtors. This will enable him to understand the nature of the transactions between them. He will be able to judge a loan/debt whether a particular debt is a time-barred one or not.
2. Advances should not be made against book debts outstanding beyond 90 days. In exceptional cases book-debts outstanding up to 180 days may be considered after obtaining special sanction from the Head Office.
3. Legal assignment should be obtained by the banker. The assignment must be in writing in the presence of a witness preferably at the office of the bank in the prescribed format. Assignment is an order addressed to the debtor by the customer directing him to pay the debt to the bank straightaway.
4. In case the banker has taken book debts as a collateral security, book debt statement should be submitted to the Head Office once in six months (March and September). Such statement should contain the following detail :

   *(i)* Book debts arisen out of bonafide transaction only should be included. Loans and advances and non-trade debts should not be classified under book debts.

   *(ii)* Book debts which are bad or doubtful of recovery for which there is any decree of any court or any dispute should not be included.

   *(iii)* Book debts should be shown at net amount after deducting earlier dues by the borrower to his debtor and after deducting discounts, commissions etc.
5. The banker should send a notice of assignment to the debtor and ensure the following :

   *(a)* Confirmation of the receipt of notice given by the debtor authorising payment to the bank;

   *(b)* Debtor's statement relating to the net amount due to the customer after making any adjustments for amount due from the customer to the debtor, cash discounts, commission etc.

(c) Undertaking from the debtor assuring that he would pay the money directly to the bank.

6. The assignment obtained by the banker should be for the whole amount and not a part of it.
7. The banker should arrange for registration of the charge with the Registrar of Joint Stock Company.
8. In case of corporate borrower where general power of attorney is executed and charge on book debts is registered with the Registrar of Companies.

## ADVANCES AGAINST SUPPLY BILLS

The Central and State Government organisations, Public Corporations and Municipalities select their suppliers of goods only after inviting tenders. Once the supplier is chosen on the basis of price, quality of goods and other terms quoted by him, the supplier is asked to despatch the goods as per the agreement entered with him. The supplier may send the goods as per the contract to the department concerned.

When the goods are received by the department, the storekeeper or an officer of the department acknowledges the receipt of the goods as per the delivery note. The delivery note is the authentic record for the despatch of goods. Once the store-keeper or any other officer concerned inspects the consignment and the goods and is satisfied with the goods, he may give a satisfactory inspection note. From the point of view of the buyer, the inspection note is the satisfactory document for the receipt of the goods. In case there has been any omission, defect in the goods received or any reduction in weight/length, it may be incorporated in the inspection note. This inspection note should be certified by the authorised officer. Thereafter, on the basis of the inspection note, a bill, in the name of the buyer, is supplied. Such bills are known as 'Supply Bills'.

It is common for the banks to advance against the Supply Bills because they would collect the money immediately after payment. In the case of other types of loans/advances, the banker may not know how his customer (borrower) would use the funds. But in the case of supply bills, the banker is fully aware of the fact that a business transaction has taken place and the borrower would get his collection in the normal course. Hence, the possibility of collecting the money is more. However, there are many risks in this kind of advance.

### Risks

1. Supply Bills are not accompanied by documents of title to goods, as the documents of title to goods like bill of lading/railway receipts would have been sent to the buyer.

2. In the case of Government and Semi-government organisations, there is no guarantee that the bills would be passed within a reasonable time. It might also be unduly delayed due to certain procedural flaws. Some bills may be returned in some sections for want of information or for petty reasons.
3. In case there are defects in the goods supplied and identified after giving the inspection note, the bills may not be passed into. Even if it is passed, it may be passed for a part-payment.
4. Since delivery note and inspection note are the basic documents, any difference between the delivery note, inspection note and supply bills for the goods supplied may be viewed seriously.
5. The possibility of a counter claim or set-off against the supplier may discourage the banker to lend against supply bills.

**Precautions taken by a bank while lending against supply bills.**

1. Supply bills are neither documents of title to goods nor bills of exchange. It is only a document stating that the goods mentioned in the delivery order/inspection note have been supplied. Hence, the banker should rely more on the honesty, integrity and experience of the customers for whom he intends to advance against supply bills.
2. Secondly, the banker should assess the buyers of such goods. If the buyer fails to pay the amount, it would be difficult to collect from the supplier. Therefore, the type of buyers should be carefully ascertained. Even if it is a Government Organisation, payment procedures may differ from officer to officer.
3. It is really necessary for the banker to understand the original terms and conditions of the contract. The banker should check whether these terms and conditions have been strictly followed by the supplier.
4. The banker should get an authorisation from the supplier that he would be empowered to collect the bill for the goods supplied straight from the buyer. Also he should get an undertaking from the supplier that he would remit the cheque/money at the bank for the settlement of debt as soon as he receives from the buyer.
5. The banker should thoroughly check the copy of the delivery order with that of the inspection note on the bill. In case of any discrepancy among them, he should clarify them.
6. The supply bills specify the quantum of the goods supplied, rate, amount and the Gross Total with tax, discount etc. The banker should examine each and see that there is no error.
7. The supply bills should have been received and acknowledged by the

buyer. It should be signed by a responsible officer acknowledged with his seal. The banker should ask the supplier to endorse this bill in his favour.

8. Adequate margin should be kept by the bank as in the case of other loans. He may maintain 15-25% margin depending upon the nature of the customer, product ,trade, experience etc.
9. The banker should send a letter to the buying department concerned conveying the information that he has advanced the supplier of such goods and asking them to remit the proceeds direct to the bank. Sending a copy of such authorisation letter given by the supplier may be appreciated by the buying department.
10. Finally, the banker should constantly monitor the payment on supply bills. If there is any delay or problem, he should inform the borrower that his advance would be cancelled. Then every effort should be made by the banker to collect the loan.

## ADVANCES AGAINST REAL ESTATES

In the recent past, there has been a tremendous increase in the demand for land and buildings in the urban and semi-urban areas as the population increases in the city and urban areas day by day. Even the prices of vacant plots are in great demand. However, the commercial banks hesitate to lend against land and buildings due to the inherrent risks toward such real estate securities.

### Risks

The banker faces the following risks while lending against real estates like land and buildings :

1. *Valuation of Properties :* Primarily, the valuation of land and buildings is very difficult because there is no standard value for such properties. For instance, a beautiful building at an exorbitant cost with all its modern amenities in a remote village may not fetch any reasonable price if offered for sale. There must be people who would be willing to buy that kind of a building at that place. Hence, bankers cannot relay upon the cost of the asset. The valuation reports of expert surveyors, architects and engineers should be called for. Even then, the resale value is something which one cannot predict exactly in the case of real estates. We cannot anticipate price increase at all times. In case the Government imposes restrictions in the construction of flats, multi storey buildings, for some reason or other, the prices may even fall.
2. *Legal Hurdles :* There may be legal hurdles in the transfer of properties. Even the Laws in this matter are complicated, as we do not have a uniform Law. Hindu Laws are different from Mohammedan Laws

particularly in relation to succession and transfer of immovable properties. When people convert themselves from one religion to other, the problem is compounded. In some States, legal restrictions are placed for transfer of lands. For instance, in Punjab, agricultural lands cannot be sold to a non-agriculturist.

3. *Ownership of the Properties/Real Estates :* It is difficult to trace the real owner of the land and buildings, particularly in an urban and semi-urban areas. Real estate transactions are carried on purely on trust. Just because a person possesses the title deeds of an immovable property, it does not mean that he is the absolute owner of the same. He may be only an agent who would have been entrusted with the responsibility of selling such land or may be just a relative/known person who is accidentally in possession of the title deeds. Hence, the banker may find it difficult to identify owner and ownership.
4. *Area and description of the Properties :* The area of land as shown by the title may also include Government lands as there is a tendency to encroach casually into the puramboke/natham (Government lands) which are kept vacant. When such persons sell their lands, these areas are also included in their title deeds. In the case of a city like Chennai, MMDA (Chennai Metropolitan Development Authority) approval is necessary for ownership lands.
5. *Land Tenures :* The Land Tenures prevailing in one part of the country is different from that of the other. The tenancy system also creates ownership to the tenant if he continues to cultivate/occupy the land continuously for more than 18 years. The land tenures are also changing frequently.
6. The commercial banks deal with short-term funds, as they may have to pay back their short-term liabilities. In case a banker is forced to take legal action against a defaulted customer, he may not be able to straight away sell the land or buildings without taking the matter to the courts. The procedure is cumbersome and complicated, particularly when tenants exist in such premises. He may take long time to recover his dues, as the security cannot be disposed off instantaneously.
7. *Expenses :* While registering the mortgage in the name of the bank, the procedure is not simple. Moreover, the customer has to incur heavy expenditure. The expenses in connection with the document security fee, encumbrance certificate, stamp duty, registration fee etc., are enormous which will reduce the quantum of advance to the borrower.

## Precautions taken by Banker while Lending against Real Estates

Commercial banks may not, by themselves, be willing to lend against the Real

Estates. But their customers may not have other kinds of securities to offer at the bank for obtaining the loan. Hence, the banks, instead of lending loans purely on personal security, may prefer to lend against landed properties. Since there is a trend in the increase of prices of lands and buildings situated in the urban and semi-urban areas, the bankers need not hesitate to lend against such immovable properties. However, they should take the following precautions :

1. When a customer approaches a bank with his formal application for a loan against land and buildings, the banker himself should satisfy himself about the status of the customer. He must quickly judge whether the intending borrower is a desirable person for such a loan facility or not.
2. The next step would be to examine the assets and liabilities stated in the application form. He should review them carefully to ascertain the background of the applicant. He may make a few enquiries with the borrower about the purpose of the loan and how he would be using the funds, assets and liabilities, if any.
3. The banker should examine the title of the property to know whether the borrower possesses an absolute title. He should examine the application to find out whether the properties are in his own name. The banker can ask for the original title deed which may be sent to his legal advisor to get expert opinion on legal matters relating to such documents. In the case of properties jointly owned, adequate care should be taken to include all joint owners in the loan application. The banker should also get a letter of declaration from the borrower assuring that the property is owned by him and is free from any encumbrance.
4. The banker should get the encumbrance certificate for atleast 13 years from the registrar office to satisfy himself whether the property is free from any mortgage or any other type of encumbrance and is not subject to any litigation.
5. The banker should estimate the value of the properties. If he has some knowledge in the area of real estates, he himself can assess the value of the property. The banker may pay a visit to the place where properties are held and have first-hand information. Lending funds purely on the basis of records may lead him into problems. Hence, the banker should arrange to get additional information thorough other sources also. In case he finds it difficult to move out of the premises, he should depute one of his officers to collect such first-hand information.

In the case of lands in urban and semi-urban areas, the value of land may be fast increasing. Hence, there may be variation in the market price of the land and the Government prices (i.e., price fixed by the Government). The value fixed by the Government can easily be ascertained in the Registrar office. With reference to market price of the land, the latest price at which the adjacent lands have been sold should be found. The banker should estimate the price of the land only on the basis of the principle, 'Market price or Government price whichever is lower".

In case the banker is not able to estimate the value, he can entrust the responsibility with an appraiser at a cost. Most banks have their own appraisers who could be deputed to estimate the value of buildings and lands. If the banker comes to know of the fact that there are tenants living in such premises, he has to be careful while lending loans. He should examine the agreement between the tenants and the landlord (borrower).

6. The banker should maintain about 40-50% margin in the case of land and buildings. He should keep in mind that he should be able to realise his loan in time. In case of need, the banker should be able to arrange to sell the properties and make all adjustments toward his loan.
7. The banker should also ask his customer to arrange for insuring the buildings or other property against all types of losses.
8. The banker should see that the property is legally mortgaged in the name of the banker and get it registered. In case of a joint stock company, it should be registered with the registrar of joint stock companies.
9. The banker should also get a promissory note from the borrower to make him personally liable for the debts.
10. The banker should get the original title deeds from the borrower and leave them in his safe custody. The banker should not part with these documents till such time the accounts are settled in full.

## MODEL QUESTIONS

**Section - A**

1. Define the term Goods.
2. How are goods classified?
3. What is an "ISI" Mark?
4. What is a warehouse?
5. What is a bill of lading?
6. What is a debenture?

7. What are fully paid-up and partly paid-up Shares?
8. What is a FDR?

**Section - B**

1. Discuss the precautions required to be taken by a banker in the case of advances made against security of goods.
2. What is a document of title to goods? What are the precautions to be taken while granting loans against documents of title to goods?
3. Discuss the merits of granting loans against Life Insurance Policies.
4. What are the risk factors involved in accepting L.I.C. policy as a security?
5. Write short notes on "Advances against Stock Exchange Securities".
6. What are the demerits of granting loans against shares and debentures?
7. Discuss the merits and limitation of granting loan against Book Debts.
8. What are the demerits of granting loans against shares and debentures?
9. Write short notes on "Advances against Fixed Deposit Receipts".
10. What are the risks that the banker has to face while granting advances against Real Estate?

**Section - C**

1. Explain what factors are to be considered by a banker while making advances against goods and document of title to goods?
2. Discuss the suitability of the following types of securities as cover for granting advances :
   *(a)* Fixed Deposit Receipt.
   *(b)* Shares and Debentures.
   *(c)* Life Insurance Policy.
3. Assess the merits and demerits of the following as security for advances :
   *(a)* Goods.
   *(b)* Real Estate.
   *(c)* Book Debts.
4. How would a bank consider an application for advances against
   *(a)* Bill of Lading
   *(b)* Life Insurance Policy and
   *(c)* Stock Exchange Securities?
5. Discuss the Real Estate as a security for loans.
6. Write short notes on
   *(a)* Insurable Interest
   *(b)* Book debts as banker's security
7. Writes short notes on

*(i)* Advances against Bills of Lading

*(ii)* Advances against Dock warrant

*(iii)* Advances against Warehouse receipts

*(iv)* Advances against Delivery Order

*(v)* Advances against Railway receipt.

# 14

# THE NEGOTIABLE INSTRUMENTS

In the modern business environment, negotiable instruments play an important role as a convenient mode of settling accounts between parties. A considerable portion of law and practice of Banking in India consists, of negotiable instruments. A negotiable instrument is primarily a credit instrument with features of negotiability. But there are also some credit instruments, which are not negotiable. For example: Postal orders and I.O.U. (I Owe You). A banker should be thoroughly conversant with the negotiable instruments, as he would mostly be dealing with such instruments during the course of his banking business. He may often have to deal with it as ; *(i)* holder for value, *(ii)* a paying banker, or *(iii)* as a collecting agent. Once he makes a mistake in such transactions, he may not be able to rectify his mistake at all and it would prove fatal in some situations. Therefore, a banker should have a fair knowledge about the theoretical and practical aspects of banking transactions.

## Definition

A negotiable instrument has not been defined adequately by the Negotiable Instruments Act, 1881. Section 13 merely indicates a negotiable instrument as a promissory note, bill of exchange or cheque payable either to order or bearer. Although the term 'negotiable instrument' has not been defined exhaustively, the characteristics of such documents have been clearly explained in Section 4, 5 and 6 of the Negotiable Instruments Act.

Justice K.C. Wills, in his book on 'Negotiable Securities' defines negotiable instrument as one the property which is acquired by any one who takes it bonafide and for value notwithstanding any defect in the title of the person from whom he took it and from which it follows." An instrument cannot be termed as negotiable unless it is such a state that the true owner could transfer that contract or engagement contained therein by simple delivery of the instrument.

## Characteristics of Negotiable Instruments

1. A negotiable instrument is a written contract for a definite amount signed by the parties therein evidencing the right to receive money. It may be used as evidence of indebtedness as they have special rules of evidence. The amount mentioned in the instrument is for a certain money payable in rupees and paise. This instrument may be considered as substitute for money as conversion is easier.

2. The instrument is payable at a definite time. It is payable on or before a stated date or at a fixed period after a stated date. However, any one can easily know the date of payment.

3. The 'Transferable character' is the essence of negotiable instrument. If a share in a joint stock company is to be transferred, a separate instrument of transfer is required. But a negotiable instrument can be transferred by one person to another even by mere delivery and in some cases by delivery and endorsement.

4. One of the special features of the instrument is that the transfer is not affected by the defects of the transferor. In the case of transfer of goods or bill of lading, when there is a defect in the title of the holder, the transferee cannot have a better title than that of the transferor. But in the case of a negotiable instrument, the situation is different. When a person acquires a negotiable instrument, he becomes an absolute owner irrespective of the defects in the title of the transferor or previous holder. The transferee need not be enquiring about the title of the transferor and previous holders because the *special feature of the negotiable instrument is that the holder in due course enjoys a better title than that of the transferor if he (transferee) takes the instrument in good faith, as the instrument is free from counter claims.* This feature is referred to as 'negotiability.'

5. In case of any difficulty even at a future date, the holder of a negotiable instrument can sue in his own name for enforcing any right or claim on the basis of the instrument.

*Note :* The term 'Negotiable Instruments' has been used in a limited sense because the law has restricted it only to Promissory Notes, Bills of Exchange and Cheques. The Act does not provide for the rights of transmission to similar analogous documents like share warrants, dividend warrants, bearer debentures, bank drafts, circular notes hundis etc. These non-negotiable instruments have acquired the quality of negotiability by the mercantile usage or by other enactments.

6. On the due date the amount mentioned in the instrument can be claimed without giving any notice to the party liable to pay. This simplifies the procedure.

7. A special procedure is provided for suits on promissory notes and bills of exchange under Civil Procedure Code. Decree can be obtained more quickly than in the case of other suits.

### Presumptions

Section 118 brings out the special rules of evidence regarding presumptions relating to the negotiable instruments. Until the contrary is proved, the following are the presumptions.

1. *Consideration :* Every negotiable instrument is made or drawn or accepted, endorsed, negotiated or transferred for consideration only. In case there is no consideration, there is no obligation of payment as between immediate parties.
2. *Date :* Every negotiable instrument bearing a date was made or drawn on such date.
3. *Time of acceptance :* Every bill of exchange was accepted within a reasonable time after its date but before its maturity.
4. *Time of transfer :* Every transfer of a negotiable instrument was made before its maturity.
5. *Order of Endorsement :* The Endorsements appearing upon a negotiable instrument were made in the order in which they appear thereon.
6. *Stamp :* A promissory note or bill of exchange is duly stamped.
7. *Holder in Due Course :* A holder of a negotiable instrument is a holder in due course. But if the instrument has been fraudulently obtained, the burden of proving that the holder is a holder in due course falls upon him.

The Negotiable Instruments Act, 1881 lists only three negotiable instruments - Promissory Note, Bill of Exchange and Cheque.

## PROMISSORY NOTES

In the case of a credit purchase or any other transaction, the debtor agrees to pay on demand or after some time by drawing a promissory note. The promissory note contains a promise to pay a certain sum of money either to him or any other legal holder of the instrument. The person who agrees to pay the money on a promissory note is called the promissor and in whose favour the promise is made is known as the promisee. A promissory note is also known as 'Pro-note' in ' the business circle. Currency notes are not deemed to be promissory notes although it is a promise made by the Governor of RBI.

A promissory note may be payable either on demand or after a definite period of time. A promissory note should be sufficiently stamped as per the Stamp Act, 1899.

Section 4 of the Negotiable Instruments Act, 1881 defines a promissory note as "an instrument in writing (not being a bank-note or a currency note) containing an unconditional undertaking signed by the maker, to pay a certain sum of money only to, or to the order of, a certain person, or to the bearer of the instrument."

**Specimen of a promissory note**

| |
|---|
| Place<br>Date |
| Three months after date, I promise to pay a sum of One Thousand Rupees only for the value received. |
| Rs.1000/- Signature<br>(Name of the Prommissor) |

## Characteristics of a Promissory Note

1. *Instrument in writing* : A promissory note is an instrument in writing. It may also be typewritten or a printed one. An instrument drawn with a pencil is risky to deal with although there is no restriction in the Act.

2. *Unconditional Undertaking* : There should be an express promise or clear undertaking by a debtor to his creditor. The debtor takes the initiative and gives an unconditional promise which is not a mere acknowledgment of debt. There should not be any conditions attached thereto with his promise. For example: "I promise to pay Mr. X or order Rs.1, 000." This is a promissory note whereas an example like "I promise to pay Mr. X Rs. 1,000 if Y gives me enough to pay the sum" is not a promissory note at all.

3. A *Certain Sum of money only* : The amount payable should be certain and not vague. The contract between the promissor and promisee is to pay a definite amount of money only and nothing else. Any note containing payment of money and anything else cannot be deemed to be a promissory note.

4. *Signed by the maker :* In the case of a promissory note, the debtor has agreed to pay by signing such note. A *promissory note may be* a *written or printed document. The document is complete only if it is signed by the promissor.*

5. *The Payer must be certain :* Section 4 clearly points out that the money should be payable to a certain person or to the bearer of the instrument. The payee may be marked, in the pronote by his name or designation. In case a promissory note is drawn in favour of a deceased person without the knowledge of his death, his legal representatives can enforce the payment.

6. *Date of the Promissory Note :* A promissory note is dated as it is made payable at or after a particular time. In order to know the due date, it is essential that a promissory note is to be dated, as the due date would be calculated on the basis of the date of the promissory note The exact date of drawing the bill maybe immaterial, as the bill may be, sometimes anti-dated or post-dated. Therefore, the date appearing on the note is deemed to be the date of the note.

7. *Rate of Interest :* The rate of interest should be calculated from the date of the promissory note until the realisation of such amount. Interest shall be calculated at rate specified on the amount of the principal money. In case interest rate is not specified in the instrument, interest should be calculated at the rate of 18% p.a. from the date on which the same should have been paid by the promissor.

8. *Maturity :* The maturity of a promissory note or bill of exchange is the date on which it falls due. Delay in presentment for payment is excused if the delay is caused by circumstances beyond the control of the holder and not due to his default, misconduct or negligence. For instance, war, riot or political disturbance. In case of reasonable delay, the promissory note should be presented within a reasonable time. However, three days of grace are allowed for these documents (Section 22). When the due date of the promissory note or bill of exchange falls on a public holiday, the instrument shall be deemed to be due on the next preceding business day. The expression "public holidays' includes Sundays and any other day declared by the Central Government by notification in the official gazette, to be a public holiday (Section 25).

## Illustration

*(a)* A negotiable instrument dated 29th Jan., 199 1, is made payable one month after date. The instrument is at maturity on the third day after the 28th Feb., 199 1.

*(b)* A negotiable instrument dated 30th August '91 is made payable 3 months after date. The instrument is at maturity on the 3rd Dec.'91.

*(c)* A promissory note or bill or exchange dated 31st August '91 is made

payable 3 months after date. The instrument is at maturity on the 3rd December, 199 1.

It should also be remembered that a promissory note or bill of exchange in which no time for payment is specified is payable on demand (Section 19).

Section 32 clearly indicates that the maker (Promissor) of a promissory note is bound to pay the amount to the holder of the instrument. The maker of the promissory note may be a single individual or more than one individual. If there are more than one individual, the liability of the promissory note may be joint or joint and several. In default of such payment of a promissory note, the promissor or promissors are bound to compensate the loss sustained by the holder.

## Parties to the Promissory Note

While dealing with the negotiable instruments, one may have to come across many parties :

1. *Drawer and Drawee :* Section 7 states that the maker of the bill of exchange or cheque is called the "Drawer" and the person thereby directed to pay is called the "Drawee." In the case of a promissory note, the drawer is the person who promises to pay the amount to the holder.

2. *Holder :* According to Section 8, the 'holder' of the promissory note or bill of exchange or cheque means any person entitled in his own name to the possession thereof and to receive or recover the amount due thereon from the parties thereto.

   The holder is a person who has the legal right to possess the instrument. Physical possession of the instrument is not absolutely necessary. When the note, bill or cheque is lost or destroyed, the holder of such instrument is the person so entitled at the time of such loss or destruction. The finder of a lost instrument is not the holder. The essential point here is that the holder must have the legal right to possess the instrument in his own name and must be entitled to receive the amount from the parties thereto.

3. *Payee :* Payee is the person to whom the money is payable. He is the person named in the instrument to whom or to whose order the money is by the instrument directed to be said (Section 7).

4. *Acceptor :* Only a bill of exchange needs acceptance. After drawing the bill of exchange, the drawer sends the bill to the acceptor for his acceptance. He may sign across the bill with or without the words "Accepted." The acceptor of the bill of exchange may have to pay the money to the holder of the bill on the due date, when presented for payment.

5. *Endorser and Endorsee :* The person who transfers the right of a Negotiable instrument by endorsement is called endorser and the person in whose favour the instrument is endorsed is called endorsee.

## BILL OF EXCHANGE

A Bill of Exchange is a common credit instrument. Section 5 of the Negotiable Instrument Act, 1881 defines a bill of exchange as 'an instrument in writing containing an unconditional order, signed by, the maker, directing a certain person to pay a certain sum of money only to, or to the order of, a certain person or to the bearer of the instrument."

There are usually three parties to a bill of exchange- drawer, drawee and acceptor. In a credit transaction, a bill is used in the following way. When 'A' sells goods to 'B' on credit, 'B' draws a bill of exchange for a specified period (say 1 month) in favour of 'A'. The bill is sent to 'C' for his acceptance. When C signs across the bill with or without the word "Accepted", he becomes the acceptor. After acceptance, the bill is sent to A (Payee) who is also the holder. He can transfer this right to any third party by endorsement and delivery. In case he needs money before the due date, he can discount the bill with a bank. Otherwise he will present the bill on the due date to 'C' (Acceptor) who will pay the amount to 'A'.

### Parties to the Bill of Exchange

1. ***Debtor and Creditor :*** When person buys goods on credit, he is a debtor and the person from whom he receives the goods on credit is called 'Creditor'.

2. ***Drawer and Drawee :*** When the creditor draws a bill on the debtor, he becomes the 'drawer' and the debtor on whose name the bill is drawn becomes the 'drawee'.

3. ***Acceptor :*** The creditor (drawer), after, having drawn the bill, sends the bill to the Drawee (Debtor) for acceptance. Once the Drawee accepts the bill, the (Drawee) becomes the acceptor.

In case the creditor wants that the bill should be accepted for payment by a more reliable person (Bank), he (creditor) may ask the Drawee (Debtor) to get the banker's acceptance. Once the banker accepts such bill, the banker will be the 'Acceptor'. On the due date, the bill will be presented for payment to the Acceptor.

4. ***Payee :*** The accepted bill will be handed over to the creditor who will receive the payment on the due date from the Acceptor. The person who is entitled to receive the money in his name is called 'Payee'.

5. ***Holder :*** Holder is a person who is legally entitled to the possession of

the negotiable instrument in his own name and to receive the amount thereof.

6. ***Endorser and Endorsee :*** If the holder of the bill needs money immediately, or at any time, he can transfer the right to someone else. The act of transferring his right of ownership to another person can be done by 'Endorsement'. The person who endorses the instrument is called 'Endorser' and in whose favour it is endorsed is 'Endorsee'.

## Essentials of a Bill of Exchange

The essential ingredients of a bill of exchange are similar to promissory note:

(1) The instrument must be in writing.

(2) It must contain an unconditional and express order to pay.

(3) It should be signed by the maker (drawer of the bill of exchange).

(4) There are usually three parties to the Bill of Exchange - Drawer, Drawee and Payee. Sometimes, the drawee and payee may be the same persons when there are two parties to the bill.

(5) The drawer should direct a certain person to pay the money. Such certain persons should accept the bill of exchange.

(6) The amount of money payable should be certain and it must be paid in legal tender. Section 5 clearly indicates that it is a contract to pay money only and nothing else as in the case of promissory note. The sum payable may be "certain" within the meaning of Section 5 and Section 4, although it may include future interest or is payable at an indicated rate of exchange.

(7) A bill of exchange may be payable either on demand or after sometime. When a bill is payable on demand, it is known as Demand Bill. If it is payable after a specified period, then it is known as Time bill. As in the case of promissory notes, the bill matures for payment three days after the day on which the bill is deemed to be payable.

(8) An order bill is one which is payable to the payee or to his order and a bearer bill is one which is payable to the bearer.

# CHEQUES

Section 6 of the Negotiable Instruments Act, 1881 defines a cheque as "a bill of exchange drawn on a specified banker and not express to be payable otherwise than on demand." A cheque is defined as a bill of exchange. Therefore, the characteristics of a bill of exchange are the same for a cheque. These are three parties to cheque-drawer, drawee and payee. The cheque is drawn only on a banker and therefore, the drawee will always be a banker.

Specimen of a Cheque

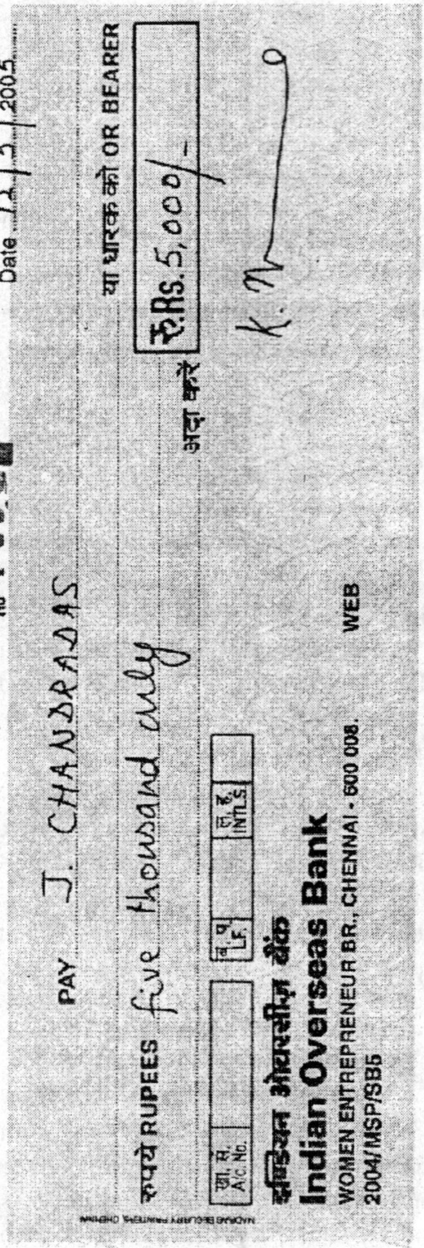

## Essential Features

1. *An Instrument in writing :* A cheque is a written order signed by the drawer. The cheque may be written with a pen or pencil. It may also be a typewritten or printed one. In practice, banks do not pay cheques written in pencil since they are capable of being easily altered. In modern times, cheque writers (special typewriters for exclusive use of writing cheques) are being used for writing cheques to avoid alterations. Although the Act has not specified the format of a cheque, the bankers normally insist that the printed standardised cheques supplied by them to the respective customers should be used. They reserve the right to refuse payment of any cheque drawn otherwise. A customer cannot design a cheque and issue it for payment.

2. *Unconditional Order :* It is an order to pay money without any condition even if the customer adds the word ' Please' preceding the word "Pay" meaning "Please Pay", it is deemed to be an order. When payment is made by the companies and public bodies, they expect the payees to sign a receipt for the record purposes. The requirement of the payee's receipt attached with the cheque makes the instrument unconditional. But if the requirement is part of the order, i.e., the banker is authorised to pay only if the payee gives a proper receipt, then the drawer's order is deemed to be conditional and the instrument is not a cheque.

3. *A Certain Sum of Money Only :* A cheque is drawn for the payment of money only and nothing else. No provision for calculation of interest can be made while drawing a cheque. It should be a definite amount stated in rupees and paise.

4. *Signed by the Drawer :* A cheque should be signed by the drawer or any person duly authorised by him. In the case of an illiterate person, his left hand thumb impression is to be affixed on the cheque in lieu of his signature. The banker should exercise great care and caution in paying cheques bearing such impressions or marks.

5. *Payee Must be Certain :* Payee is the person who is entitled to receive money from the bank. Payee may be an individual, firm, body corporate or any other institution as the case may be. A cheque may be payable to a certain person or order or bearer. If it is a bearer cheque the banker will pay the cheque to anyone who presents it for payment through the counter. Even a finder of the lost cheque may encash it. But if it is an order cheque, the banker takes adequate precautions to ensure the payment to the right person. A cheque may also drawn payable to "Self or order," which means payable to the drawer himself. Similarly, a cheque may be drawn without mentioning the payee's name at all. *e.g.*, "Pay cash." This is to be construed as a bearer cheque.

6. *Date of the Cheque :* A cheque should be dated, as the payment will be made by the banker on or after such date. A cheque may be post-dated or anti-

dated. From the point of view of a banker, a post-dated cheque is one which bears a date later than the date of presentation for payment. An anti-dated cheque is one which bears a date prior to the date of presentation. A cheque should be scrutinized by the banker. If it is a post-dated, the banker should not pay the money. He may ask the customer to present the cheque on or after the date appearing on the face of the cheque. In the case of antidated cheque, if it has been in circulation for more than 6 months from the date of the cheque, it becomes a stale cheque. A stale cheque will be dishonoured by the banker. In case of undated cheque, the customer himself may write the current date. A banker can return an undated cheque, as he is not sure of the date of issue.

7. *Amount :* The amount of the cheque should be clearly mentioned in words and figures. Section 18 says, "If the amount undertaken or ordered to be paid is stated differently in figures and in words, the amount stated in words shall be the undertaken or ordered to be paid." However, in practice, the banker will return the cheque if there is difference in words and figures.

8. *Specified Banker :* A cheque is a bill of exchange drawn on a specified banker only and not on any other individual, body, corporate or otherwise. The cheque should contain particulars relating to the name of the bank, branch at which it is issued, address of the branch etc., to enable the holder to present the cheque for payment.

9. *Payable on Demand :* A cheque is always payable on demand although the drawer of a cheque has not specified the time or period of such payment in the cheque. The cheque should be presented to the bank for payment within a reasonable time.

Section 64 clearly points out that promissory notes, bill of exchange and cheque must be presented for payment to the maker, acceptor or drawee thereof respectively, by or behalf of the holder. In default of such presentment, the other parties thereto are not liable thereon to the holder. In the case of a cheque, it should be presented for payment within a maximum period of six months from the date of the cheque. Presentment for payment must be made during the usual hours of business and within banking hours (Section 65).

A promissory note may be payable in instalments. But a cheque should be payable at one time. The banker should either honour the cheque or dishonour the cheque.

A cheque must be presented at the bank upon which it is drawn. In fact it should be drawn at the same branch at which the customer has the account. If a cheque is not presented for payment within a reasonable time of its issue and thereby any loss is suffered through the delay, the drawer is discharged to the extent of such damage, that is to say, to the extent to which such drawer or person is a creditor of the banker to a larger amount than he would have been if such cheque had been paid (Section 84). A cheque should be presented within 6 months from the date of issue but what is a reasonable time depends on the nature of the instrument, the usage of trade and the facts of a particular case (Section 84(2)).

## DRAFTS

Draft is an instrument issued by the bank to its customers on receipt of full value received. It is payable at branches of the bank wherever it is mentioned. It is otherwise cash readily available to the customer. It is also a security paper for the banks.

Draft and banker's cheque are one and the same excepting for the fact that drafts are payable outside the center of the issue. Otherwise, locally payable drafts are called Banker's cheque.

### Features of the draft

1. If the sum of the draft crosses the limit of 50,000, two authorised signatures are required.
2. Currency is payable to anyone but draft is payable only to a specified person.
3. Validity of the draft is only for 6 months. It can be revalidated beyond that. After confirmation. it can be either cancelled or encashed.
4. Draft can be endorsed to another person subject to the provisions of Negotiable Instrument Act.
5. Countermanding of the draft is not permitted in case of any dispute arises because of the assurance given by the bank.
6. Duplicate draft can be obtained, if the draft is lost as there is no restriction imposed for the same.

## MODEL QUESTIONS

**Section - A**

1. What do you mean by Negotiable Instrument?
2. Define a cheque.
3. Define bill of exchange.
4. What is an unconditional order?
5. What is a promissory note?
6. Who is a payee?
7. Bring out the specimen of a promissory note and a cheque.
8. What do you mean by a draft?

**Section - B**

1. Define a Negotiable Instrument and explain its characteristics.
2. Describe briefly the characteristics of a promissory note.
3. Bring out clearly the characteristics of a cheque.
4. Write about the parties a person may come across while dealing with Negotiable Instruments.
5. State the presumptions relating to negotiable Instruments.
6. Explain the features of draft.

**Section - C**

1. What is a Bill of Exchange? What are the essentials of bills of exchange?
2. Give the specimen of a cheque and explain its essential features.
3. What are the essential features of a cheque?
4. Distinguish between a bill of exchange and a cheque.

# 15

# CROSSING AND ENDORSEMENTS

## CROSSING OF CHEQUES

In the early years cheques were invariably drawn payable to the bearer. Crossing of cheques originated only in the 18th century, as the open cheques were liable to great risks in the course of circulation. Many times the clerks in the clearinghouse were assaulted and robbed off the open cheques. Gradually the practice of crossing developed inside and outside the clearinghouses. However, only in 1858, crossing was legally recognised in England.

The significance of crossing is that a crossed cheque should be presented through the customer's account only. Direct payment through the counter will not be made by the banker. Even if a crossed cheque is stolen and fraudulently converted, the culprit can easily be identified.

A crossing is a direction to the banker that payment should not be made through the counter. *The object of crossing is to ensure the payment being made to the right person.* There are two kinds of crossing:

*(a)* General Crossing

*(b)* Special Crossing

**Definition: (General Crossing)**

Section 123 of the Negotiable Instrument Act, 1881 defines a Crossing as "Where a cheque bears across its face an addition of the words "and company" or any thereof, between two parallel transverse lines, or of two parallel transverse lines simply, either with or without the words "not negotiable", that addition shall be deemed a crossing, and the cheque shall be deemed to be crossed generally."

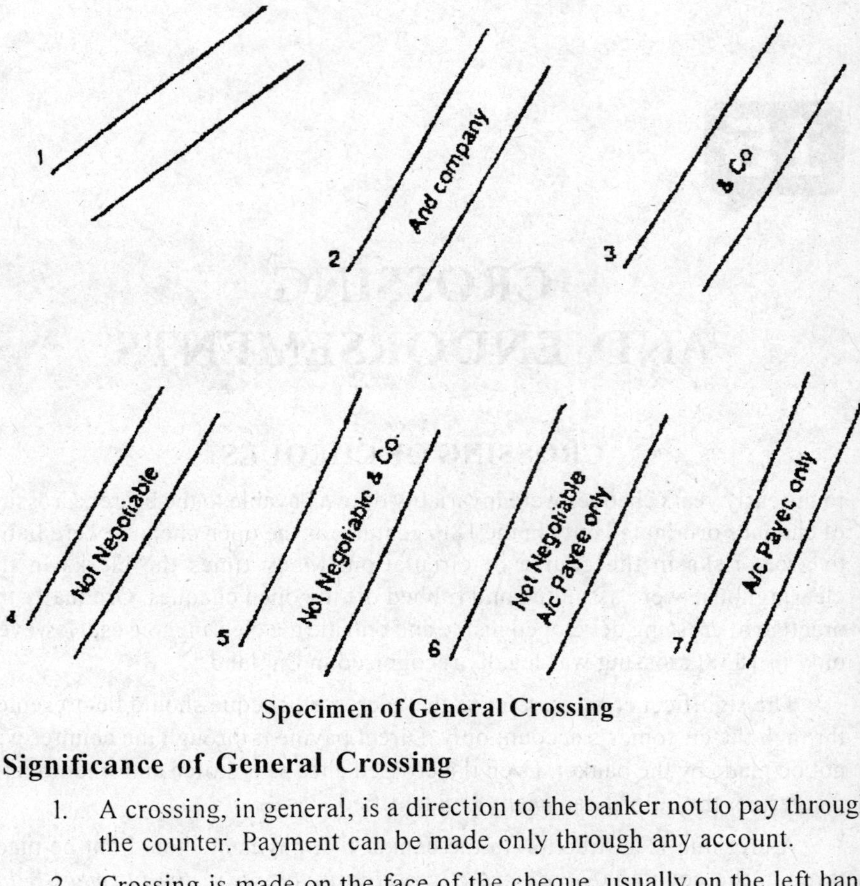


**Specimen of General Crossing**

## Significance of General Crossing

1. A crossing, in general, is a direction to the banker not to pay through the counter. Payment can be made only through any account.
2. Crossing is made on the face of the cheque, usually on the left hand top comer of the cheque.
3. General Crossing may be made as per the illustrations given above.
4. The two lines contemplated in Section 123 should be parallel only and not crosswise or in any other manner.

## Definition : (Special Crossing)

According to Section 124, a special crossing is defined as "where a cheque bears across its face an addition of the name of a banker, either with or without the words "not negotiable" that addition shall be deemed a crossing, and the cheque shall be deemed to be crossed specially, and to be crossed to that banker."

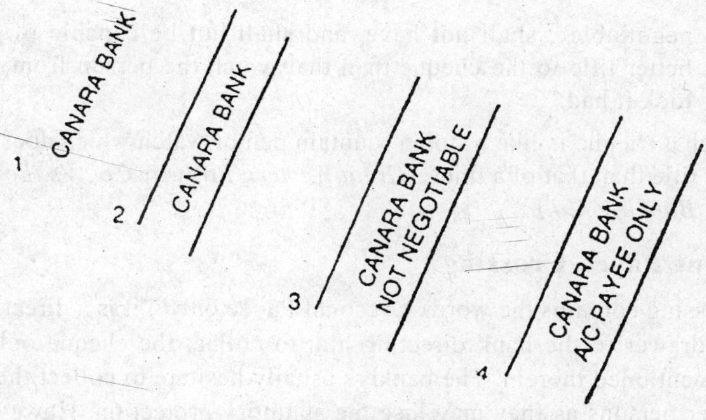


**Specimen of Special Crossing.**

## Significance of Special Crossing

1. Special crossing contains the name of the bank within the lines. In some cases the name of the bank itself might appear without the parallel transverse lines. Even in this case, it is considered as a special crossing.
2. In the case of a cheque marked with the name of a bank, the cheque should be presented for payment only through the bank.
3. Special crossing makes the cheque still safer as the fraudulent person would find it more difficult to convert it as the banker whose name mentioned in the cheque is likely to know the customer.

## Not Negotiable Crossing

Section 123 and 124 permit the use of the words "Not Negotiable" in the general and special crossings. This serves as the same purpose as in the case of "Payees Account only." These words "Not negotiable" and "Account Payee only" do not make the cheque non-transferable but takes away one of the two attributes of negotiability of the instrument which is an important character of a negotiable instrument, i.e., transferability free from equities. An illustration would help to understand the meaning:

'A' has issued a cheque in favour of 'B. ' 'C' stole the cheque from 'B' and gave it to 'D' for a valid consideration. 'D' received the cheque from 'C' without the knowledge of the fact that 'C' had stolen it :

(*i*) If it is a cheque *without* 'Not negotiable' crossing, 'D' will be a holder in due course and have valid title though 'C' does not have a title to the cheque.

(*ii*) It is a cheque with "Not negotiable" crossing then 'D' cannot enjoy an absolute ownership. Section 130 says, "A person taking a cheque crossed generally or specially bearing in either case the words "not

> negotiable", shall not have, and shall not be capable of giving, a better title to the cheque than that which the person from whom he took it had."

Such a cheque is like a stolen fountain pen or watch which does not have a better title than that of a thief. *(Great Western Railway Co., Vs. London and County Banking Co.).*

## Account Payee Crossing

If a crossing contains the words "Account Payee only", it is a direction given by the drawer to the bank directing him to collect the cheque only for the payee mentioned therein. The bankers usually hesitate to collect the cheques for other persons as they may lose the statutory protection. However, if the amount is small bankers collect such crossed cheques for their trusted customers. In fact this type of crossing is not recognised by the Negotiable Instruments Act although such type of crossing prevails in the usage.

## Double Crossing

If a cheque is crossed specially in favour of two bankers, it is known as "Double Crossing." A cheque cannot, ordinarily, have two special crossings. If a bank does not have a branch at a place of paying banker, another bank's name may also be used in the crossing in which case the other bank will act as an agent for the collecting bank. Section 127 says, "Where a cheque is crossed specially to more than one banker, except when crossed to an agent for the purpose of collection, the banker on whom it is drawn shall refuse payment thereof."

## Safest Crossing

As early as in 1957, the Council of Institute of Chartered Accountants in England and Wales referred to the combination of "Not negotiable" and "Account Payee" crossing as the safest crossing. This type of crossing secures the advantages of both. A cheque may be crossed by any one before it is made payable.

Crossing, being a material part of a cheque, cannot be obliterated or removed. However, the crossing of a cheque can be cancelled only by the drawer. He should also write "Pay Cash" followed by his signature. If a paying banker pays an erased crossed cheque, he will be held liable if any problem arises afterwards. Section 89 gives protection to the paying banker. "Where a cheque is presented for payment which does not at the time of presentation appear to be crossed or to have had a crossing which has been obliterated, payment thereof by a person or banker liable to pay, and paying the same according to the apparent tenor thereof at the time of payment and otherwise in due course, shall discharge such person or banker from all liability thereon;

and such payment shall not be questioned by reason of the instrument having been altered or the cheque crossed."

The banker is liable to pay the instrument if the obliteration of crossing is not apparent and the payment is made in due course.

## Endorsement

The word "Endorsement" is derived from a Latin word 'indorsum' meaning at the back.' This means that endorsement may be made at the back of the instrument. But the Act states that endorsement may be made:

*(i)* By signing at the back or face of the instrument; or

*(ii)* By signing on a slip of paper attached thereto, called "Allonge",

or

*(iii)* By signing a stamped paper intended for endorsement and by delivery.

The person who endorses a negotiable instrument is called 'Endorser' and in whose favour it is payable is known as 'Endorsee.'

## Definition of Endorsement

As per Section 15 of the Negotiable Instruments Act, 1881, Endorsement is defined as "When the maker or holder of a negotiable instrument signs the same, otherwise than as such maker, for the purpose of negotiation, on the back or face thereof or on a slip of paper annexed thereto, or so signs, for the same purpose, a stamped paper intended to be completed as a negotiable instrument, he is said to endorse the same, and is called the "endorser."

The transfer of ownership of a negotiable instrument may be made in two ways :

1. *By Mere Delivery :* The transfer may be made by mere delivery of the instrument to whom it is to be transferred. This may be done in the case of an instrument payable to the bearer (Section 47).
2. *By Endorsement in the Instrument :* Endorsement is a method by which the holder signs at the back of the instrument and hands over the instrument to whom it is to be paid. Thus, the ownership is transferred. While a bearer instrument can be negotiated by mere delivery, an order instrument requires endorsement and delivery (Section 47 and the last part of Section 46).

Delivery may be either actual delivery or constructive delivery. In the case of actual delivery, the endorser hand overs the instrument to the endorsee or to his agent. But in the case of constructive delivery, the endorser advises his bank to transfer the instrument to the endorsee's credit. The illustration is given in Section 47.

**Illustration : (Section 47)**

*(a) Actual Delivery :* 'A,' the holder of a negotiable instrument payable to the bearer, delivers it to 'B's agent to keep for 'B.' The instrument has been negotiated.

*(b) Constructive Delivery :* 'A,' the holder of a negotiable instrument payable to bearer, which is in the hands of 'A's banker who is at the time the banker of 'B', directs the banker to transfer the instrument to 'B's credit in the Banker's account with 'B.' The banker does so and accordingly now possesses the instrument as 'B's agent. The instrument has been negotiated, and 'B' has become the holder.

The endorsement is deemed to be complete only when it is delivered to the transferee with an intention of transferring the rights. Before delivery, the endorser may revoke the contract, by cancelling endorsement. Transfer can also be made, as stated in the last part of the definition (Section 15), by a written document signed by the transferor. If it is assigned so, then it does not come under the purview of 'negotiation, 'but it comes under the provisions of the Transfer of Property Act. One of the important differences between negotiation and assignment is that in the case of negotiation, the transferee becomes holder in due course if he takes the instrument in good faith and for value regardless of the title of the transferor whereas in the case of an assignment, he does not become automatically the holder in due course. He does not have a better title than that of the transferor even though he takes the instrument in good faith and for value.

*In the case of Indian Government Securities, an endorsement made on the back of the instrument only is valid.* (Section 6 of the Indian Securities Act, 1886).

In the case of a bearer negotiable instrument, the mere signature on the back of the instrument constitutes an endorsement. An endorsement by a rubber impression or in any other form of facsimile signature is valid at law. But the bankers do not accept them in practice. An endorsement in pencil, although it is quite valid legally, it would be difficult to establish the fact at a later date as alteration is possible.

Although the law permits endorsement on the face of the instrument, invariably endorsements are made on the back of the instrument. Any number of endorsements can be made. In case there is no space for further endorsement, a slip of paper known as 'allonge' is attached to the instrument, as stated in Section 15 and further endorsements may be made on it. But the first endorsement on the allonge should be made in such a way that the first half of such endorsement be made in the instrument and the latter half in the allonge; similarly the signature of the endorser.

Endorsements may be made in the vernacular language also provided the parties understand it fully. An illiterate person may endorse by putting his left hand thumb impression in the presence of certain other person who should sign it as a witness.

Endorsement should be made by all payees. For example, if a cheque is made payable to more than one payee, all must endorse. The endorsement is valid even if the endorsements have been made by them on different dates but before the due of the instrument. *(Seshi Reddi Vs. Venkata Subbayya, 1953).*

An endorsement made by a minor is valid but the endorsee can enforce his rights only against all parties except the minor.

An endorsement should be made for its entire amount. But if part of the instrument has already been paid, endorsement for the balance amount may be permitted as per Section 56. But a note to this effect should be shown in the instrument. Section 56 states: "No writing on a negotiable instrument is valid for the purpose of negotiation if such writing purports to transfer only a part of the amount appearing to be due on the instrument; but where such amount has been partly paid, a note to that effect may be endorsed on the instrument, which may then be negotiated for the balance."

The effect of endorsement is that the property therein, together with the right of further negotiation passes to the endorsee.

## Duration of Negotiability

According to Section 60 of the Act, "A negotiable instrument may be negotiated (except by the maker, drawee or acceptor after maturity) until payment or satisfaction thereof by the maker, drawee or acceptor at or after maturity, but not after such payment or satisfaction.

The negotiable instrument may be negotiated till such a time the maker, drawee or acceptor discharges the instrument. A cheque may be in circulation for a period of six months and afterwards it becomes stale.

## Who May Negotiate?

According to Section 51, "Every sole maker, drawer, payee or endorsee, or all of several joint makers, drawers, payees or endorsees of a negotiable instrument may, if the negotiability of such instrument has not been restricted or excluded as mentioned in Section 50, endorse and negotiate the same."

Negotiation may be made only when it is not restricted by Section 50 of the Act. The maker or drawer should possess the instrument lawfully and the payee or endorsee should be a holder of the instrument. A person who is not a party to the instrument cannot negotiate, *e.g.*, a finder of the lost cheque or a thief.

## Legal Consequences

Section 50 states, "The endorsement of a negotiable instrument followed by delivery to the endorsee the property therein with the right of further negotiation; but the endorsement may, by express words, restrict or exclude such right or may merely constitute the endorsee, an agent to endorse the instrument, or to receive its contents for the endorser, or for some other specified person."

In addition to the meaning 'transferring the title' for endorsement, there are other meanings as referred by a Judge in a South African case, *National Bank Vs. Patterson.* They are:

(1) Every signature appearing on the back of any negotiable instrument may purport to receipt of the value of the instrument.

(2) Signature identifies the individual or endorser.

(3) A signature at the back of the instrument signifies that the transfer is made by him with an intention of undertaking the liability.

## Forged Endorsement

A forged endorsement is one in which the signature of the endorser is forged. The validity of such endorsement depends on the nature of the instrument as to whether it is a bearer instrument or order one.

If it is a bearer instrument, as endorsements may be just by delivery even without signing at the back, forgery does not invalidate such instrument. The holder in due course of a negotiable instrument can exercise his right to receive the money from acceptor, maker or any one prior to him. For example, A endorses a bearer instrument in favour of 'B'. 'C' steals it from 'B' and endorses it to 'D' for valid consideration. 'D' becomes holder in due course. He can enforce his rights against 'A' and 'B' although 'C' does not have a title.

But if it is an order instrument, a holder of such instrument with forged endorsement cannot transfer its title to the endorsees. If endorsed, the endorsee cannot exercise his right as a holder in due course. However, the true owner's right is not affected. For example, A endorses an order instrument in favour of 'B'. 'C' steals it and endorses it to 'D' for valid consideration. Although 'D' is a holder in due course, he cannot get any title to the instrument. The true owner 'B' can enforce the right and claim money from 'A' even if 'D' had claimed the money earlier from 'A'. 'B' can also claim the money from 'D' if D had received payment from 'A.' According to Section 41 "an acceptor of a bill of exchange already endorsed is not relieved from liability by reason that such endorsement is forged, if he knew or had reason to believe the endorsement to be forged when he accepted the bill."

In the case of an order cheque, the banker cannot be held liable just because he makes payment of a cheque with forged endorsement. The paying banker gets protection under Section 85 which reads as follows:

"Where a cheque payable to order purports to be indorsed by or on behalf of the payee the drawee is discharged by payment in due course."

In the same way a bank gets protection under Section, 85 A towards the payment of a bank draft.

The endorser creates the legal consequences as follows:

(1) The endorser transfers the title of the instrument in favour of the endorsee and the endorsee acquires the properties in the instrument and enjoys further right of negotiation.

(2) The endorser guarantees that the document is genuine and all signatures prior to his endorsement are genuine.

(3) The endorser undertakes to pay if the instrument is dishonoured.

(4) The instrument may be endorsed in favour of an agent. In case of the death of the principal, the endorsement has been made in favour of an endorsee: (1) Specific purpose; (2) Collecting of instrument, does not invalid. The Law of agency cannot be exercised in this case as in (case of *Mohthireddy Vs.' Pothvireddy,* A.I.R., 1963, A.P., 313.

## Types of Endorsement

In addition to the meaning transferring the title for endorsement, endorsement is broadly classified into:

(1) Blank or General endorsement.

(2) Full or Special endorsement.

(3) Partial endorsement.

(4) Conditional endorsement.

(5) Restrictive endorsement.

(6) Sans Recourse endorsement.

1. *Blank or General Endorsement :* If the endorser signs his name only on the back of the instrument without writing the name of the payee (the person to whom it is payable), it is called 'Blank Endorsement or General Endorsement [Section 16 *(i)*]. By doing so, he has transferred the title in favour of the endorsee. As the name of the endorsee does not appear in the endorsement, an endorsement in blank is very risky. The finder of such instrument can easily encash it.

A blank endorsement converts an order instrument into a bearer one, transferable by mere delivery. Section 54 of the Act points out, "Subject to the provisions herein after contained as to crossed cheques, a negotiable instrument endorsed in blank is payable to the bearer thereof even although originally payable to order."

An endorsement in blank may be converted by its holder into full endorsement by writing his name or payee's name above the signature. He can do so even without becoming a party to such endorsements.

2. *Full or Special Endorsement :* In the case of full endorsement, the name of the payee should be specified with the endorser's signature.

*For example :*

Pay to Ranjan or order

(Sd/-) Gopal

An endorsement without the words 'or order' also means the same.

Section 16 *(i)* states : "If the indorser signs his name only, the endorsement is said to be "in blank," and if he adds a direction to pay the amount mentioned in the instrument to, or to the order of, a specified person, the indorsment is said to be "in full", and the person so specified is called the "indorsee" of the instrument.

3. *Partial Endorsement :* Partial endorsement is one when part of the amount mentioned in the instrument is endorsed in favour of the endorsee. While endorsement is to be made for the full amount, partial endorsement is permitted when part of the amount has already been paid on the instrument (Section 56). A note to this effect should be shown in the instrument.

4. *Conditional Endorsement :* A conditional endorsement, also known as qualified endorsement, is one wherein the endorser imposes certain conditions on his endorsement.

*For example :*

Pay to Raman on his signing the enclosed document.

(Sd/-) David

According to Section 52 of the Act, "The indorser of a negotiable instrument may, by express words in the endorsement exclude his own liability thereon, or make such liability or the right of the indorsee to receive the amount due thereon depend upon the happening of a specified event although such event may never happen."

A negotiable instrument cannot be drawn conditionally; but an endorsement may be made conditionally. The endorser's liability arises on the happening or not happening of a specified event as stated in the endorsement.

If things happen contrary to the conditions specified therein, the endorser's liability is extinguished. However, all parties prior to his conditional endorsement are liable to the endorser. The conditional endorsement is applicable only between such endorser and endorsee.

5. *Restrictive Endorsement :* If the endorser restricts further endorsement either by express words or by restricting further negotiation, the endorsement is known as 'Restrictive Endorsement.'

*For example :*

Pay Kannan only

Pay John or order - Notice of dishonour not required.

Section 50 of the Act states about the restrictive endorsement. This endorsement either restricts further endorsement or allows the subsequent endorsees to deal with the instrument in the manner directed.

6. *Facultative Endorsement :* In the case of conditional endorsement, the endorser imposes certain conditions and excludes his liability in a negotiable instrument. In the same way, he can give up some of his rights. If the endorser, while making such endorsements, gives up his rights, the endorsement is called 'Facultative endorsement.'

*For example :*

Pay Kannan or order - Notice of dishonour waived

(Sd/-) David

Ordinarily the endorsee is liable to give notice of dishonour to all the parties so that he could hold them responsible for payment of money. But in the above case, even if the notice is not served on the endorser, David, he is liable to the holder, if the instrument is dishonoured.

7. *Sans Recourse Endorsement :* The phrase 'Sans Recourse' means without recourse or without reference. If the endorser intends to exclude his own liability in the endorsement from all subsequent endorsers, he may use this type of endorsement.

*For instance :*

Pay Shankar or order without recourse to me

(Sd/-) David

The second paragraph of Section 52 states, "where an indorser so excludes his liability and afterwards becomes the holder of the instrument, all intermediate endorsers are liable to him."

## Illustrations as Given in Section 52 of the Act

(1) The endorser of a negotiable instrument signs his name, adding the words—"Without recourse." Upon this instrument, he incurs no liability.

(2) 'A' is the payee and holder of a negotiable instrument. Excluding personal liability by an endorsement "without recourse," he transfers the instrument to 'B' and 'B' endorses it to 'C', who indorses it to 'A.' 'A' is not only reinstated in his former rights, but has the rights of an indorsee against 'B' and 'C'.

The original holder, 'A', having endorsed the instrument in favour of 'B', 'B' to 'C', has again become the holder. If the bill is dishonoured, 'A' has the right to recover the money from prior parties, 'B' and 'C.' But A himself, being the prior party, he is liable to all of them. Just as 'A' is having the right to sue the previous endorsers, 'B' and 'C' also have the right to sue 'A' in any other type of endorsement.

But the second para of Section 52 gives exclusive right to 'A'. In case A has resorted to sans recourse endorsement he may exclude his liability but he will be entitled to sue the prior parties. In short, A cannot be held liable and recover the money. This principle is known as 'Circuiting of action."

## MODEL QUESTIONS

**Section - A**

1. What is the objective of crossing?
2. State the significance of General Crossing.
3. Give the specimen of General Crossing and Special Crossing.
4. What is the advantage of Double Crossing?
5. Distinguish between negotiation and assignment of a negotiable instrument.

**Section - B**

1. Define crossing. Explain the several types of crossing bringing out clearly their significance.
2. What do you understand by the term "Not Negotiable Crossing"?
3. Write short notes on :

   1. Account payee crossing.

   2. Double crossing.

   3. Safest crossing.
4. Explain with illustration the ways through which the ownership of negotiable instruments be transferred.
5. What is an endorsement? What are the requisites of a valid endorsement?
6. What is a forged endorsement? Does forgery invalidate the instrument? Explain.
7. Write short notes on :

*(a)* Facultative endorsement.

*(b)* Sans recourse endorsement.

**Section - C**

1. Define endorsement. Explain the various types of endorsements.
2. Explain the significance of general and special crossing.

16

# PAYMENT AND COLLECTION OF CHEQUES

## PAYMENT OF CHEQUES

When a customer issues a cheque, it is an order to the banker directing him to pay according to his mandate. It is a statutory obligation on the part of the banker to honour customer's cheques. But it is an obligation subject to certain conditions like availability of funds, drawing cheques properly, etc. The obligation duty is only to the drawer of the cheque and not to the holder. If he fails to pay the cheque issued by the customer, he may have to compensate the loss as stated in Section 31 of the Negotiable Instruments Act, 1881.

Section 31 says, "The drawee of a cheque having sufficient funds of the drawer in his hands properly applicable to the payment of such cheque must pay the cheque when duly required so to do, and, in default of such payment, must compensate the drawer for any loss or damage caused by such default."

A banker must deal with the payment of cheque carefully. His position is like that of sitting in between the devil and the deep sea. If he honours a cheque by mistake the money is lost and at the same time, if he dishonours the cheque without sufficient reasons, he is to compensate the drawer for the loss suffered by him. The paying *banker* should take the *following precautions before honouring a cheque :*

1. *Proper Form of a Cheque :* The banker should see whether the cheque presented at the counter is the one which he had supplied to the customer. The bankers can refuse the payment of any cheque drawn otherwise. Another view

is that the banker may not be justified in refusing payment if a cheque form supplied to another customer is used. *(Bihta Co-operative Development and Cane Marketing Union Ltd., and Another Vs. Bank of Bihar Ltd., and Others).* However, a note in the cheque book states, "No blank cheque forms from this book should be given to others even if they represent themselves as customers of the bank and under no circumstances whatever cheques to be given to unknown persons in exchange for cash."

2. *Date of the Cheque* : A banker should see whether a cheque has been properly dated. If it is a post-dated cheque, he should not pay the cheque. He may ask the customer to present the cheque on or after the date appearing on the face of the cheque. But if it is a stale cheque, he may return the cheque. In case the cheque bears no date, the banker may return the cheque, as he is not sure of the date of issue of the cheque.

3. *Language* : A cheque should be drawn in a language to be under-stood by the banker. In India, cheques are drawn in English or in the local language. If the banker is not able to understand the language, he may refuse the payment.

4. *Crossing* : He should see whether the cheque is crossed. If it is an uncrossed cheque, payment may be made through the counter. If it is a crossed one, he should advise the customer to present the cheque through his account.

5. *Amount* : The amount of the cheque should have been clearly mentioned in words and figures, adding the word "only" or drawing a line after the amount in words. He should not leave any space anywhere as fraudulent insertions or alterations are possible. Although Section 18 suggests the payment of amount stated in words, when there is a discrepancy between words and figures, the banker will return such cheques in the normal practice.

6. *Sufficient Funds* : Before honouring the cheque, the banker should essentially check the customer's account and ensure whether there are adequate funds to honour the cheque. In fact, the banker has to honour or dishonour the cheque. He cannot make part payment. The banker should also see whether he had agreed for an overdraft or cash credit to enable him to pay the cheque. For the purpose of computation of balance, the customer cannot expect a banker to adjust from any other account maintained by him either in the same branch or in any other branch. However, the minimum balance maintained in a current account or savings account as the case may be, can be used for payment of cheque. The banker cannot dishonour a cheque for want of minimum balance in any account. In case there is no minimum balance, he is empowered to charge the customer with incidental charges. Payment for cheques should be made in the chronological order. In case two cheques are presented simultaneously through clearing and if the balance in the customer's account is just adequate to honour one of the cheques, he must honour such cheque

accordingly. The banker cannot treat them as one demand as they were presented together and dishonour both.

7. *Signature :* At the time of opening an account the banker obtains specimen signature of the customer. He retains it with him carefully. Before paying any cheque, the banker should scrutinize the customer's signature and see whether it tallies with the specimen signature. Normally he does the scrutiny when there is a doubt about the genuineness of the signature. If he finds any difference, he should refuse payment. Even in the case of joint account a bank should verify the signature of the parties concerned and even if one of the signatures is forged, he will be held liable for the payment of such cheque. If need be, the cheques should be examined with help of ultra violet rays/special lamps. As a person's signature is likely to change over a period of time, fresh specimen signatures of the customers may be obtained periodically.

8. *Banking Hours :* A banker should be careful to pay the money only during the banking hours. Section 65 points out "Presentment for payment. must be made during the usual hours of business and if at a banker's, within banking hours." 'Banking Hours', in this context, means the period of time during which the public transact banking business. The bankers would be held liable if he makes payment before or after the banking hours.

9. *Mutilated Cheques :* A mutilated cheque is one which is torn into pieces. The banker should see whether it is torn with an intention to cancel it. If the material part of the cheque has been torn, he should refuse payment. In case there has been damage at the corner without any damage to the main contents, the cheque may be paid. In case he has doubt about the genuineness of the instrument, he can clarify with the customer.

10. *Endorsement :* The banker should see whether the endorsements are regular. In case of irregular endorsements, cheques should not be paid.

11. *Countermanding Order :* The banker should also verify whether there is any countermanding order from the customer. A countermanding order is an instruction or request from the customer to stop payment of the cheque. The banker should note the following in this regard.

*(a)* The order should be in writing and should include the payee's name, amount of the cheque, cheque number and other particulars, if any.

*(b)* In case of telegraphic or telephonic countermanding, the banker can only postpone payment and cannot refuse payment. The banker has to wait for the written confirmation.

*(c)* The banker should not accept countermanding order from the payee of the cheque. It is only the drawer who has the right to countermand. Therefore, the payee should contact the drawer in case the cheque is lost or stolen. However, depending upon the status of the payee and, other circumstances, the banker must postpone the payment.

12. *Material Alteration :* A cheque is drawn by the customer with a clear direction to the banker to pay a certain sum of money only to a certain person. A change in the mandate can be done only by the drawer. Any alteration made therein without the knowledge of the drawer affecting the rights and liabilities of the parties should be deemed as material alteration.

A material alternation is one which substantially changes the rights and liabilities of the parties or any of the parties to the instrument; or

*(a)* which substantially changes the rights and liabilities of the parties or any of the parties to the instrument; or *(b)* which changes the identity and legal character of the instrument; or *(c)* causes it to speak a different language from that it originally spoke; or *(d)* changes the business effect of the instrument changing any of the following: *(i)* date, *(ii)* amount, *(iii)* place, *(iv)* number of parties *(v)* removal of crossing, *(vi)* converting the order instrument into bearer one.

A casual look at the "Instructions to the customers" printed on the wrapper of the cheque book reveals the following:

1. Cheques should be written in good quality permanent ink or typed in pinpoint typewriter only. While writing, reverse carbon should be used on the cheque to prevent fraudulent alternations.

2. Cheques should be drawn both in words and figures distinctly commencing as near the printed words "Rupees" and "Rs." as possible adding the words, so as to leave no space for fraudulent insertions or alternations.

3. Any alternation in the cheque should be confirmed by the drawer with his full signature.

## Examples of Material Alternation

1. *Date :* The date is an integral part of the cheque. Any change in the date may be made with an intention to postpone the limitation period. A cheque can be in circulation only for 6 months. If six months have lapsed from the date of the cheque, it becomes a stale cheque and the banker will not pay such cheque.

Similarly, a post-dated cheque may be altered to make it appear a current cheque. A postdated cheque is one which bears a date later than the date of presentation at the bank. Such alternations without the authorisation of the drawer is invalid.

In case a cheque is originally dated 29th February '05 (non-existent date) and is altered to 1st March '05 without the signature of the drawer, the banker will not pay the cheque although the cheque is presented on 4th March '05. The banker will consider this change as material alteration.

2. *Amount :* The amount Column of the cheque is an important component of a cheque. The customer should write the amount clearly in 'words' and

'figures'. If there is any difference between words and figures, the banker will not pay the amount and he will return the cheque with the remark 'Amount in words and figures differ'. In case the banker finds that the amount in words is less than the amount mentioned in figures, and pays such lower amount, the customer cannot find fault with the banker.

If the alteration is apparent, a banker will not honour such cheques. However, if the banker pays such cheque, he will be held liable and will not get the statutory protection. If an alternation has been skillfully executed in such a way that the banker cannot find out, the banker can escape from his liability as he is innocent. However, if the customer has drawn a cheque carelessly, leaving blank spaces and if some unscrupulous person has taken advantage of such a situation, the banker cannot be held liable.

3. *Place :* The cheque should be drawn at the specified branch of the bank. If the consumer has used any other cheque leaf other than the one supplied to him, the banker will not honour the cheque. In case the place of payment is altered, it is considered to be material alternation.

4. *Number of Parties :* A customer may draw cheque in the names of more than one person. Strictly speaking, all should jointly present the cheque for payment at the bank. However, a banker may pay to one of the parties if the cheque is signed by all the payees. But if any of the payee's name is removed or added without any authorisation of the drawer, it amounts to material alteration and such cheque should not be paid.

5. *Removal of Crossing :* If crossing is to be removed, the drawer can cancel the crossing by writing across 'Pay Cash' with his full signature. Such cancellation of crossing enables the holder of the cheque to receive cash through the counter.

6. *Converting an Order cheque into a Bearer cheque :* The significance of the bearer cheque is that the banker can pay the amount of the cheque to any one who presents such cheque for payment. But if it is an order cheque, the banker should ensure that the cheque is paid to the right person. While a bearer cheque may be converted to an order cheque, an order cheque can be converted into a bearer cheque only by the drawer. If any other person converts an order cheque into a bearer one, with out the authority of the drawer, it becomes material alteration.

## Alternations permitted by Law

1. The Negotiable Instruments Act of 1881 permits the following :

(a) As per Sec. 125, open cheque/ uncrossed cheque can be crossed by any one for safety. General crossing may be converted into a special crossing.

(b) Sec. 47 permits any holder to convert blank endorsement into endorsement in full.

(c) Sec. 20 of the Negotiable Instruments Act permits any one to fill the blanks in the instrument. For example, if a cheque is undated, the holder can insert the date. The banker will not dishonour the cheque on the ground that the hand-writing/ink used is different.

2. If an alteration does not affect the fundamental character of the instrument, it may be called as immaterial alteration. For example, the word rupees mentioned twice, and then, one is cancelled.

## Steps to prevent Material Alternation

In a busy world, neither the customer nor the banker has leisure time to scrutinize what has already done. Hence, a customer may carelessly draw a cheque and a banker may honour such materially altered cheque, leading to legal problems. The following steps may be undertaken to arrest the material alteration :

## Steps to prevent Material Alternation

1. The customers should be educated about the careful usage and drawing of cheques.
2. The cheque is made of a special paper which should prevent the use of chemicals.
3. The cheque should be printed with a polished surface. In the event of erasure of particulars, it would be immediately noticed by any one.
4. The ultra-violet lights are being used in most of the banks to detect any alteration. All branches are to be provided with such detective devices to check the alterations.

## Circumstances in which a Banker should Refuse Payment

There may be certain special circumstances in which a banker should refuse payment :

1. *Defective Title :* The customer may issue cheques to any person. The banker is not expected to know of the person presenting the cheque for payment. In case of an order cheque, the payment should be made to the person mentioned therein. When the banker notices that an order cheque is presented by some one else other than the payee, without endorsement, he should refuse payment.

If a cheque which has already been countermanded by the drawer is presented for payment, the banker should refuse payment. But in the case of a request made by a person claiming to be a payee to stop payment of a particular cheque, and if such cheque is presented, he should postpone the payment. He may pay the cheque after making proper enquiries. In certain cases, the banker may have certain genuine doubt about the title of the party presenting a cheque, especially when it is drawn for a disproportionately large sum. The banker may have to confirm with the drawer and then only he should decide.

2. *Notice of Death, Insanity or Insolvency :* When the banker receives a formal notice about the death, insanity or insolvency of the customer, the banker should stop operating the account till some executor or administrator is appointed.

A banker might also come across the obituary column or an advertisement in a newspaper about the death of the customer. He may also take this as a notice and stop paying the cheque. But in the case of joint account, he need not stop payment as long as one of them is surviving. However, if the cheque bears the signature of the deceased joint account holder payment should not be made. The banker has to take care to see that he is not carried away by the rumours.

When the customer is adjudicated as insolvent, the banker should not pay his cheques. But the cheques presented prior to the date of adjudication order are considered to have been paid properly if the banker did not receive any notice of insolvency petition. In the same way the banker is justified in refusing payment when he comes to know of the insanity of a customer. He must get the confirmed news of the mental incapacity of his customer.

3. *Countermanding Order :* The banker should stop the payment of a cheque issued by his customer if he has received any instruction or request from his customer to stop the payment of a particular cheque. If any cheque is presented, he must check the payee's name, amount of the cheque, cheque number and other particulars, if any. If he receives such cheques he should not honour such cheque. As a precautionary measure the banker should get the countermanding order from his customer in writing. In the meantime if the message is received through telephone or telegram, he can postpone such payments.

4. *Garnishee Order :* A garnishee order is an order issued by the court directing the banker to stop payment from a particular customer's account. . *The issuance of a garnishee order prevents the banker from paying away a balance up to the total amount for which it is made unless the claim of the judgment creditor has been satisfied.*

5. *By Injunction :* When there has been a dispute relating to certain funds, an injunction order may be passed to freeze a bank account till such a time the matter is settled.

6. *Notice of Closure of accounts :* When the customer intends to close his bank account, he may send a notice specifying a date on which he would close the account with the bank. The notice is given to the bank to enable the holder of cheques to encash them before such a date. The banker should not pay any

cheque presented on or after the date given in the notice. In the same way the banker will also close an undesirable customer's account after giving a reasonable notice. No cheques should be honoured after this date. If the customer fails to close his account within a reasonable time from the date of notice the banker can close the account and send the balance, if any, to the customer.

## COLLECTION OF CHEQUES

The primary function of a commercial bank is to receive deposits and lend them for profit. In addition, he undertakes the responsibility of collecting cheques on behalf of the customer as an incidental function although there is no legal obligation on the part of the banker to collect cheques for his customers.

When a customer receives a cheque, there are two options before him. He should go either to the branch at which the cheque has been issued and encash the cheque or send the cheque through his own bank for collection. As the former is difficult, the customers resort to the help of the bankers to collect their cheques. Thus, the banker has to collect the cheques for his customers and this is an indispensable service rendered by the banker to his customers.

Bankers normally collect either by presenting cheques to the drawee bank across the counter or through clearing. Most of their cheques are collected through clearing houses.

### Clearing Houses

"Clearing" is a simple arrangement through which a bank exchanges cheques drawn on other banks for those drawn on it. In the absence of such clearinghouse, the bankers would be faced with the problem of exchanging their cheques with innumerable banks. Moreover, they may have to deal with larger amount of cash.

Clearing houses are established in most of the cities where the volume of cheques is large. The Reserve Bank of India or State Bank of India act as a clearing house. At places where neither has got a branch, one of the associate banks of State Bank of India situated at the nearby place supervises the clearing. The total amount payable to other banks and the total amount receivable from other banks are computed and presented at the clearinghouse. The difference between the total amount receivable and payable is computed. Depending upon the balance, the bank may either issue a cheque or receive a cheque to settle the account. This arrangement results in considerable saving of time and cost.

While collecting a cheque, a banker acts either as :

*(i)* Holder for value; or

*(ii)* An agent of the customer.

## Holder for Value

On many occasions, the banker is entrusted with the responsibility of collecting outstation cheques. A cheque cannot be collected immediately. It may take two or three days for the banker. In case of outstation cheques, it may take even a week for him to collect the cheque. However, in order to accommodate his customer, the banker may,

*(i)* Pay the customer in anticipation of collection of cheques;

*(ii)* Credit the customer's account;

*(iii)* Allow him to withdraw the money from the bank.

In the above cases, the banker acts as holder for value. When a cheque is paid in and the bank expressly or impliedly allows the customer to draw against the cheque before it is cleared, the banker is a holder for value. In practice, the banker will get an undertaking from the customer to reimburse if such cheque is dishonoured.

According to Sir John Paget , a banker becomes holder for value in any of the following circumstances :

*(a)* By lending further on the strength of the cheque;

*(b)* By paying over and above the amount of the cheque or part of it in cash or in account before its effects are cleared;

*(c)* By agreeing, either then or earlier, or in the course of business, that the customer may draw before the cheque is cleared;

*(d)* By accepting the cheque in allowing reduction of an existing overdraft or some other indebtedness;

*(e)* By giving cash over the counter for the cheque at the time it is paid in for collection.

## Holder in Due Course

According to Sec. 9, "Holder in due course" means any person who for consideration became possessor of a promissory note, bill of exchange or cheque if payable to bearer, or the payee or indorsee thereof, if payable to order, before the amount mentioned in it became payable and without having sufficient cause to believe that any defect existent in the title of the person from whom he derived his title".

1. A person who obtains a negotiable instrument should have got it for valid consideration. In the absence of valid consideration, he cannot become a holder in due course. For instance, if a person has received a cheque as a gift, he cannot become a holder in due course. Similarly, if any one has received a cheque to complete an ill-legal act, he cannot be a holder in due course.

2. He must possess the negotiable instrument before the maturity date. In case of a promissory note or a bill of exchange, a person who receives a bill on the maturity date does not become holder in due course. A holder of a post-dated cheque can claim the right of holder in due course.

3. One should have received the negotiable instrument in good faith and without negligence. If any one has already known about the defect of the instrument and receives this for valid consideration, the possessor cannot claim to be a holder in due course. Even if he has received it in good faith (without knowing the defect in the instrument), but was negligent, he cannot become holder in due course, as he should have taken reasonable care to check the defect.

## Privileges of a Holder in Due Course

1. *Free from all defective title* : The defective title of the previous endorsers, if any, will not adversely affect the rights of the holder in due course. For example, A issues cheque to B, and C steals it from b and endorses to D for valid consideration. In case D has received the cheque in good faith and with out negligence, he can pass on the same to others by endorsement. He can exercise his right with all the previous parties although no consideration was paid by C. One it passes through the holder in due course, the subsequent parties can recover the amount of the instrument from all the previous parties.

2. *Better Title* : The holder in due course obtains a better tile to the instrument than that of a true owner.

3. *Rights not affected* : When an inchoate (incomplete) instrument is completed with a larger amount than it was intended by the maker, the right of the holder in due course to receive the money is not affected. Even the defective title of the previous endorsers will not affect his individual rights. The drawer of a negotiable instrument cannot claim invalidity of the instrument against him.

4. *Enforcement of fictitious Bill* : Where the drawer and payee of a bill are fictitious persons, the holder in due course can hold the acceptor responsible for the payment of bill provided he can prove that the signature of the supposed drawer and first endorser is the same.

5. *No effect on absence of consideration present of unlawful consideration* : Even if an instrument is obtained by fraud, or by means of an offence or for unlawful consideration, the holder in due course can obtain such payment.

6. *Estoppel against denying original validity of instrument* : As per Sec. 120 of the Negotiable Instruments Act, no party either a maker of a promissory note or drawer of a bill of exchange or cheque and acceptor is permitted to deny the validity of the instrument as originally made or drawn.

## Collecting Banker as Agent

If a banker credits the customer's account or pays the customer after collecting the cheque, he acts as an agent of the customer.

The relationship between the customer and bank is that of principal and agent. The bankers, while collecting cheques belonging to other persons, are exposed to tremendous risks. If the banker collects a cheque to which his customer has no title, the banker can be held liable to the true owner for "conversion." Conversion is defined as "unlawful taking, using, disposing or destroying of goods, which is inconsistent with the owner's right of possession."

According to Hart's law of banking (4th edition, p. 606), "conversion means wrongful intermeddling with the goods of another for the purpose of taking them away from party entitled to them."

The banker is engaged in collecting large number of cheques. It would be practically impossible for him to examine every cheque whether it contains forged endorsement or not. To facilitate him, Section 131 was introduced.

## Non-liability of Banker Receiving Payment of Cheque: (Section 131)

"A banker who has in good faith and without negligence received payment for a customer of a cheque crossed generally or specially to himself shall not, in case the title to the cheque proves defective, incur any liability to the true owner of the cheque by reason only of having received such payment."

As in the case of paying banker the protection available to the collecting banker is also conditional: Section 131 affords valuable protection to the collecting banker. The banker is not liable to the true owner for conversion even though his customer's title is defective, provided the following conditions are fulfilled :

*(i)* It is a crossed cheque;

*(ii)* He has received the payment as an agent for collection, and not on his own behalf as a holder;

*(iii)* He has collected the cheque for a customer; and

*(iv)* He has collected the cheque in good faith and without negligence.

1. *Crossed Cheques Only :* The banker can claim statutory protection only in the case of crossed cheques. If he collects an open cheque, this protection is not available to him. Consequently, he is liable to the true owner. The banker should only collect crossed cheques. Bankers themselves cross cheques that come into their hands for collection. This would help them only to the extent of safety of such cheques. These cheques cannot be stolen or encashed. However,

such crossing can not give protection to the collecting banker under Section 131 unless the cheques have already been crossed before reaching the hands of the customer.

2. *To Receive Payment as an Agent :* The banker can claim protection under Section 131 only when he has received payment as an agent of his customer and not as a holder for value. If the banker pays money across the counter for such cheques, he has taken it for granted that he is holder in due course by satisfying the requirements in Section 8. If so, he cannot claim protection under Section 131. But the banker's position is not very unsafe. He gets protection from the Explanation to Section 131 which was added in 1992 whereby the collecting banker can claim protection even in cases where the customer's account has been merely credited with the amount of the cheque before receiving payment thereof.

Explanation to Section 131: "A banker receives payment of a crossed cheque for a customer within the meaning of this section notwithstanding that he credits his customer's account with the amount of the cheque before receiving payment thereof."

3. *For Customer's Only :* Section 131 can give protection provided the banker collects the cheque on behalf of his customer only. If the banker collects a cheque for a person other than his customer, he cannot get the statutory protection although the cheque is crossed. A customer is one who maintains some sort of deposit account with the bank irrespective of the duration and state of account, whether debit or credit. It should be remembered that a customer of one branch is not a customer of another branch of the same bank.

*4. To Receive Payment in Good Faith and Without Negligence :* Section 90 of the English Bili of Exchange Act, on which the Indian Negotiable Instrument Act is modelled, explains 'good faith' as an act supposed to be done in good faith if it is done honestly. But in some cases where a banker may become suspicious and fails to enquire into it fearing that his suspicions may prove to be correct, it can be said that he has acted dishonestly and so not in good faith.

Negligence may also be stated as the omission to do something which a reasonable man guided upon by considerations which ordinarily regulate the conduct of human affairs would do, or something which a prudent and reasonable man would not do.

However, it would be difficult to draw a boundary line. Lord Sankey's observation will reveal clearly the position of a bank: "In my view a bank cannot be held liable for negligence merely because they have not subjected an account to microscopic examination. It is not to be expected that the officials of banks should also be amateur detectives. It is difficult to define the degree of negligence which would render them liable. Many factors have to be taken into consideration, the customer, the account and the surrounding circumstances. Though it is difficult to draw the line, the problem upon which side of the line a particular case falls does not present such difficulties."

## Negligence can be classified into Three Types

1. Opening an account without proper reference;
2. Failure to enquire when fiduciary relation exists between the customer and drawer or payee of the cheque.
3. Failure to enquire the surrounding circumstances in spite of unusual nature of collection.

## 1. Opening of Accounts

The requirements of absence of negligence is not limited to the actual act of collecting the cheque. The banker should have taken adequate care while opening accounts for new customers. The bankers following an established practice of obtaining an introduction for their new customers before opening an account with them. All bankers follow this practice to establish the bonafides of their customers. The bankers should also follow-up and verify such references and should be satisfied with it. An account may be satisfactorily operated by a customer for some time and later on he may convert a cheque. If the banker had not taken adequate care while opening account, he may be charged with negligence.

*(a) In Ladbroke Vs. Todd,* A thief opened an account with a stolen cheque after forging the endorsement of a payee. The bank collected the cheque. The thief withdrew the amount. The bank lost the statutory protection because no introduction was obtained for opening the account.

*(b)* The banker should also enquire and record the name and the nature of profession or business and other particulars of the employer of a customer while opening the account, as he may be held negligent if he collects for him cheques, payable to his employer. *(Savory & Co. Vs. Lloyds Bank Ltd., (1932.)*

Two clerks working in Savory & Co., stole bearer cheques belonging to the company. They drew cheques payable to third parties. One clerk was having an account in his own name and the other in his wife's name. The stolen cheques were deposited in these accounts. Savory & Co. charged the bank for conversion on the following grounds that the bank did not make proper enquiry about :

*(i)* The customer's employment particulars and

*(ii)* The customer's husband's name and employer's name at the time of opening the account.

*(c) In Guardians of St. John's Hampstead Vs. Barclay's Bank Ltd., (1923),*

a customer opened a fictitious account, giving his real name as the referee He gave an impressive introduction. When the problem of conversion arose, the banker lost the statutory protection due to his failure to follow-up the references where the referee is unknown.

*(d)* A banker cannot defend himself even though there is inadequate staff. In *Crumplin Vs. London Joint Stock Bank, Pickford, J.,* said, "It is no defence for a bank to say that they were so busy and had such a small staff that they could not make enquiries. If they could not make enquiries , when necessary, they must take the consequences."

## 2. Collecting Cheques for the True Owner

The banker should collect cheques for the true owner. The banker has to be very careful while collecting cheques as the possibility of collecting cheques for others are more.

While dealing with partnership accounts cheques belonging to a firm may be collected for the active partner.

## 3. Surrounding Circumstances

*(a)* If the surrounding circumstances give reason for suspicion and warrant an enquiry, the collecting banker should make enquiries before collecting cheques.

*(b) Endorsement :* The collecting banker should verify the regularity of endorsements on the cheques collected by him. In case of a stolen cheque with irregular endorsement was collected, the banker would be held liable for conversion.

## Crossed Cheques Only

In the case of special crossing, the banker whose name appears on the crossing alone is authorised to collect the cheque. If some other banker collects the cheque negligently without taking note of such crossing, he would be liable for conversion and for having acted negligently.

## Collection of forged cheques :

The collecting banker may receive 3 kinds of defective instruments:

*(a)* Where the drawer's signature is forged;

*(b)* Where the payee's signature is forged;

*(c)* Where the amount of the cheque is raised or altered.

The banker has to be careful in all these cases. Although Section 18 suggests the payment of amount stated in words, when there is a discrepancy between words and figures, the banker will return such cheques in the normal practice.

## MODELQUESTIONS

**Section – A**

1. What do you mean by payment of cheque?
2. What are mutilated cheques?
3. What is material alteration?
4. What is a Clearing House?

**Section - B**

1. Can a banker refuse payment of a cheque? If so, under what circumstances a cheque may be dishonoured?
2. Can a Banker honour a cheque that is materially altered?
3. Who is a holder in due course? What are the privileges enjoyed by him?
4. Write short notes on :

   *(a)* Garnishee Order.

   *(b)* Countermanding Order.

**Section - C**

1. On what points should a banker satisfy himself before honouring a cheque presented for payment?
2. Discuss in detail the role of the collecting banker as :

   *(a)* Holder for value.

   *(b)* An agent of the customer.